Caste, Entrepreneurship and
the Illusions of Tradition

DIVERSITY AND PLURALITY IN SOUTH ASIA

The **Diversity and Plurality in South Asia** series, wide in scope, will bring
together publications in anthropology and sociology, alongside politics and
international relations, exploring themes of both contemporary and historical relevance.
This diverse line in the social sciences and humanities will investigate the plurality
of social groups, identities and ideologies, including within its remit not only
interrogations of issues surrounding gender, caste, religion and region, but also
political variations, and a variety of cultural ideas and expressions within South Asia.

Series Editor
Nandini Gooptu – University of Oxford, UK

Editorial Board
Christophe Jaffrelot – CERI/CNRS, France
Niraja G. Jayal – Jawaharlal Nehru University, India
Raka Ray – University of California, Berkeley, USA
Yunas Samad – University of Bradford, UK
John Zavos – University of Manchester, UK

Caste, Entrepreneurship and the Illusions of Tradition

Branding the Potters of Kolkata

Geir Heierstad

ANTHEM PRESS

Anthem Press
An imprint of Wimbledon Publishing Company
www.anthempress.com

This edition first published in UK and USA 2019
by ANTHEM PRESS
75–76 Blackfriars Road, London SE1 8HA, UK
or PO Box 9779, London SW19 7ZG, UK
and
244 Madison Ave #116, New York, NY 10016, USA

First published in the UK and USA by Anthem Press 2017

British Library Cataloguing-in-Publication Data
A catalogue record for this book is available from the British Library.

ISBN-13: 978-1-78527-187-8 (Pbk)
ISBN-10: 1-78527-187-3 (Pbk)

This title is also available as an e-book.

The King and the merchant settled on a riverbank and engaged in spiritual practice, chanting the supreme hymn to the Goddess.

When they had fashioned an earthen image of her on the riverbank, the two of them worshiped the Goddess with flowers, incense, fire and libations of water.

Devi Mahatmya 13.9–10

CONTENTS

FIGURES

ACKNOWLEDGEMENTS

This monograph is about Kolkata's Kumartuli and its inhabitants. It is their histories, life and work I try to relate. Thus, it is to them I must express my gratitude first and foremost. Outside Kumartuli a number of people have been important to my work. Afraid of missing someone out, I will restrict my thanks to Arild Engelsen Ruud, Lars Tore Flåten, Kenneth Bo Nielsen, Swastika Dhar, Anne Waldrop, Pamela G. Price and Rudraprasad Sengupta. Beyond my work other people have been equally important, and I wish to express my thanks to Bjørg, Embla and Nokkve: *Cholo*, let's go skiing.

TRANSLITERATION
AND TERMINOLOGY

Bengali words are written in italics on first use and subsequently given in roman font. Words are not spelled with the inherent vowel 'a' when it is not pronounced. Diacritical signs are not used as they disturb the reading.

Kumar or *Kumor*:[1] This denotes both 'potter' and 'the potter caste'. However, in present-day Bengal in general, and in Kumartuli in particular, the Kumars do not make very many pots – they make murtis or images in the form of unbaked clay statues. And while the dictionaries present 'potter' as one of the meanings of 'Kumar', this is not necessarily what Bengali-speaking people associate with the term. To them, the word generally refers to makers of unbaked clay statues of gods and goddesses. Consequently, I will mainly use the word 'Kumar' and not the regular translation 'potter'. 'Kumar' will thus denote a maker of clay images.

Kumbhakar:[2] While 'Kumar' denotes a maker of images, it also denotes a caste. However, there are Kumars, as people who make images, who not belong to this caste. As a consequence I will use the more formal term *Kumbhakar* to refer to the caste. The word 'Kumbhakar' can be translated as 'maker of (*kar*) rounded vessels (*kumbha*)'.

Malik:[3] The Kumars of Kumartuli can be divided roughly into two groups, labourers and Maliks. The latter is a term used in Kumartuli to denote owners of workshops. Most of the informants given voice in this book are Maliks and they will frequently be referred to as such, especially when it is necessary to distinguish between the image-makers in general and the workshop-owners.

---

1 কুমোর [kumōr] n. a potter, a claymodeller (Samsad Bengali–English Dictionary 2000: 242).
2 কুম্ভকার [kumbhakār] n. a potter; a person who makes clay pots by hand (Samsad Bengali–English Dictionary 2000: 242).
3 মালিক [mālik] n. a proprietor (*fem.* a proprietress, a proprietrix), an owner; a master (*fem.* mistress), a lord (Samsad Bengali–English Dictionary 2000: 863).

Murti:[4] This word has several meanings; in this book it refers to a statue or image. Why not stick to that translation? Often when Kumars are mentioned in works in English, they are said to be makers of *idols*. In one way, it is idols they make – conceptualizing an idol in terms of something 'that is the object of excessive or supreme devotion, or that usurps the place of God in human affection' (*OED Online* 1989). However, 'idol' often has a negative connotation, as '[a]n image or similitude of a deity or divinity, used as an object of worship: applied to those worshipped by pagans' (ibid.). To Bengalis, 'murti' denotes an image or a statue in general. In Kumartuli, where they manufacture both religious and profane statues and reliefs in various materials, this is a good term. However, in more formal discourse there is always a reference to the making of *thakur murti*, a representation of a god, or to *pratima*,[5] which more directly refers to a representation of a god.

Jati:[6] This is another word with a multitude of meanings. In the context of this book, the word is used interchangeably with the word 'caste'. Thus, caste and jati are distinguished from *varna*. See Chapter 2 for an elaborate discussion on this topic.

---

4 মূর্তি [mūrti] n. a body; an incarnation; an embodiment; an image; a form, a shape, a figure, an appearance (Samsad Bengali–English Dictionary 2000: 876).
5 প্রতিমা [pratimā] n. an icon; an image; an idol (Samsad Bengali–English Dictionary 2000: 678).
6 জাতি [jāti] n. multiple meanings like birth, origin, sort, class, race, genus, caste, nation, people, tribe (Samsad Bengali–English Dictionary 2000: 396).

Prologue

THE DURGA PUJA BUSINESS

Cars, trams, buses, autos, rickshaws, taxis, trucks and bicycles are all pushed aside, immobilized by the sheer number of people in the streets and alleys of Kolkata. Roads are closed, pavements get broadened and fenced off, and the traffic police work overtime. It seems like no one stays at home, that everyone is outside in public; aeroplanes and trains arrive in the city crammed with people and depart empty. It is Durga Puja time: a time for all to visit the makeshift temples that sprout everywhere and offer prayers to the goddess. It is about new clothes, spending time with family and friends and devouring plate after plate of hot and sweet delicacies. It is the annual joyous state of emergency that seizes all Bengali Hindus and lasts for five days.

The autumnal celebration is known as both *Durgutsab*, the Festival of Durga, and *Durgapuja*, the worship of Durga. In the centre of attention is Ma Durga, the mother goddess.

Ma Durga – the victorious killer of the atrocious deity Mahishasur. Ma Durga – flanked by her four children. Ma Durga – with her unparalleled beauty, her all-conquering strength.

Uniquely linked to this occasion are provisional tent-like structures called *pandals* that are built to house the goddess. Members of the iron worker caste have become drummers, *dhakis*, beating the *dhak* (drum). Loud music crackles from countless speakers. Decorative religious placards and commercial advertisements fashioned from numerous multicoloured light bulbs adorn streets and buildings. Never-ending streams of smiling people flow gently from pandal to pandal, or visit the royal houses, *rajbaris*, which have opened up their *thakur dalan*, or in-house temple, to the public, providing a glimpse of bygone days. Stalls sell fast food, slow food, toys, soft drinks, ice cream, clothes and fruit. Theme-based pujas abound, with pandals that resemble a pyramid, a house of cards, a fishing village, a volcano or a tsunami memorial. Ma Durga appears in various guises within them – as a pharaonic queen, as the Queen of Spades, as tribal art that glows like shining metal. Cultural events take place on makeshift stages on every second street corner: recitation of known and unknown poems, dance performances, bands playing old and new songs, a woman singing songs of Rabindranath Tagore, known as *Rabindrasangeet* – all blaring through loudspeakers competing with each other.

Ma Durga, made of unbaked clay on a frame of wood and straw, has been painted and dressed with a beautiful sari and adorned with glittering costume jewellery. Her four children and the demon-like Mahishasur, also made of unbaked clay, are painted and dressed – brought to life by the Brahman, worshipped and adored by the Hindus. In the words of the famous Hindu monk Swami Vivekananda:

Putula punjo kare na hindu	The Hindu does not worship an idol
katha mati diye gara	made of wood and clay
Mrnmaya majhe cinmaja dekhe	Within the earthenness he sees consciousness
haya jaya atma-hara	and loses himself in it

Robinson 1983, my revised translation.

The worship and the festival. Both are inseparable (Figure P.1).

Cutting through these various aspects and activities, Ma Durga, as manifested in the statues called *murtis*, is still the central focus for both worship and competition. Among the commitees arranging the pujas there are competitions regarding all apsects of the pujas, and among the most prestigious are those concernings these murtis; to win a prize for the best Durga murti is something every organizer desires. A beautiful murti always attracts attention and appreciation. Gifts and food, friends and entertainment aside, it is Ma Durga who has entered the city to show us that in the end good conquers evil even when it seems totally impossible.

Durga Puja is perhaps the single most important event that unites and defines the majority of Bengali Hindus. Some scholars have written about the puja as a cultural practice (Banerjee 2004) to be investigated in itself as an interesting feature of the region. Some have approached it within an anthropological framework (Östör 2004), using the puja as a point of departure to investigate the society at large. While walking more or less aimlessly with and without friends through Kolkata's pujascape I started to wonder about the politics of Durga Puja, and remembered some short references to how Durga Puja was historically used as an anticolonial and anticlass medium (Banerjee 1989). Later, when researching the main subjects of this work, the potters of Kolkata's Kumartuli district, I found a few paragraphs concerning popular or folk resistance:

[In] the [Durga] puja images […] the divinities were often moulded according to certain types that were to be seen in the surrounding society. The god Kartika (son of Durga) was a favourite character for the 'kumors'. The style of moulding his image changed according to the

Figure P.1 Durga Puja 2006 at Baghbajar. Photo by author.

fashions prevalent among the foppish *babus* of Calcutta in different periods […] the clay-modellers never lost the chance of a jibe at the rich and the religious leaders, just like the *kobi-walas* [poets] who never hesitated to hit out at their patrons whenever there was an opportunity. The clay *sawngs* [parodic imitations] which were part of the Durga Puja festivities provided them with such a chance. (Banerjee 1989: 128–30)

Back in the puja streets, immersing myself in the ubiquitous pandal-hopping, enjoying the beauty and joy and bustle of the festival, appraising the murtis, some questions arose. What are the stories of these magnificent and versatile murtis that end their life in the River Ganga? Who are the artists behind them, the creators of the main focal point of every pandal? What are their – the artists'– stories?

The Old World

I visited Kumartuli for the first time during the Durga Puja of 2000. On later visits to Kolkata I often tried to make at least one visit to the alleys of Kumartuli, to the Kolkata beyond busy markets, heavy traffic, hawkers, beggars and shopping malls.

Through the years I read whatever writings I chanced upon about the neighbourhood. And my curiosity was further fuelled by small notes like:

> Kumartuli. Or the potters' hub. This area in north Calcutta has remained as vital to the [Durga] festival today as it was in the late eighteenth century. [...] Not much has changed since then. (Banerjee 2004: 65–6)

And:

> Kumartuli is the only surviving colony of artisans in the heart of north Calcutta and one of the oldest anywhere in the city. (Dutta 2003: 52)

Then it got even more intriguing:

> In Kumartuli, next to Sonagachi where the sex workers still ply their trade, the goddess [Durga] is crafted from straw and silt from the river, and adorned with glittering jewels fashioned from tinsel, gold and silver foil, and *shoal* pith. It is believed that a little clump of mud from the threshold of the whores is generously mixed with the rest of the silt for good luck. (Chatterjee 2004: 64)

For me Kumartuli started to materialize into an anthropological cornucopia, with its political agitation hidden in the sculptures made for the main Bengali religious festival, the old, never-changing hub, the 'believed' cultural practices with a tantric flavour and the existence of commercial websites like Kumartuli.com (www.kumartuli.com). This (seemingly?) time-capsuled society, I thought, must truly be the kind of (unreliable?) anachronism that makes for good anthropology.

I made up my mind – I would make the small neighbourhood of potters, thriving in a Kolkata that attempts with a good degree of success to become one of the most important Indian centres of information technology, my new fieldwork site.

Thus, armed with fuzzy concepts of coded politics in an old caste-based neighbourhood producing the murtis needed for the main Bengali Hindu puja, and with ideas about rituals containing sexual undertones in the age of web-based marketing, I returned to Kumartuli in early 2006. Within a few hours I understood that this is not what Kumartuli is all about – at least not any longer (and it probably never was).

A New World

The Kumars are hard-working businessmen, and a few businesswomen, claiming an identity as artists in a tough and economically strained local and global market. Artistic entrepreneurship is highly appreciated if time and funds allow scope for such extravagance. Ritual practices are largely nonexistent where the making of the murtis is concerned. Fibreglass and plaster of Paris are important mediums, especially for murtis that are exported. Old caste categories and stories remain unknown to ordinary Kumars. Politically, they attempt to achieve various development goals through organized labour committees, as well as by voting in local and state elections.

The scanty paragraphs I had read about the Kumars seemed insufficient, providing a totally wrong, idealized and static image of these so-called image-makers. I soon understood that I had to seek the history of these rural caste-artisans working under local patronage, who had over time become urban artists in a global market, in order to understand and tell the Kumars' stories.

In Aristotle's *De Anima* the faculty of image-making is an important aspect of what makes human beings different from other creatures (Napier 1992: xxi). While Aristotle referred to image-making as a process of the mind, not as a physical and economic activity, it is a business for the Kumars. The contemporary image-makers of Kumartuli have crafted a profession out of their capabilities of imagination. Initially, this was not the reality among the Kumars. Their trade as producers of clay images involved little imagination at first; they copied what was widely accepted as a traditional style of depicting Durga, often using the same mould for the face for many years. After the 1930s, the demand from the market changed and innovative designs became popular. Then the faculty of imagination became one of the most important assets for Kumars who wished to succeed in their work. This can be described as a modernistic development, when artisans were replaced by artists in their own right. There are no simple definitions that place 'artisan' and 'artist' in two different categories: the distinction between the two remains fuzzy and permeable. At this point, it is sufficient to add that while both the Kumar artisans and the Kumar artists are engaged in the production of symbolically saturated objects, the latter represent a new kind of self-reflexivity in connection with their work that is often associated with a modernity that has made 'tradition' an object of the past.

Moreover, the modernity that emerges among the Kumars does so in a context where caste is an assertive source of self-representation. Young and old, they all say the same thing – that working with clay, making the murtis, is in their blood (*rakte acche*). It is not necessary to go to school to learn artistic skills, as these come to them naturally. The activity of murti-making has surrounded them from birth; it has been and is in the air they breathe. Again, it is part of their heritage and it runs in their family (*bangsher dhara*) as an inherited quality, as a natural skill that differentiates them from others. So, when one observes a murti, one also gets a glimpse of a self-claimed innate quality of the maker as a *Kumbhakar*, a member of the potters' caste.

Kumbha karuti (kore) kumbha kar is an old Bengali saying known to many Kumars. *Kumbha* means 'pot', *karuti (kore)* means 'making', and *-kar* means 'creator/maker' – thus the saying translates as: 'One who makes pots is one who is of the potters' caste.' At present in Kumartuli, the Kumbhakars are mainly *murtikars* (image makers) – and they still identify themselves with reference to what they do and make. They are who they are because of what they do and create. This tautological aphorism ties the Kumars and their work into a self-identifying entity. An important part of their cultural identity is invested in the creation of murtis.

Interestingly enough, it is caste as profession that is mainly evoked in the context of Kumartuli. While caste endogamy is still dominant, aspects of ritual purity (concerning especially hierarchy) that usually define the ideology of the caste system are rarely seen. 'Caste' with no or few notions of opposition between the pure and the impure might be regarded as a misnomer (at least to the Dumontians), but according to the Kumars' conception this is not the case. In contemporary Kumartuli, caste affiliation is an asset. The purchase of murtis from a caste Kumar assures customers that they have bought a 'proper' murti with a genealogy going back to prehistoric times.

Thus, in Kolkata's Kumartuli the stories of indigenous modernities seem to be concealed behind tradition. Among the potters inhabiting the shanty-like, earth-floored workshops of the caste based neighbourhood, the history of a modern and economically neoliberal-minded India unfolds.

And here are some stories of how these potters of Kumartuli transformed caste into a brand for the purposes of marketing their products in the competitive art business of selling sculptures. To contemporary potters, caste is in their blood, caste is about being creative and independent artists and caste is about business as they engage in a competitive market to sell their artworks. In Kumartuli, caste has become a commodity.

Chapter 1

ON KUMARS, MODERNITY, CASTE AND COMMODIFICATION

This is a portrayal of the Maliks among the Kumars of Kumartuli in the Indian megacity Kolkata.[1] The Maliks are the owners of the workshops and studios that make the images used in the numerous pujas – worship ceremonies – within and outside of Bengal, of which Durga Puja is the most important. In general, the Kumars work as makers of unbaked clay images, and in Kumartuli they form a caste-based neighbourhood. In fact, 'Kumartuli' means 'the potters' neighbourhood' and is the last of Kolkata's larger neighbourhoods still dominated by a single caste working within their 'traditional' caste profession.

Thus, they might seem like survivors of a long-lost tradition, a secluded group untouched by modernity, a capsule that has resisted time and development (Fabian 1983, Wolf 1997 [1982]). At least this is how they are usually represented (Banerjee 2004). It is as if time-travel is possible after all: 'Just visit Kumartuli where time has stood still.' This strange impression paves the way for a new understanding of caste in the twenty-first century: caste as a commodity. I establish this through a study of how Kumars understand and practise caste. Further, by means of empirical descriptions I seek to develop the theory of caste as both an analytical and a descriptive device.

In order to understand the world of the Kumars, it is necessary to understand the histories out of which contemporary Kumartuli emerges – histories that that Kumars of today use actively in their business. Based on the Maliks and their families' own stories and recollections, I present and analyse the transformation of this group of Bengali caste-based potters from regular village artisans into highly esteemed urban artists. Emphasis is placed on how they constitute or present themselves through oral histories of their past and present lives as image-makers.

---

1 Also known by its former name Calcutta.

My major concern is to depict and analyse the meaning of caste in a society and context where caste has had a more hidden impact, while also exploring how this impact has changed (Searle-Chatterjee and Sharma 1994, Gupta 2004, Khare (ed.) 2006, Chandra, Heierstad and Nielsen 2015). This approach is contextualized within an understanding of the Kumartuli Kumars as a highly modern community for the most part, even as the specific form this modernity takes should be described as partly alternative, indigenous and western (Gaonkar 2001, Narayan Rao, Shulman and Subrahmanyam 2003, 2007, Chatterjee 1993, Gupta 1998). The Kumars of this book are immersed in a modernity that is not only a product of the European Enlightenment and capitalism, but also encapsulates processes and practices where high degrees of self-reflexivity, historicity, subordination of tradition and presentness mark out a new understanding of self, history, tradition and contemporary society. Further, the development of various practices connected to caste in Kumartuli are epitomized in what I label the *commodification of caste*, through which caste affiliation is used as a marketing brand.

Caste is often described as something that is *done to you* (e.g., Searl-Chatterjee and Sharma 1994). This is also indeed the case for many of the Kumars, especially many among the younger generation of clay artists, who talk about how they were pressured into their caste's occupation by their seniors. However, caste is also something that *one can do*. In Kumartuli a large number of the artists use their caste affiliation to sell their religious status as traditional, real and genuine. Through the logic of the market and capitalism, many Kumars use their caste background as a label or a brand. Thus, caste is both different from and more than a central principle of everything Indian, from social organisation and ritual practices to political practices and economic structures. Caste both confines action and catalyses change.

With the prevailing importance of Durga Puja among the Hindus as both a religious event and a profane festival in West Bengal in general, and Kolkata in particular, the makers of the religious clay statues so central to it have gained a new self-understanding. As artisans they might be potters spinning the potter's wheel while belonging to the lowest of the four groups above what was called the untouchables of the old hierarchy. But with degrees from art colleges, Internet competency and an increasing understanding of global business and marketing, some of them have no problem in annually adding several new pages to their newspaper scrapbooks documenting their work – as well as to their PC-folders containing radio and TV-clips from interviews they have given about it.

A casual visit to Kumartuli does not easily reveal this reality. Functionally dressed labourers, usually wearing only *lungis*, pieces of simple cloth wrapped around the waste, sit on the mud floors of the ramshackle workshops, making murtis with their hands, using some pieces of bamboo covered with straw and clay. Kumartuli is among the oldest caste-based neighbourhoods in Kolkata and it looks like it. This is, however, an illusion; an illusion of tradition.

The histories of the Kumars of Kumartuli, as told by themselves, structure this book, but it is always the individuals of today who recollect and tell their stories. Thus, these contemporary image-makers present themselves through the stories that I, an outsider, asks them to remember. Their daily work and the conditions under which they do it forms the second empirical pillar of this study. While modernity and capitalism might seem distant from daily life and work in Kumartuli, the empirical material from the Kumars' actual activities shows that modernity and capitalism perhaps are the best terms to describe and analyse the recent changes Kumartuli has undergone and the neighbour-hood's present condition.

The fundamental process of making the murtis has not changed profoundly through the centuries. But their form, and the characteristics of their buyers has changed significantly. From historically being purchased by the rich elite, at the end of the nineteenth century the images increasingly became sold market style to neighbourhood puja committees. Almost simultaneously the common perception of how the face of Durga should be moulded changed, and few follow the traditional style. And for the last seven decades she has borne a resemblance to mortal women such as the neighbourhood beauty, a beloved actress or a well-known foreigner. The arrangements of the various figures in the scenes depicted in the pandals are also experimented with. From their initially relative rigid features and postures, there are now murtis made under the label *art bangla* where artistic freedom is next to total. Features, postures and decorations traditionally foreign to Durga and the accompanying figures are now commonly incorporated into the work.

Such changes, from the new ways of marketing murtis to the stylistic disjuncture just described, are defining trajectories in the present day Kumars' self-representation as artists. The Kumars of Kumartuli that I came to know are far from static tantric artisans doomed to having to hide their political viewpoints in their work. Rather, they are modern artists, creators who use caste in order to recapture a market that they feel has progressively slipped out of their control.

Still, one is struck by the defining feature of Kumartuli that is its caste-based identity as a neighbourhood. Is there not a contradiction in terms between the 'hereditary profession' and the 'role of modern artist' of the Kumars? As with everything else concerning analysis and theory, this depends on definitions. What is meant by caste and modernity? Throughout this book I will seek to establish, if not a short and congruent definition of caste, then at least a theoretically founded understanding of the concept that fits the territory

I experienced during my fieldwork. To say that caste is tradition while the rejection of caste demarcates the entry of modernity represents a common mistake within much of the ethnographic and theoretical scholarship on South Asia. First, such an assumption represents a misunderstanding of the role of caste and how the caste system functions. Secondly, it represents a confusion of analytical levels, as it makes little sense to say that a caste society relates to an egalitarian society as tradition relates to modernity. In the case of Kumartuli, caste is practised within the context of a neighbourhood of modern artists.

My point of departure is the uncontroversial claim that caste is only one possible source, among many others, of social organisation and self-representation (Dirks 1992). Upon studying the history of Kumartuli over the past century it also becomes evident that belonging to the caste of Kumars is transformed from an identity regulating marriage, commensality and labour into an emblem under which products are sold. This notion of caste and its transformation bears a resemblance to processes of commodification also found among some other ethnic and indigenous groups such as the Zulus of South Africa and Aboriginals of Australia (Comaroff and Comaroff 2009).

Comprehending the Kumars

Kumartuli is a caste-based community with an unambiguous modern *ras* or flavour. This combination of seeming opposites of a caste-based artist community with a modern mindset does seem intriguing and worthy of study.

The importance of caste is unambiguous; the profession of murti-making in Kumartuli is largely an inherited one for the Kumars. People from other castes are also engaged in the work no doubt, and this has been common for more than one hundred years, but these others constitute a minority. At first glance at least, caste as an inherited profession among the Kumars appears to be a central feature of Kumartuli.

Most Kumars have a very conscious understanding of who they are as clay artists, and of their reputations and the cultural importance of their work. As a necessary part of their work they relate to various styles of images, ranging from 'traditional Bangla-style' to 'modern art-er-style'. Moreover, they have a shared understanding of when the break with tradition took place and what it consisted in. The combination of these two aspects – self-reflexivity and historical awareness of the break from tradition – is what many social scientists argue constitutes modernity.

An important aspect of this book concerns the long transition of the Kumars from being artisans working mainly in patron–client relationships to becoming modern artists showcasing their goods and abilities in a highly competitive market. Thus, what I present and analyse is a section of the genealogy of this trajectory among the Maliks belonging to the *jati*[2] Kumbhakar. As a point of departure in the study of caste, Louis Dumont's analysis of caste in *Homo Hierarchicus* is used, as it is considered a landmark study in the literature on the Indian sociology of caste. As such, it is also contested. Important names in this dialogue are Dipankar Gupta (2003), R. S. Khare (2006), Searl-Chatterjee and Sharma (1994) and Nicholas B. Dirks' two works *The Hollow Crown* (1987) and *Castes of Mind* (2001). Writ large, the general critical stance can be summed up as follows: 'Orientalist versions of India's essence and anthropological representations of the centrality of caste have conspired to deny Indians their history and their historicity simultaneously' (Dirks 1992: 76).

Thus, there existed an understanding of caste as the totalizing principle for everything that happens in India, for everything Indian. Secondly, caste is still often seen as the opposite of modernity. Where does that leave the Kumartuli Kumars, a group of business-minded artists working within their caste-based occupation in a neighbourhood defined by their caste's presence? Have the meanings and implications of caste changed during the last decades? Is the common depictions of modernity in social sciences wrong?

Given that Dumont's notion of caste and its implications have been highly contested, it seems likely that using the traditional sociology of caste would turn out to be unsatisfactory. Thus, in order to approach the reality of the modern caste-based image-makers, a second notion of caste seems necessary. I will return to this later.

Modernity is an elusive concept. Modernity can be a period in art, a belief in the possibilities of science, an attitude towards the world and so on. Within anthropology, following philosophers and sociologists, modernity is mainly approached as an attitude and practice (Appadurai 1996, Miller 1994). Still, the elusiveness of the concept is especially evident when one tries to use modernity as an attitude. Modernity is often portrayed as the western Enlightenment's triumph of reason (at least the conviction that reason in the end can triumph), but this is only one side of the coin. Also the opposition of faith to reason that soon followed the emergence of European rationalism and capitalism is part of what should be understood as modernity. A key feature of this opposition is the position given to imagination. Overarching this intrinsic contradiction (Simmel 1978, Miller 1994) of reason versus imagination is the process of self-reflexivity and a radical sense of 'presentness' (Miller 1994). Tradition loses its quasi-natural status and custom no longer provides all the

---

2 The term *jati* is ambiguous. As noted in the section on *Terminology*, I use it in a strict sense as being synonymous with 'caste', not as denoting birth, origin, kind, sort, class, etc.

answers (Miller 1994). One result is often a historical awareness, a sensation that the time one lives in is different from the past. In fact, the very experience of the existence of a tradition is a result of this presentness that often is a hallmark of modernity (Rudolph and Rudolph 1984 [1967]). When I use modernity as a comparative concept, it is especially the emphases on historicity, self-reflexivity and presentness that are important in order to map the many 'alternative modernities' that exist (Gaonkar 2001). Further, I follow the likes of Sudipta Kaviraj, who argues that we 'should expect modernity not to be homogeneous, not to result in the same kind of social processes and reconstitution of institutions in all historical and cultural contexts' (2005: 138).

Portraying the Kumars and analysing caste through a concept of modernity is part of an argument that caste and modernity do not encompass two incommensurable and opposing sets of values. But we need a more detailed understanding of modernity as context and caste as a set of flexible practices before the concept of commodification can be explained. Let us consider context first.

Making Modernity the Context

Let me turn to Dilip P. Gaonkar, a teacher of rhetoric and cultural studies, in order to grasp the descriptive and analytic importance of modernity or modernization as a theory. In the history of ideas, modernity was, according to Gaonkar, '[b]orn in and of the West some centuries ago under relatively specific sociohistorical conditions' (2001: 1). But at present it is not a phenomenon limited to the West, as it has been 'awakened by contact; transported through commerce; administrated by empires; bearing colonial inscriptions; propelled by nationalism; and now increasingly steered by global media, migration, and capital' (ibid.).

Gaonkar asserts that 'modernity is best understood as an attitude of questioning the present' (ibid.): an attitude that is defined by its dual character of the early capitalist bourgeois and its opponents, initially in the aesthetic realm. Modernity is thus twofold.

First, in an idealized description of a 'modern' individual, there is the 'growth of scientific consciousness, the development of a secular outlook, the doctrine of progress, the primacy of instrumental rationality, the fact–value split, individualistic understanding of the self, contractualist understanding of society' (Gaonkar 2001: 2). Such an understanding is, for example, evident in Barbra Harriss-White's writing on caste and corporatist capitalism, where she defines modernization as 'the rational organisation of economy and society' (2003: 176). The cognitive transformation behind such comprehensions of modernization is often said to originate at a time during the Enlightenment when the West witnessed 'the emergence and institutionalization of market-driven industrial economies, bureaucratically administrated states, modes of popular government rule of law, mass media, and increased mobility, literacy and urbanization' (Gaonkar 2001: 2). Parts of this understanding of modernity are also connected to the growth of science since the Enlightenment and the belief that science could provide us with an objective and pure knowledge of the world. In fact, Bruno Latour states that science was instrumental in constituting modernity (1993). Science has been able to create the impression that it is not affected by culture, that it is a separate ontological sector. The belief in this second ontological reality and the possibility that we can approach it through the scientific method denies the existence of the hybrid nature of all kinds of knowledge and knowledge's various objects. Latour's conclusion is consequently that we have never been truly modern, since there is no completely separate ontological sector available to us through science. However, Latour writes that people's belief in the reality of objective science marks them as modern. While modernity as the existence of a new ontological sector accessible through science is impossible and has never existed, the *attitude* of belief that it is a possibility, or even a reality, is characteristic of modernity.

Second, against this bourgeois and idealized outlook came a reaction in the late eighteenth century. This movement, dominated by its aesthetic wing, focused on 'the cultivation and care of the self [...] self-exploration and self-realization were its primary concerns [... and] a high premium was placed on spontaneous expression, authentic experience, and unfettered gratification of one's creative and carnal urges' (Gaonkar 2001: 2). Reason was scrapped and imagination took its place as the guiding star. Aesthetic and moral boundaries should be transgressed or subverted, and everything, including 'the demonic, the artificial, and the fugitive' (Gaonkar 2001) should be scrutinized.

It is in this 'twin matrix' of bourgeois reason and its opposing child imagination that the modern self is made and unmade (ibid.: 3). It is not a coincidence that the beginning of modernity corresponds with the growing importance of transcontinental trade.

Both reason and imagination have their light and dark sides. Reason, as a part of societal modernization, is split between promises of prosperity, democratization, better technology and so on, on the one hand; and alienation and despair in a disenchanted world of meaningless routines on the other. Imagination, as part of cultural modernity, is divided between a positive outlook on the aesthetic and creative enjoyment of modernity, as a spectacle of speed, novelty and effervescence on one side; and the absence of morality in a world of facades on the other (Gaonkar 2001: 9).

Thinkers on modernity have approached the dark and light sides of the dual character of modernity. Habermas discards Weber's negative description of modernity and wants to rehabilitate the project of modernity by revivifying reason as agency with many forms and voices (Bernstein 1985, Habermas 1987). Foucault does not see reason and its twin rationality as being subject-centred, since it can never escape from relations and the effects of power – reason is entangled with power (Gaonkar 2001: 10–11, Foucault 1980). Thus, Foucault turns to cultural modernity and argues that modernity entails both a form of relationship to the present and to oneself. It is a sort of outside position from which one can interpret oneself as an object, like Baudelaire's dandy who sees himself as a work of art. Modernity is thus not an epoch, but rather an attitude of critical self-reflectivity and questioning of the present through which a historical awareness becomes manifested. There is an experience of a break or caesura with the past, which is seen as tradition. It is this kind of attitude that has gone global according to Appadurai (1996), Gaonkar (2001) and Miller (1994). And its various manifestations in time and space present us with 'alternative modernities'.

Arjun Appadurai in his highly influential *Modernity at Large* (an important source of inspiration for Gaonkar) approaches modernity slightly differently, as he emphasizes how electronic media and migration are important globalized features of modernity. The notion of modernity as dual in the above sense and the thesis of its emergence being a result of the age of Enlightenment in the West are pronounced in Appadurai's work. In India, modernity is something coming from the outside – something that changes 'the *work of imagination* as a constitutive feature of modern subjectivity' (Appadurai 1996: 3). His emphasis on the mobility of signs is also important in the case of the modernity of Kumartuli. Through the flows of signs and knowledge, localized people can imagine and sometimes actualize different lives, they come to 'seek to annex the global into their own practices of the modern' (ibid.: 4). But is this attitude necessarily a univocally Western product?

In much writing on modernity there is a striking consensus concerning its source and genealogy. In Western social theory, modernity as we know it today is usually seen as an offspring of Western centres of economic and political power (Kaviraj 2005: 138). The rest of the world came to be influenced by modernity due to its contact with Europeans, especially through the latter's colonial enterprises. It is as if the West 'had some unique historical advantage, some special quality of race or culture or environment or mind or spirit, which gives this human community a permanent superiority over all other communities' (Blaut 1993: 1). Blaut, a professor of geography, describes this understanding as Eurocentric diffusionism and argues that it is one of the most powerful beliefs concerning world history and geography. He writes further:

> The belief is both historical and geographical. Europeans are seen as the 'makers of history'. Europe eternally advances, progresses, modernizes.

The rest of the world advances more sluggishly, or stagnates: it is 'traditional society'. Therefore, the world has a permanent geographical center and a permanent periphery: an Inside and an Outside. Inside leads, Outside lags. Inside innovates, Outside imitates. (Blaut 1993: 1)

While Blaut readily exaggerates and uses meaningless categories in his book ('third world historians', 'Indian feudalism'), he also pinpoints something important, namely that one should be extremely alert when anyone attempts to fix the origin of an worldwide attitude or practice such as 'modernity' accurately in time and space (something one could argue that Blaut does). As such, he follows others who recognize early and alternative modernities, such as Abu-Lughod (1998) and Eisenstadt (2003). Akhil Gupta is more moderate when he notes: 'To speak of modernity is less to invoke an empirical referent than a self-representation of the West' (1998: 36). This renders modernity as the prototype of and the measure of the social progress of the West (Hall 1992: 313), consciously built on a difference with another like the Orient (Gupta 1998: 36). However, it has become increasingly evident that what is needed is to broaden the history of modernity beyond Europe (Chakrabarty 2007) and to introduce a few more beginnings.

Indian origins

Sheldon Pollock addresses the difficulty of precisely identifying the 'caesura of modernity' (2006: 8), as it is difficult for most thinkers on modernity to describe what came earlier, e.g., the pre-modern condition, especially in the case of South Asia. The caesura or division is fuzzy and permeable; elements ascribed to modernity are not all entirely unknown to pre-modernity. Pollock states that

> European modernity and South Asian premodernity are obvious uneven and not absolute categories; the former displays premodern features, the latter modern ones [...] Not only did Indian 'premodernity' contain elements of European modernity, but in some key areas of culture [...] it might even be said to have provided a stimulus to the development of that modernity. (2006: 9)

While Pollock agrees that the discussion of the existence of early, multiple or alternative modernities is legitimate, he is not primarily concerned with the enterprise of finding an Indian modernity. His subject is mainly differences between 'culture-power practices and their associated theories [...] that came into being in modern Europe and the world of South Asia before the arrival of these practices and theories on the heels of European expansion' (2006: 9–10). These practices in the South Asian context he calls premodern, without fretting too much over definitions of 'premodern' and 'modern'. While Pollock is aware of the difficulties of identifying the advent of modernity in South Asia with European influences, this is nevertheless exactly what he does.

While Western colonialism and capitalism undoubtedly have made an immense impact worldwide, the genealogical origin of every 'alternative modernity' is not self-evidently linked to them. In an Indian context the colonial encounter definitely played an important role in shaping modern attitudes within the country's own population (Appadurai 1996, Chakrabarty 2003). But in order to be empirically and theoretically consistent, one can never take the genealogical thesis of (exclusively) Western influence for granted. In societies like India, with a pre-colonial history of modernity, modernity's encompassing attitudes might very well be latent among a number of its inhabitants even when they are not pronounced, in the sense that there might exist indigenous models for modern attitudes. This is convincingly argued by Velcheru Narayana Rao, David Shulman and Sanjay Subrahmanyam in their *Textures of Time* about history writing and historical awareness in pre-colonial times (2003). The latter work extends the argument of their earlier collaborative work *Symbols of Substance* (1992), where they describe the emergence of a new, nontraditional South Indian elite, and *When God is a Customer* (1994), where they approach the rise of the individual and the public sphere (Chekuri 2007). All these works explore the experience of early modernity in South Asia before the consolidation of colonial rule (Narayana Rao et al. 2007).

It should be noted that this is a rather difficult enterprise, since the search for other modernities that lie outside European history tends to imply seeking and finding Europe in other histories – in this case, in India. The definition of modernity is thus based on a peculiarly Western conception of it. However, the opposite approach, which denies 'the other's' historical awareness, self-reflexivity and so on, through narratives of manifestations of a Western modernity going global in step with colonialism and capitalism, is more problematic. Without entering into the discussions of absolute beginnings, historical and ethnographical work concerning the existence of markers of Western modernity, such as historicity and self-reflexivity, prior to any encounters with the West, is important. This represents no denial of the sociohistorical particularities of Western modernity (Pollock 2007); rather it redefines the ground upon which we understand our experience of modernity by drawing our attention to the historical and ethnographical contexts outside the Western world. Akhil Gupta notes that 'modernity *may have* been instituted as a global phenomenon through colonial capitalism' (1998: 9, italics added), but stresses that in this process it was 'resisted, reinvented, and reconfigured in different social and historical locations' (ibid.). He further emphasizes that multivalent genealogies of modernity in a country like India are an important aspect of modern life as such. Gupta argues convincingly that the present modernity in post-colonial India is mainly a result of colonization, as well as of more recent Western discourses on nationalism and development (1998). However, he should probably have been more radical in his development of the notion of multivalent genealogies of modernity, as some recent scholars are.

Narayan Rao, Shulman and Subrahmanyam (2003) take the supposed lack of historical awareness of pre-colonial India and the neglect of local historiographical traditions as their point of departure and argue for the existence of an indigenous notion of history (a view found also in Guha 2002, Lal 2003 and Chakrabarty 1997). The trio refer to the existence of a group of professional scribes in South India, *karanams*, who in fact represented a genuine indigenous historiographical tradition. In order to be able to approach and understand the history written by the karanams, one has to discard Western notions of history as a specific genre. The karanams' history writing came in a variety of genres and is accessible as historiography only through the use of the 'subgeneric markers' available to the indigenous or educated reader, who will understand what is factual, historical information as opposed to fiction. The markers are labelled 'texture' and through a correct reading of a variety of writings in various genres composed by the karanams, the authors show how markers such as a small shift in tempo, an emphasis on numbers, a new down-to-earth narrative tone and so on, indicate the communication of factual history to the reader, within the frame of a genre that was not originally used to carry such information. Thus, this special historiographic tradition developed no specifically new 'historical' literary genre. Instead it used already existing ones, but added textural changes to mark the jumps between parts with fictional and factional information, between invention and empirical recollection. The writers themselves are also visible in these texts, for they usually sign the work (which is new) – thus a certain form of personhood or individualistic authorship emerges as an important part of this early modernity. The karanams are evidently individuals approaching historical material as factual incidents and communicating their information through a consensual historiographic method based on texture (a view substantiated from another South Indian point of view by Mattison Mines (1994)).

In the context of this book it is important to note the existence of an early modernity in South Asia that has been lost to generations of readers and academics. The literature reviewed by Narayan Rao, Shulman and Subrahmanyam has, in their own words,

links to older historiographical modes in South Asia, but also constitutes a new departure; in a sense, it marks the arrival of a certain kind of 'modernity' in the far south, beginning at a point far in advance of the benchmarks [of modernity] usually cited. The new sense of the past belongs to a wider series of diagnostic features, which include striking individualism, a new sense of the human body and its possibilities, a common political culture that cuts through the boundaries of collective ('religious') identities. (2003: 264)

To assert that modernity must be understood as an 'embedding of conditions within modern governmental modes' (Chekuri 2007: 393) that are solely European in their origins and exported to India on the wings of colonialism (Narayan Rao et al. 2007: 426) is highly problematic. As Alexander Woodside states concerning China, Korea and Vietnam in his *Lost Modernities* (2006), rationalization processes in those countries' bureaucracies were what we would label modern today, even as they took place independently of each other and of Western influence. Moreover, they were separate from aspects of European modernity like capitalism and the industrial revolution. Such aspects were peculiar to Western modernity, something that Gaonkar as well notes (2001); in other places modernity took different shapes.

Nevertheless, one finds the same degradation of the role of tradition in these contexts as well, combined with the attitudes of self-reflexivity and historicity and being in the present that characterize modernity – a break, a caesura, however fuzzy the border might be, that applies to the entire population. And in order to grasp a theory of modernity as a comparative tool, it is exactly the existence and experience of a break or caesura that is important. Through such breaks, whatever their origin – whether from a belief in rationality of the western Enlightenment or due to the establishment of a bureaucracy – a new self-understanding might be manifested, as the break creates a sense of historicity. A sensation of having a 'tradition' (Rudolph and Rudolph 1984 [1967]) emerges, which makes a new kind of self-reflexivity possible as 'the other' becomes part of one's own society. Thus, when Gupta writes that modernity consciously builds on a difference with an other like the Orient (Gupta 1998: 25), he should also add that the difference might well be located within any given society itself. The sensation of difference, of a break or caesura, is perhaps the most important feature of modernity, as in many cases this transformation contains the possibility of changing the society dramatically.

Modernity is not an attitude that comes about in an entire population during the night, like the upgrading of computer software at one's workplace. Even as its consequences change the society completely, it takes time; it is a slow, gradual process that will never be finalized in any way. In the same way as there exist no purely modern societies, there has never existed a purely premodern society. There is always a continuum: there are times when modernity as an attitude and practice dominates and periods when it does not.

Consequently, the narrative of modernity as related by the likes of Habermas (1987), Gaonkar (2001) and Miller (1994) denies 'others' their own modernities, modernities that a growing number of researchers at present are bringing to light. To accept this does not imply a denial of the vast impact on Indian society made by the Western colonial powers. European governmental, educational and scientific modes not only transformed India, but also themselves changed as a consequence. Instead, it makes us aware of that historicity, the self-reflexivity of the individual and so on also have their own indigenous roots. Changes took place in India prior to the introduction of Western modernity, changes that made the subjects aware that something new had happened that constituted a break from the past (Narayan Rao et al. 2007). Modernity must be seen as 'more manifold than is often assumed [… and the changes it brings] may occur independently of one another, as a multiplicity of developments' (Woodside 2006: 1).

Moreover, as Gupta states, Indian modernity is different because 'the *fact of difference* itself is a constitutive moment that structures the experiences of modernity' (1998: 36). What constitutes this difference varies greatly from continent to continent and from society to society. In Western modernity there was the perceived victory of reason, so often invoked with reference to the Other(s), as well as an opposing trend of belief in the power of imagination (Gaonkar 2001). A new kind of historical awareness and self-reflexivity was part of this attitude. An important aspect of such differences, breaks or caesuras that goes together with modernity is that they enforce self-reflexivity. Further, there are different ways of being modern (Gupta 1998) that might constitute central parts of local groups' self-representation. Localized groups like the Kumars of Kumartuli have their own histories and experiences of being and identity.

Questions about modernity as an exclusively European phenomenon are not limited to academic theorizing about historical particularism. The answers have a bearing on our understanding of other aspects of various societies and their peoples, like the conceptualization of caste.

Caste between Structure and Practice

Anthropological studies of India have been dominated by discussions of caste. Béteille sees this privileging of the ritual aspects of society as being a consequence of the stress on difference and contrast in anthropology (1991: 33). The result is that Indian society to a large extent has been 'epitomized' in terms of caste (Burghart 1990: 264). An India dominated by 'caste hierarchy fulfils the need for a single and powerful organising image which enables people in the west to think about a particular non-western society' (Searl-Chatterjee and Sharma 1994: 2). According to Appadurai, this image 'capture(s) internal realities in terms that serve the discursive needs of general theory' (1992: 45). While no one denies the historical and contemporary importance of caste, its role in Indian society has been reconsidered, especially since the late 1980s (e.g., Dirks 1987, Searl-Chatterjee and Sharma 1994). Caste is now mainly seen as one (historical) cultural trait among many within Indian society, and not as the visible manifestation of a fundamental ideology underlying it as a whole. The role of caste system(s) is to a certain extent an empirical question. Before we enter that territory, let us start with a (nominal) description of what caste in fact generally implies. This detour is taken in order to contextualize the subsequent discussion of the Bengali variety of the caste system and to make the entire caste-nomenclature meaningful.

Short depiction of the caste system and the Bengali case

The word 'caste' is of Portuguese and Spanish origin, *casta*, probably denoting something unmixed or pure, and it was used in the sense of race, lineage or breed (Dumont 1980 [1970]: 21, OED Online 1989). In the Indian context it was the Portuguese who first used it from the middle of the sixteenth century, in the sense of tribe or race, according to one source applied mainly to the lowest classes in contradistinction to their overlords (Dumont 1980 [1970]: 347). While the first descriptions differed greatly, depending on whether they referred to the fourfold division into *varnas* (discussed below) or to occupational groups like jatis, no special emphasis was given by the Europeans to the hierarchical organisation that we currently label 'the caste system' (Dirks 2001: 20). The first extensive work on the caste system, *A Description of the Character, Manners, and Customs of the People of India and of Their Institutions Religious and Civil*, was published as late as 1816 under the name of the Abbé J. A. Dubois (1992). The book was in large part based on a manuscript written by Père Coeurdoux in the 1760s (Dirks 2001: 21). As the first work on the subject, it became influential for the British and other orientalists' understanding of the caste system.

Without entering into the scholarly discourse on the caste system at this point, it is enough to state that as the knowledge of Indian society increased among the Western colonialists, the term 'caste' came to denote the hierarchical system of hereditary groups, the jati system. Roughly speaking, these groups were distinguished from, and related to, one another by the following characteristics: *separation*, including endogamous marriage and the practice of commensality rules; *division of labour*, each group having a profession; and *hierarchy*, which ranks the groups as superior or inferior to each other (Dumont

1970: 21). Such a hereditary group is in India called a jati, with the image-makers featured in this book belonging to the Kumbhakar jati. There are numerous jatis in India, of both Hindus and Muslims. Every person has been ascribed to such a group and, usually, the prestige accruing to one's jati is also self-ascribed. The systems through which the groups related to each other were limited to smaller territorial districts, with great variation in the composition and hierarchical positions that existed throughout India (Dumont 1980 [1970]).

On a more general level there is a separation of five groups; the four varnas and those not belonging to any of these, usually labelled 'the untouchables' or 'the dalits'. From old Sanskrit scriptural texts such as the *Manu Dharma Sastra*, we learn about the four varnas into which all Hindus are sectioned. These are the Brahman or priest, the Kshatriya or warrior-chief, the Vaisya or merchant and the Sudra or menial. In terms of ritual purity, the Brahmans are superior to the others, followed by Kshatriyas, Vaisyas and Sudras respectively, with the Dalits at the bottom or outside as the impure and inferior.

There is a general confusion regarding whether the word 'caste' should denote 'jati' or 'varna'. While scholars are mostly unified in agreeing that 'caste' is equivalent to 'jati', this is not so outside academic circles. Thus, one often reads sentences such as 'Phool Kumari belongs to that group of nearly 240 m Indians who have been traditionally kept out of the Hindu caste system' (Pandey 2008), which is from the article 'Caste shadows over school cook row' at BBC Online. Here caste refers to the varna system and the woman mentioned is a Dalit, and as such she is kept out of the varna system. But she has with all probability been born within a jati (this is not mentioned). Thus, as caste should refer to the jati and not to the varna, she is not 'kept out of the Hindu caste system' – she only belongs to the lowest rank of it.

Returning to the caste system as such, when we turn to Bengal, the situation is different. A general introduction to the caste system here will emphasize that in terms of the varna system only the Brahman and Sudra are indigenous to contemporary Bengali society (Sanyal 1981: 36, Davis 1983: 52–53). The Kshatriyas and the Vaisyas are not present. In this way the Bengali system bears resemblances to the better known South Indian 'tripartite division of Brahman, non-Brahman and Adi-Dravida' (Davis 1983: 53).

As such, there is no actual varna system as mentioned above. Instead there is a great number of jatis arranged hierarchically. Still, at least in scholarly works, it has long been common to discuss the Bengali jati-system with reference to varnas (e.g., Risley 1891, Sanyal 1981). Even as the Brahmans are often referred to as the *varnasreshta* or the highest varna, the Brahmans are also considered a jati, albeit the highest one. Historical texts show that the system has been rather flexible, with several jatis and sub-jatis moving up in the hierarchy (Sanyal 1981). But going by the prevalent tradition of the last two centuries, the jati-system in Bengal can be divided into six (or seven) groups. These are as follows: (a) the Brahmans, (b) the Baidyas and the Kayasthas, (c) the Nabasakh castes, (d) the castes ranking between the Nabasakhs, (e) the Ajalchal castes and (f) the Antyaj castes. All of the last five groups can be placed among the Sudras. One could also add the non-Hindus, the *mlecchas*, as a seventh group, but they can also be placed in the other lower jatis.

At the top of the hierarchy are the Bengali Brahman jatis. There are several ways of dividing these groups. One way is to divide them into five groups according to geographical origin. Another, more practical way, is to see the Brahmans as either clean or unclean. The clean ones are the *sat* ('good, unpolluted') Brahmans,[3] while the unclean are *patit* ('fallen') Brahmans, who have violated the code of conduct by acting as priests for the unclean groups among the Sudras.

In the same way, the Sudras can be divided into two groups, the *sat* Sudras and *asat* ('polluted') Sudras. Satsudras are also named *uttamasankara*, denoting the best or the highest stratum of *sankara* or mixed castes, or as *jalcharaniya*, which refers to the fact that water (*jal*) served by them is acceptable (*acharaniya*) to the Brahmans. The *satsudras* consist of the Nabasakh castes and the intermediate castes ranking between the Nabasakhs and the Ajalchal castes. The Nabasakhs were formed by nine (*naba*) branches (*sakh*) of the clean Sudras, but now the rank includes at least fourteen jatis. Among these were the Baidyas and the Kayasthas. The fourteen jatis who are usually included in the Nabasakhh rank Gandhabanik (spice-selling, druggist and grocer caste), Sankhabanik/Sankhari (shell-cutting caste), Kansabanik /Kansari (brazier caste), Tambulibanik/Tambuli (trading caste), Sadgop (agriculture caste), Tantubay/Tanti (weavers), Modak/Moyara (confectioner caste), Napit (barber caste), Tili (oil-presser caste), Malakar/Mali (garland maker and flower caste), Karmakar/Kamar (metal worker caste), Kumbhakar (potter caste), Barui (*pan* or betel leaf with areca nut, cultivator caste) and Madhunapit (confectioner caste) (Risley 1891a and b, Sanyal 1981: 115).

While the Baidyas and the Kayasthas are said to belong ritually to this group, their social position is much higher than the remaining twelve jatis (Sanyal 1981). As mainly landholders and professionals, they have gained an elevated position in the society and differ from the rest of the 'nine branches'-group who are mainly artisans, agriculturalists and traders. Thus, to complicate the picture even more, the Baidyas and the Kayasthas are often grouped

---

3 Also known as the *Sadbrāhmans*.

together with the Brahmans to constitute the higher caste group or *uchcha-jati*. Some of the Baidyas and the Kayasthas are known to have started using the sacred thread as the sign of being second-born. All jatis of the Nabasakh group share the right to offer a Brahman water and are entitled to services from the clean Brahmans in their religious functions. The next lower rank belongs to the intermediate castes (d), which can offer a Brahman water (*jalcharaniya*) but are served by unclean Brahmans.

The remaining groups are all unclean Sudras. The Ajalchal castes get their name from the fact that a Brahman will not accept water from them (*a* = not, *jal* = water, *chal* = acceptable). At the same time they are served by the unclean Brahmans. The Antyaj castes are the untouchables or *asprsya*: A touch from these can pollute not only the persons of people belonging to higher ranks, but even the sacred water of the River Ganga.

Almost all the jatis are subdivided into endogamous units, and these sub-jatis are variously known as *sreni*, *samay*, *asram* or *thak*. Again, the various srenis within a single jati are arranged hierarchically, but their positions are not as fixed as that between the jatis. Srenis are known to compete with each other for a superior position. Among the Kumbhakars, as for many other jatis, the srenis have probably been formed on the basis of technological differences or territorial affiliation. Bara Bhagiya and Chhota Baghiya are for instance two among several (historical) srenis of the Dhaka (capital of present Bangladesh) Kumbhakars, which are distinguished primarily because the former produce both black and red pottery and the latter make exclusively red pottery. The Bara Bhagiya is further divided into two groups, one specializing in black pottery and the other in red pottery (Risley 1891a: 518, Sanyal 1981: 22–23). Further, Kumbhakars in Bengal and Orissa belonged to various srenis which only existed locally. Thus, there were no Bara Bhagiya and Chhota Baghiya srenis outside the Dhaka area (Risley 1891a: 518–20). It should be added that this is according to historical material and ethnographical information collected around the end of the nineteenth century. As discussed later, at present there is little knowledge among the Kumbhakars concerning these divisions.

Each of the endogamous units was further divided into exogamous units called *gotras*. Gotras are patrilineal lineages that are mainly relevant with reference to marriage. When the size of the srenis or jatis, when it was undivided, was not large enough to guarantee that marriage always took place across the gotra sections, there were no divisions into gotras.

As noted earlier, the Kumbhakar jati belongs to the clean Sudras of the Nabasakha group. Thus their position is respectable and has been so for a long time (Risley 1891: 524). An interesting comparison that shows the great geographical variations of the caste system comes from the Sungaria and

Gadheria districts in the former Central Provinces. There the Kumars used to keep donkeys and pigs, which are regarded as impure:

> Sir D. Ibbetson said of him [the Kumar]: 'He is a true village menial; his social standing is very low, far below that of the Lohar [blacksmith] and not much above the Chamar [tanner]. His association with that impure beast, the donkey, the animal sacred to Sitala, the smallpox goddess, pollutes him and also his readiness to carry manure and sweepings.' (Russell 1916 Vol. 4: 6)

Also Bengali variety of the jati hierarchy has varied throughout history. The Baidyas and the Kayasthas are just two of many groups who have climbed to a more elevated position.

Hitesranjan Sanyal, in his historical study of social mobility in Bengal, argues that caste mobility has been a ubiquitous feature in the social life of Bengal (1981, 1971). Typically the process of caste mobility started with a change of hereditary occupation, usually to agriculture, since there earlier was an abundance of potentially arable land. The Sadgops represent such a group. They are an offshoot of the pastoral Gop or Goala caste who broke away from the main jati before the middle of the sixteenth century. Their switch to agriculture was only 'the starting point of rise to eminence' (ibid.: 75). Through extending their activities to trade, they established control over the land they had put under the plough. Thus, leaders from the group acquired political power at the local level. Later on the group also ventured into trade and worked as officials of the state and the big *jamidars*.[4] Members of the new group also made achievements in the fields of religion, and from dissident Gop families came popular saints like Syamananda and the founder of the influential Kartabhaja sect, Aulchand. In the process, they changed their jati affiliation by adding *sad* (*sat*, 'clean') to their name, thus becoming Sadgops. Control over land and political power together with the religious achievements of the Sadgops resulted in an elevation in their social prestige also within the society at large. Their separate identity as a unique jati was validated when the Sadgops were included among the Nabasakha jatis. Thus, from their starting position as members of a jati from whom a Brahman would not accept water, and who needed unclean Brahmans to perform their religious services, the dissidents were able to create a separate caste with a high social standing and a higher level of ritual purity among the Nabasakhas. While the Sadgops

---

4 জমিদার n. a landowne r, a zemindar, a landlord (Samsad Bengali–English Dictionary 2000: 390), also revenue collector.

represent a very successful example of upward mobility, it is not unparalleled. Many other groups have changed occupations to form new jatis and their position within the social and religious hierarchy has changed. Some, like the unclean Brahmans, have fallen, while others, like the Sadgops, have climbed. At least in the case of Bengal it seems that control over land or other kinds of economic advancement, combined with political power, initially raised a group's social standing; only secondarily has the ritual and religious position been raised accordingly.

Sanyal approaches the caste system as a system of hereditary occupational groups with a monopoly. The ritual and religious aspects are important, but always secondary. Thus, he writes: 'Security of livelihood in a non-competitive and hereditary system of economic organisation appears to have been one of the major reasons why different *jatis* remained loyal to the caste system' (Sanyal 1981: 26), and in this way secured their sustained existence in a village-based society. While this perspective is highly debatable, as we soon shall see, Sanyal is still able to communicate the Bengali version of the caste system as a system where mobility was integrated. With this in mind I will turn to the debates concerning the roles given within the caste system and the practices this entailed.

Conceptualizing and contextualizing caste

Caste has fascinated and interested orientalists and scholars for more than two centuries, and as a result the number of works concerning the subject is vast. Among all the works produced about caste, Dumont's *Homo Hierarchicus* (1980 [1970]) holds a unique position. Some argue that it represents something entirely new in terms of its approach to and understanding of the caste system, while others assert that it represents the culmination of preceding attempts (Khare 2006). Whichever stand one takes, Dumont's *Hierarchicus* is a good place to start when entering a discussion on how to approach and understand the caste system, as it provides for both looking back at earlier works and for looking forward to the subsequent debates and standpoints. In addition, the present work is not a study of the history of the caste system but rather a study of a piece of the caste system as it is practised in urban Kolkata in the twenty-first century. As such, this is not the place to provide another evaluation of the history of caste studies (e.g., Béteille 2005 [1996], Cohn 2004, Appadurai 1992, Dirks 1987 and 2001). So, let me begin with a discussion of Dumont.

Dumont's work with all its faults and limitations is still among the most important when one sets out to understand what caste is (or was) all about. It is an authoritative work, which is frequently cited even though over four decades have passed since its publication. Dumont still has a lot to teach most of us. While Dumont's work is not a dead horse in many ways, to frame the understanding of caste that this book promotes on a partial critique of Dumont is a valid and well-travelled road. In addition, due to *Homo Hierarchicus'* elevated position in the sociology of caste, it is also pedagogically a valid method. If students read anything at all about caste in their curriculum, it is often centred on Dumont's work. *Homo Hierarchicus* is a sort of the lowest common denominator when it comes to anthropologically informed knowledge about the caste system.

One major contribution to anthropological studies of caste made by Dumont has been his encouragement to make us 'think of caste in terms of ideology rather than in terms of empirically observable groups of people having some kind of essential identity' (Searl-Chatterjee and Sharma 1994: 6), and thus to enable us to 'escape from fruitless debates about whether caste has changed its "essential" character in the modern period' (ibid.: 9). What goes without saying is that caste as a set of essential characteristics, like specific practices of endogamous marriage and commensality rules, naturally changes according to changing circumstances across time and space. This is also the case, as I shall describe in later chapters, when it comes to the Kumars of Kumartuli. Being a caste-based professional in a caste-based neighbourhood of twenty-first century Kolkata has with all probability changed dramatically during the locality's 250 years of history. Consequently, to state that commensality rules as they were practised in the retired image-maker Niranjan's youth have been abandoned says little about the present caste system as such.

But what does Dumont imply in terms of the caste system as ideology? It should be noted that there is no valid way to give a brief account of Dumont's views without neglecting many important aspects; his analysis is too multi-faceted and complex for such an endeavour. Thus, the following account is partial and emphasizes mainly aspects that are important for my arguments.

Dumont, critiques and alternatives

Late professor Louis Dumont (1911–1998) was a French anthropologist who started his career working in India on concepts like holism and hierarchy (1980 [1970]), and who moved later to studies of national variants of individualism as an ideology mainly in the West (1986, 1994). With Claude Lévi-Strauss among his early mentors, Dumont belongs to the school of French structuralism. His work has made contemporaries like Edmund Leach, David Schneider and Stanley Tambiah mention him as one of the most prominent anthropologists of the second half of the twentieth century (Madan 2006a: vii). While Dumont left an extensive production of academic articles and books, it is his

Homo Hierarchicus, originally published in French in 1966 and translated into English in 1970, and then republished in a extended version in 1980, which stands as his single most influential work on the caste system. At this time Dumont had already spent much time in India, starting with his first fieldwork in 1949 and 1950 among the Pramalai Kallar caste in Tamil Nadu. In 1957 he launched and edited in collaboration with David Pocock entitled *Contributions to Indian Sociology. Homo Hierarchicus* was in many ways the culmination of many years of caste system studies undertaken by Dumont.

To Dumont, caste (jati) is a 'state of mind which is expressed by the emergence [...] of groups of various orders generally called "castes"' (1980 [1970]: 34). Thus the question of what caste is should be understood using the notion of the 'fixed principles' of the system which govern its 'fluid and fluctuating' elements (ibid.). The elements are the castes, internally divided in many ways and hierarchically arranged. As these systems vary empirically, according to which castes are present, how they are organized and how they behave relationally in space and time, Dumont sets out to describe the system as an ideology. In this sense, the system of castes as a system of ideas and values rests on common principles, making it possible to speak of '*the* caste system as a pan-Indian institution' (ibid.: 35).

The best way to describe the caste system is as a hierarchy; it is not as simple as 'a linear order going from the highest to the lowest' (Dumont 1980 [1970]: 39), arranging all castes with one group above and one below (except the one at the top and the one at the bottom). But empirically this is not valid, since in many cases it is impossible to provide a definite place in the hierarchy for many castes (an important insight that many Dumont critics miss). Thus, we have to emphasize that the hierarchical system in the ideological sense is ranked by principles that can be reduced to a specific structure. This structure consists of oppositions. The main opposition that structures the caste system Dumont that points to is that between the ritually pure and the impure:

> *The whole is founded on the necessary and hierarchical coexistence of the two opposites* [...] This fact is of extreme importance, since it transports us at once into a purely structural universe: it is the whole which governs the parts, and this whole is very rigorously conceived as based on an opposition. (Dumont 1980 [1970]: 43, italics in original)

It is this opposition – pure/impure – that is not 'the *cause* of all the distinctions of caste [... rather] it is their *form*' (Dumont 1980: 45). Thus Dumont still manages to separate the domains of the empirical and the ideological in his hierarchy of value, which demands that the pure and the impure are kept apart.

Another important point for Dumont is that the caste hierarchy as holisti-
cally conceived is relatively independent of 'natural inequalities or the distribution of power' (1980 [1970]: 20): it is independent in the sense that the ritual
status of the caste system encompasses power. There is a distinction between
power and hierarchical status (1980 [1970]: 37). This grants the Brahmans the
highest position in the society (ritual status), while the Kshatriyas as the ruling
class and power-holders are accommodated within the hierarchical caste system (Khare 2006: 18). It is exactly this subordination in ideological terms of
power to status that distinguishes the Hindu caste system from other seemingly
similar structures (Dumont 1980 [1970]: 216, Searl-Chatterjee and Sharma
1994: 3).

We are thus left with a description of India where ritual status based on
the superiority of the pure to the impure is the ideology that encompasses
almost everything. This provides the Indians with a holistic way of thinking.
The other possibility would be the individualistic way of thinking (Dumont
1980: 9). Dumont also equates holistic societies with traditional ones and individualistic societies with modern ones (ibid.), and his necessary conclusion
is: 'India represented a premodern mode of thinking and social organisation'
(Searl-Chatterjee and Sharma 1994: 4). This is a topic that will be further
discussed later in this chapter.

Before I turn to the critiques, it is important to note that the rigid and
unchanging structuring of the caste system does not deny that 'territory or
locality [...] intervenes at the level of the concrete manifestations of the caste
system' (Dumont 1980 [1970]: 36). Thus, at the empirical level on the ground
there exist many caste systems, but ideologically there is only one.

Critiques of Dumont's theory of the caste system have been and still are
plentiful (for a few recent overviews, see Khare (ed.) 2006, Gupta (ed.) 2004,
Parry 1994, Searl-Chatterjee and Sharma (ed.) 1994,). While a few have taken
a positive stand (Madan 2006b), most of those working on caste have responded
negatively to at least parts of his theory. The multitude of attacks and critical comments are impossible to reproduce in the context of this book. What
follows are a few common and relatively contemporary critiques relevant to
the overall project of this book. While Dumont's shift towards the ideological
aspects of caste and his emphasis on the rules or structure that constitute the
various empirically observable groups is an important new approach (Searl-
Chatterjee and Sharma 1994), in other aspects Dumont might be seen as representing an approach that dates back to the early colonial orientalists (Dirks
1987). In this latter respect he does not represent something new, but rather
stands at the end of an old theoretical and methodological line.

A major problem with Dumont is that to some extent he reproduces the
viewpoint concerning caste often described as Brahmanical (Gupta 2004,

Parry 1994, Dirks 1987). Brahmans were given a larger than legitimate role in the conception of Indian society, and Dumont also provides us with a view on the caste system that privileges Brahmans and their conceptions of purity. Surely, hierarchy as informed by the pure–impure dichotomy has an impact on the caste system, but caste assertion and dignity makes caste itself as important by providing discrete identities that lead to the articulation of multiple and contesting hierarchies (Gupta 2004: vii). This has probably always been so, even as colonialism did make a difference in privileging the Brahmanical view. In contemporary India, ritual dominance does not 'determine the nature of caste interaction [...] the pure hierarchy [...] is left unattended on the wayside' (Gupta 2004: ix). Castes that were seen as 'sudra-like' in status have empowered themselves politically and economically, often based on caste identities. The pure and encompassing hierarchy of Dumont perhaps became a reality for a short period after the colonial encounter, but now it 'stands bereft of empirical support from practically every quarter of Hindu India' (Gupta 2004: x). Before the consolidation of colonial power and its understanding of caste, the hierarchy that was expressed on the local level was the one that had economic and political power behind it (ibid.). The view of caste groups other than the Brahmans on the caste system and the hierarchy was and is different. Dumont is said to have

> failed to see that each caste valued itself highly and had deep pockets of ideological inheritance from which it could draw continuous symbolic energy for both political activism and economic competition. (Gupta 2004: x–xi)

This critique is substantiated by Sanyal's description of social mobility in Bengal that I cited above. It seems evident that the Brahman notion of hierarchy was never as encompassing as scholars often tend to assume; assertive caste identities were and are not controlled by Brahmanical and, I may add, Dumontian renditions. The encompassing (Brahmanical) ideology depicted by Dumont does in some ways deny Indians any agency, denying that they can act based on their distinct caste identities in opposition to the pure hierarchy posited by the Brahmanical ideology (Searl-Chatterjee and Sharma 1994). At this point it is important to note that this critical understanding of Dumont is based on empirical material on contemporary castes that was not available earlier. Dipankar Gupta states:

> It would be incorrect to rush to the conclusion that castes have changed in contemporary India. What we should acknowledge instead is that contemporary transparencies have brought to light aspects of caste

previously darkened by imperfect lenses. Caste has not changed, but the
potentialities that were always there within this stratificatory system are
now out in the open, and in full view. [...] Castes cannot change intrinsi-
cally as long as they are fundamentally founded on identities that draw
their substance from a rhetoric of natural differences that are imbued
with notions of purity and impurity. (2004: xix–xx)

As we shall see, the rhetoric of natural differences is something that is often
communicated by the Kumars. Their membership in the clay-working caste
is something that is 'in their blood', it comes naturally to them. This is even
so in a time when only a minority of them choose to pursue the occupational
specialization connected to their caste. What we are left with is a Brahmanical
notion of caste and hierarchy that is a contested proposition among other jatis
and not a central principle. Through placing other (non-Brahmanical) groups
at the centre of our studies, different sets of values and hierarchies will emerge.
Searl-Chatterjee and Sharma actually argue that we should regard caste in
terms of a system of action (flexible and mutable) or as a collection of modes
of action, as something people 'do' or is 'done to them' if they are Dalits, upon
whom restrictions are imposed by others (1994: 9). Identity, so often mentioned by Gupta (2004), emerges in certain situations and is complementary
to a perspective on action. Thus, we can follow Dumont by discarding debates
concerning changes and variations in 'essential' characteristics. On the other
hand, instead of approaching caste as an encompassing pure hierarchy, one
can see caste as providing assertive identities and motivations for action. This
approach is also described by Michelutti, who shows how the Yadavs use their
caste affiliation to argue for their position in politics because politics is in their
blood (2004). The result on the ground is multiple hierarchies informed by a
great number of ideologies where the Brahmanical distinction between the
pure and the impure is not the sole, or even a major, value.

The relation between ritual status and power is another contested point in
Dumont's work. Again, this is seen as part of the Brahmanical notion of pure
hierarchy. That status does not follow power creates a disjunction. Dumont's
description of how the Brahmans stood above the rest in the Indian society
with a special reference to the Kshatriya rulers is not shown to be substantiated in any convincing way (e.g., Dirks 1987). According to Robert Parkin, this
'devaluation of the Kshatriya's allotted place in Hindu thought has caused
Dumont more problems than anything else' (2003: 160).

Historically informed approaches often view notions of the caste system
in the light of former, often British, colonial, descriptions and analyses. The
extreme stance taken by Bayly is that the caste system was more or less created by the British in colonial times (1999), even as she importantly draws

our attention to the ethnic-like features of caste in post-colonial India that make it a modern phenomenon. A more consensual position is that 'colonialism *did* make a difference [… and that the] way British officials understood caste obviously also affected the way caste was practised' (Gupta 2004: xii). A central example is how the British gave the Brahmans 'a larger than legitimate role' (ibid.) in the Indian society. This is viewed as the reason why the Brahmans were seen as superior in the hierarchy, since their own perception gave them that position. Another aspect is the all-encompassing role given to caste and religion. An important work in this critical tradition is Bernhard S. Cohn's article on the role of colonial census-making as it concerned caste and its impact on how we came to understand the caste system (2004). One of Cohn's students, Nicholas Dirks, has also worked on the role of colonialism in how caste came to be both understood and practised (1989, 2001). Moreover, Dirks states that socioeconomic features other than caste made and continue to make an impact in India. Notions of home-place, family, artistic capabilities and, more recently, level of education were and are additional sources of identity and markers of self-representation that motivate practice (Dirks 1992, Beteille 2005 [1991]. The role of pure hierarchy gets diminished while at the same time the caste system becomes one among many possible sources of identity and motivations for action.

Caste today

It should be clear by now that 'caste' or 'the caste system' does not denote a simple ideology, set of practices or essential traits that lend themselves to easy description. Because it is such a highly contested concept, it is difficult to provide a unified description of what caste means. However, a few insights from the above discussion will certainly help us.

First, and perhaps less controversially, the caste system in the empirical sense has been and is continually changing. Common correlates of caste such as inter-dining restrictions and occupational specialization find little empirical support today. As Béteille (2002) has noted in his discussion of the phenomenon of caste-free occupations, caste and occupation did not neatly dovetail in the past either (Gupta 2004: xix). Commensality rules should not be considered to be totally ignored at present: '[it is] just that spaces for such strategic moves are more limited now than what was true generations back' (ibid.). And just as the colonial understanding of caste affected the way caste was practised through privileging Brahmanical notions (Dirks 1987, Parry 1994, Gupta 2004), urbanization has also affected the practice of caste (e.g., Kolenda 1986 in Searl-Chatterjee 1994). Approaching caste armed with a set of essential characteristics is thus necessarily going to be rather fruitless.

From this it follows that any representation of the caste system, be it ideological or empirical, is of necessity partial and subject to the contributor's own position. In short terms, any representation is grounded in time (historically) and space (geographically). Thus, the caste system as a set of ideas and values structured by hierarchical oppositions is an analysis of a limited set of cases from a few limited periods in a few restricted areas of India. As a partial description and theory it is not necessarily wrong, but as a holistic description it certainly is. This is perhaps the major mistake made by Dirks in *The Hollow Crown*, where he tends to simply replace the Brahman with the Kshatriya and thus reproduce the holistic structure of Dumont (Gupta 2004).

Caste should not automatically be given priority when it comes to identity formation among Indians. Several studies over the last few decades demonstrate convincingly that the priority granted to caste is largely of British colonial origin (Cohn 2004, Dirks 2001). Empirically speaking, the role given to caste by individuals and groups varies enormously. Empirical studies of the caste system that attempt to establish a given number of fixed traits that define it are evidently fruitless (Gupta 2004), along with ideological studies setting out to provide us with a pan-Indian set of values and ideas. Caste is, as Jayaram (1996) states, tremendous flexible.

Still, empirical studies concerning the role given to the caste system, as well as caste-notions that are acted upon, provide us with the necessary means to approach caste comparatively. Even while the caste system (as well as modernity) is recognizable all over the Indian subcontinent this does not mean it represents the same thing to every group. Yes, there is an important element of hierarchy in any depiction of the caste system and sometimes egalitarian forms might also be found (Parry 1974, Searl-Chatterjee and Sharma 1994), which together with notions of purity have been and sometimes still are motivating certain behaviours, like marriage. But the hierarchy is most often viewed differently if one takes the view of a different group than the Brahmans (like colonial orientalists and Dumont) or Kshatriyas (like Dirks). Thus, one has to ask in each case what motivates certain actions, and to what extent these is part of an assertive caste identity (Searl- Chatterjee and Sharma 1994 and Gupta 2004). Only through such an approach might we reach an understanding of caste system(s), which are more attuned to other important aspects of caste than the one described by Dumont.

Dumont insisted that 'caste as a system of relations of a particular kind exists or does not exists; [and] it does not change' (Madan 1999:479 in Khare 2006: 17). Consequently, 'genuine caste can exist only in that synchronic [ahistorical], traditional [non-modern] India, and only as long as the ideology of hierarchical opposition holds supreme' (Khare 2006: 17). The caste system in the Dumontian sense is thus largely nonexistent in the context of contemporary India and Kumartuli. While we have established an alternative to Dumont's 'genuine caste', it is time to briefly approach *commodification*.

Commodification and Authenticity

Commodification designates the process through which something, anything, gains economic value. It is generally understood that an increasing number of arenas enter into exchange systems, most notably those of capitalism and neo-liberalism. These arenas are not necessarily directly connected to the material process of appropriation of nature to satisfy human beings' wants and needs (Harvey 1999). Today body parts and human lives have a price tag, art is all about investing in turbulent times and wombs are for rent (Nash 2000). Culture has also become, if not an outright commodity, then at least com-modified. This is especially so within the tourist industry (Cole 2007), where descent and ethnicity are essential parts of the packages sold by mainly, but not solely, minority communities in ethno-parks. It is the *ethnoprise* of *ethno-commodities* (Comaroff and Comaroff 2009).

Culture, identity and ethnicity are brought into the market. This is often done through an explicit emphasis on representing something authentic that outsiders and insiders alike can savour (ibid.), of something that someone has sought to monopolize (Harvey 1999 and 2002). Uniqueness is often important in commodification processes as it connects to exclusive control.

Caste is traditionally linked to subsistence, to occupation. As such it might seem strange to emphasize how caste is used by the clay-workers to sell arte-facts made of clay. In South Asia economical transactions (and exploitation) were to a large extent dialectically connected to the caste system.

As the upcoming narratives will show, within the Bengali tradition of image-making the Kumars had no monopoly on production. Further, with the advent of community pujas and the subsequent production of readymade religious clay statues for sale at the local bazaar, the competition between pro-ducers became detached from their caste background. And, as I shall argue throughout this book, commodification entails features different from those connecting caste with occupation. In the Kumartuli of today branding, mar-keting, place and caste identity are brought together.

Fieldwork in Kumartuli

'You have insects in your head [laughing]. Just like me [knocks his index-finger on his head] – insects in the head, coming all this way to Kumartuli to ask questions about our history', said the senior Niranjan, during one of our talks that took place during my fieldwork. I spent nine months in the field in the course of five visits, starting from March 2006 and lasting until autumn 2007. In addition, over the last fifteen years I have visited Kolkata several times and spent a total of around two years in the city. I crisscrossed this part of Kolkata using *egaro numbar bas*, bus number eleven, i.e., walking on two legs, in order to get a feel for its various streets, buildings, *paras, tolas, tulis*, neighbourhoods, back alleys, *bajars* (markets), *ghats* (river beds), parks, communities and ponds. For me it has been a lot of talking while walking. I have my favourite tea shops in the various parts of this area where tea sellers know what I like. I have friends living here whom I can visit whenever I feel the need for some *adda*, chatting, or a rest. I know the shortcuts through the alleys and the cultural fabrics of the various areas. Furthermore, I know enough Bengali to make simple conversations and do interviews; something not quite common for foreign visitors to Kolkata and Kumartuli, who usually never talk to the Kumars and who the Kumars feel are out of reach of contact. This combined knowledge of Kolkata's cityscape and history, as well as Bengali, made my access to informants in Kumartuli a rather easy one.

The independent Maliks and their families became my main informants. This largely leaves out their labourers and other residents of Kumartuli with different occupations. While I have talked to numerous people in Kumartuli, I conducted in-depth interviews with 20 persons, of which three were females. This group of informants ranged age-wise from 17 to 86 years. Six male artists can be said to constitute the core informants, with whom I spent most time at work and at their homes.

In addition, I talked to some of the workshop labourers and people working in Kumartuli who were employed in other professions connected to idol-making (e.g., dress and adornment makers). I have also visited Kumars working outside Kumartuli.

It is Kumartuli as a neighbourhood that to a certain extent defines my informants, together with their occupation as independent artists. While some of the workshop-owners live within Kumartuli, nowadays most of them have their family homes outside.[5] The size of the workshops varies. Some are little less than a small shelter by the road, making the road the major place for actual work, whereas others have large buildings that can accommodate many workers and produce large murtis.

Open-ended interviews about memories of the past and perceptions of the present, and recollections of stories that the elders tell, are central to this project. The language of most of the interviews was Bengali, although a small number

---

5 I lived in Maniktola, which is less than 3 km away to the southwest of Kumartuli, during most of my fieldwork.

were done in a combination of English and Bengali (for the sake of both the informants and me). Again, the majority of interviews were accomplished with the help of my research assistant. My own skills in Bengali make it possible for me to carry out interviews, but in too simplified a way to be satisfactory. However, while working with the assistant, I also took part in the Bengali conversation. Almost every interview was recorded. Translation and transcription of the interviews was carried out both with and without the assistant. Working with the assistant during transcription made it possible to delve more deeply into the various meanings of words, sayings, rituals and their objects and so on, as the topics could be discussed in depth as they occurred in the recorded interviews.

Being familiar with the process of making the idols is crucial. Since the Kumars identify themselves through their work, it is necessary to develop a good understanding of what they are actually doing. In addition, a lot of information is embedded in the process, like the changing attributes of the idols and the Kumars' relations to 'their' god Bishwakarma. Most of the Malik artists do not make the actual murtis. Their work is to decide a murti's appearance, often in collaboration with the customer. Traditionally, however, they should at least make the most important parts themselves, which are the fingers and the face. This is however not always the case any longer. Young Kumars who want to join the profession themselves, or who are asked by their fathers to do so, must usually learn the process. They will spend much time making small statues and portraits, thereby acquiring the needed knowledge. Due to my fragmented fieldwork, the fact that I am already adult and, perhaps most important, a saheb, it was difficult for me to take part in the actual process. Since the main informants did little clay work themselves on an everyday basis, it never happened naturally that I engaged in the practice of making murtis. However, I spent time with them learning the process, what the labourers are supposed to do and what to expect from them. I learned how to evaluate the quality of work and appreciate various styles. In this aspect, I participated in the work of the Maliks.

There are few academic works on the Kumars. Two unpublished PhD theses on Kumartuli in English have been submitted, while there is supposedly one in Bengali. The two English theses are Beth Goldblatt's economically oriented study, *The Image Makers of Kumartuli. The Transformation of a Caste-Based Industry in a Slum Quarter of Calcutta* (1979) and J. D. Robinson's study *The Worship of Clay Images in Bengal* (1983), which centres on iconographic development and religious practices. While both theses provide reliable ethnographic information from dissimilar points of view, both lack a theoretically grounded analysis. Newspapers have for the last three or four decades written more and more about Kumartuli. This represents the largest collection of texts on Kumartuli. I, however, was more interested in talking with the Kumars.

On oral history

Within anthropology, oral history resembles the ethnographic interview in general, as diachronic studies have enjoyed waves of popularity throughout the history of anthropology. In this way anthropologists have always been interested in oral history. My emphasis on oral history derives from the prominence I gave to the Kumars' history as they told it themselves in the ethnographic interviews I did. Sidney Mintz emphasized that the anthropologist records individual histories in order to understand the cultural patterns of a society as exhibited through the representative teller's worldview. Thus, the anthropologist 'must have a conception of how people are at once products and makers of the social and cultural systems within which they are lodged' (Mintz 1990 [1979]: 302). The ethnographic interview encapsulates oral history, which in this book is seen as a special attention to historical accounts given by the informants as explanations of their society or life world. The histories they tell constitute a counterhistory. As such, the stories are approached as being culturally embedded in the present-day world. Thus, oral history provides more than information from living witnesses to supplement the data provided by the classic written sources with its dominant actors, and opens up both the history and the current period of common people (Wachtel 1990: 1). And the 'common people' traditionally approached by the anthropologists were usually without writing. Their history was of necessity oral. This is not the case for the Kumars. They live in a society where writing has existed for at least two thousand years. Still, it is only during the previous century that the Kumars have become literate. But whatever little that is written *about* them has not been not written *by* them. Their histories are still very much oral.

Oral stories, their traditions, form and content, provide us with one of many possible perspectives on a given society. They both reveal and enact local attitudes, but not through simply representing 'a "slice of life"; [since] the attitudes and actions, fears and fantasies, they depict are not raw data' (Blackburn 2007: 419). Almost a century ago Franz Boas described oral history as a form of native ethnography in a much cited paragraph. In his attempt to provide

> a presentation of the culture as it appears to the Indian himself [he] spared no trouble to collect descriptions of customs and beliefs in the language of the [Kwakiutl] Indians, because in these *the points that seem important to him are emphasized*, and the almost unavoidable distortion contained in the descriptions given by the casual visitor and student is eliminated. (Boas 1909:309, italics added)

Moreover, oral stories present us with reflections or commentaries abstracted from everyday life that are 'shaped according to local narrative conventions and taste [... they] both reflect and reflect upon society' (Blackburn 2007: 420).

As living sources, the informants possess 'unlike inscribed stones or sheaves of paper, the ability to work with us in a two-way process' (Thompson 1988: 149). This signifies what Gold, following the anthropologist C. Nadia Seremtakis, means when she writes that 'oral history is a natal event, an emergent process having much in common with performance' (Gold 2002: 80). The 'reflective insights of retrospection' (Thompson 1988: 148) make oral history different from traditional history. Recollections made during interviews become new or born-again. They are coloured by the processes and by the context of telling. This can easily be noted when informants, during interviews, add that they 'never have told this to anyone before. It has been too painful, but this is the truth – you should know about it' (Gour 2005: 3rd interview). As an outsider, one can get access to recollections that informants will not reveal to insiders. Conversely, many try to hide certain recollections; there is always a degree of *impression management* (Goffman 1971 [1959]) at work. The stories or recollections of the past are in this way not purely records of the past, they are also alive in the present. An old anthropological orthodoxy concerning such historical approaches based on oral history is that they are out of place, since the history of people without a textual tradition 'is only an elaborate commentary on the [...] structure we see before us' (Shryock 1997: 22). Moreover, Shryock mentions Peters (1967) as going even further in denying people without written records a history, since their 'oral tradition – which might not be a tradition at all – is too lively to be used as evidence of a past which is truly *behind* us' (ibid.). This highlights the difficulties concerning the use of oral history: at the same time as it is a social commentary on contemporary events, it brings to light events from the past. Truly, oral history provides us with histories as they are seen, heard and experienced on the ground among the people who tell them. So what kind of history are we able to get concerning a past that is truly behind us?

An important step is to understand that recollections or memories 'offer multiple and conflicting versions of the same event [providing us with] a more robust, multidimensional reality – giving access to polysemy, multiple meanings that may challenge dominant discourses' (Gold 2002: 82). I have not attempted to create a univocal story, but will let the informants' voices be heard with their conflicting stories. According to Shahid Amin, one should not counterpose local remembrance against authorized accounts and, I will add, one version against another, as traditional historians do (1995). Instead, by putting the contradicting versions on display, one can enhance the 'possibilities of arriving at a more nuanced narrative, a thicker description' (ibid.). Some dates turn up, like that of Independence and the subsequent Partition in 1947. Others can easily be found, as when Gandhiji or Netaji made a certain speech at a given place, or as named politicians were in charge. A historical framework will be given, but the various recollections of the lived experience of a given period in Kumartuli will not be counterposed against this framework. The recollections must be seen as adding to the framework, bringing it to life.

Among the Kumars there is also a conception of what their own stories constitute with reference to a more general history. Thus, let us turn to the indigenous categories for the stories they tell. In a Bengali context history is often referred to as itihas.[6] As Östör writes:

> Itihasa is no philosopher's stone for turning out facile interpretations [... it] does not offer a chronology or even a history of the past in the western sense, rather it is the account of past fragments arrested in the social process of the present. (1984: 22)

While itihas might well be used to refer to academic history in the western sense, there is another sense of the word, a sense that does not necessitate a chronology, even though it is often present; or necessitate a given point on a consensual timeline, even though this also often occurs; or require a proper demarcation from what in an academic setting might be described as legend or myth. Itihas in the vernacular sense can thus be seen as rather similar to ethnography (Östör 1984: 14), as both practices bring to light 'both a model of action and a model for action [following Geertz (1973)], a series of representations and interpretations that may reveal the structures and processes of social relations, the categories that shape and are shaped by practices' (Östör 1984: 21). In this depiction of itihas we find similarities with Boas's suggestion concerning oral stories.

In the field I often initially presented myself as working on the Kumars' and Kumartuli's history. I often asked whether the given informant could tell me anything about kumarer itihas or kumartulir itihas. A frequent reply was that 'Kumartuli's itihas... I do not know that much, but I can tell you a galpa[7] [story]'. Then they went on to talk about the antiquity of their jati or Kumartuli, before the 'interview' went into more specific areas with new stories depending on the direction of the informants' discourse and my questions. In this way, most Kumars referred to their histories as [in Östör's description], stories. Thus, when they narrate their past it is through (re-)telling stories. In this I experienced a certain reluctance to enter the field of history. Among most contemporary Kumars, itihas is probably mainly seen as the work of academics (like me), a large project of a certain group of professionals. Still, when the

---

6 ইতিহাস is the Bengali word.
7 গল্প. The word is also used for fictitious narratives, but it is not in this sense that the Kumars use the word in the context of narrating their past.

Kumars refer to galpa and not itihas as the term depicting what they tell me, I see the stories as the fragments that the Kumars bring into the present; it is these multivocal fragments combined that make up their itihas. The Kumars' conception of itihas differs thus from the description given by Östör. The difference might be explained by the time span between his works in Bishnupur in the 1970s and mine, and the fact that Bishnupur is a town on the periphery while Kolkata is very much in the centre of West Bengal. Among the Kumars there is a clear conception of history as an academic subject taught at schools and universities; thus they equate itihas with academic history. Galpa as used by the Kumars corresponds more to Östor's description of itihas. This might very well be a result of modernity.

In this way, the Kumars approvingly provided me with their stories so that I could write their history. And while this history might only provide a very partial, distorted and polysemic picture of a multidimensional past, it reveals some of the priorities made by contemporary Kumars when they describe their own heritage. Oral history, perhaps more than regular academic history, provides us with a society's own perspectives and as such their own evaluation of what makes them who they are at present. Accordingly, when a Kumar's story is retold in this book it is not merely a story describing the past. It is equally important to understand the story as a reflection upon contemporary everyday life.

Kumartuli and the world

As spending time in the workshops learning the method of making clay statues and doing in-depth interviews constitute the major methodological approaches of this work, it would be easy to create an image of Kumartuli as an isolated and self-sufficient neighbourhood. However, the changes that have made Kumartuli into what it is at present cannot be understood without a proper appreciation of the wider context of the Kumars. While a thorough description and analysis of the vast networks that the Kumars are a part of lies outside the main focus of this book, a few notes on these networks must be mentioned.

The artists represent a group in terms of caste, occupation, religion and so on and thus are a part of larger systems involving the society as a whole. Investigating the interlinking of castes has been a common feature in much Indian anthropology, which seeks to demonstrate the functions and ritual importance of this type of organization of society. A memorable example is *Village India* edited by McKim Marriott (1955). Further, the systems that the Kumars form a part of do not concern only exchange of status and other objects of art or ritual significance. Mundane matters of modern life such as education, news, technology, sources of inspiration like movies and so on also constitute flows within the system in which the Kumars live.

Furthermore, the Kumars do not constitute a singular, homogenous group. The various individuals represent highly differentiated points of convergence in various flows. A simple illustration is that while some Kumars have cable television and broadband internet access at their homes, others have only a radio and hardly any knowledge of what the internet is. While some have an education at university level, others cannot even read properly. Consequently, within the small area of Kumartuli there lives a group sharing a caste and occupation, but which otherwise is highly complex.

To link the group studied to wider systems of exchange is now common within anthropology. While anthropologists had 'a tendency to treat societies [...] as if they were islands unto themselves, with little sense of the larger systems of relations in which these units are embedded' (Ortner 1984: 142), this is not the case any longer. The occasional works that view societies as lacking a larger context are at present in something of an unclassifiable freak category, to paraphrase Ortner (ibid.).

The 'field' of the fieldwork has as a result changed, and even as fieldwork remains the hegemonic practice within the discipline (Gupta and Ferguson 1997: 3), there are today many examples of how this practice encapsulates the new field. The new landscape that constitutes the field is described by Appadurai in the early 1990s as follows:

> As groups migrate, regroup in new locations, reconstruct their histories, and reconfigure their ethnic 'projects', the *ethno* in ethnography takes on a slippery, nonlocalized quality, to which the descriptive practices of anthropology have to respond. The landscapes of group identity – the ethnoscapes – around the world are no longer familiar anthropological objects, insofar as groups are no longer tightly territorialized, spatially bounded, historically selfconscious, or culturally homogenous. (Appadurai 1991: 191)

Even as the geographical 'field' of this study can be described in terms of a limited number of streets and buildings on a map, the community of informants is not territorially fixed and stable, since it consists of a changing set of convergences of flows from local and global networks of people and knowledge (Appadurai 1991). Still following Appadurai, a major question that needs to be addressed is 'what is the nature of locality, as lived experience, in a globalized deterritorialized world?' (1991: 196).

Thus, with the stories of the present day Maliks as the core, modernity and caste form the major layers through which the investigation will take place. The knowledge that they take part in larger systems that reach far beyond the few streets lined with half-finished murtis and workshops that makes up the physical and geographical field of Kumartuli will always be between the lines.

As noted above, I am an outsider in Kumartuli, in terms of my native country, education, economy and appearance. This book will not be available to the great majority of my informants since it is written in English for mainly academic readers. It represents a sort of knowledge that is not synchronous with the knowledge of the Kumars, even as it claims to contain small parts of it. This is a fact that the informants are aware of. Only a few asked if they would get a copy, concrete evidence that I did what I told them I was doing. No one ever believed that I could help them in any way, except one younger person who asked me about my opinion on how to make Kumartuli more attractive for foreign tourists. In short, my role as a fieldworker, and what to expect from me, was understood by my informants.

In my attempt to convey, contextualize and interpret the Kumar Maliks' models of their world, I believe it is imperative that I provide space to their own voices, even though these are translated into English. It is my hope that through this strategy the knowledge which the Kumars gave me concerning their life remains theirs even in a book carrying my name.

An Outline of the Book

The main aim of this book is to provide a more complete set of narratives of the image-making Maliks of Kumartuli in a theoretically informed analysis. Throughout the fieldwork a number of features have repeatedly appeared as significant traits of the life and work of Kumars. I have chosen the four most common characteristics that recurred as important topics in their self-representation. First, there is the common self-presentation of the Kumars as innovative artists. Second is the importance given to their concept of the ancestral home or *adibari*, be it in former East or West Bengal. Third is the economic situation with reference to seasonal work, the necessity of borrowing money and the high degree of professionalism with which the art business is run. And fourth is the impact of higher education among the younger generation of Kumars. These four topics are further described as they develop historically.

The following chapter (Chapter 2) provides an introduction to the field of study, the present-day Kumars of Kumartuli. Their social organisation and demography will be dealt with, together with their work and the various pujas they create their images for. I discuss Kumartuli's history, contextualized within an introductory history of Kolkata and Durga Puja based mainly on the secondary literature. Then I turn to the narratives of the Kumars concerning both their origins and their lives in the nineteenth century through to the beginning of the twentieth century. Durga Puja is given special emphasis here, as throughout the book, as this puja is the basis of the existence of Kumartuli, as well as being Bengal's most important puja in terms of size and popularity. An important feature in the Kumars' narratives of bygone days is their self-representation as constitutive elements of society.

The famous image-maker Gopeswhar Pal and the role of innovation are central topics of Chapter 3. Roughly speaking, this period around 1920 represents the settlement of modernity among the Kumars. Gopeswhar's new approach to design epitomizes the transformation of the work and the market of clay modelling. From this change in the hitherto relatively conformist iconography, the Kumar as artist starts to take shape. This period also witnesses the growing popularity of communal Durga Pujas, *sarbajanin*[8] *durgutsab*.

As a central topic in the histories of the Kumars, the recollection of past days, mention of the Partition of India in the wake of Independence in 1947 recurs in most discourse with the Kumars. Thus, Chapter 4 is mainly about Partition stories. Partition meant the arrival of East Bengali Kumars who settled in Kumartuli as image-makers. Even though they belonged to the same caste, this created a divide in the local society which is still visible. Notions of ancestral home, or *adibari*, are seen as more important than caste affiliation. Partition is a tidemark in the history of Kumartuli and a central event in the self-representations of the Kumars.

A detailed presentation of the economics of Kumartuli is given in Chapter 5. The focus is on the late 1960s and the 1970s with nationalization of private banks, the Naxalite insurgency and the unionization of wage labourers. While both the introduction of a market for the sale of murtis in the early decades of the century and increased popularity of pujas after Independence changed the economics of murti making, the 1970s represent an important period in the memory of the contemporary image-makers. The development of a small-scale art industry made it possible for the more successful workshop-owners to provide their children with access to higher education, thereby paving the ground for the commodification of caste.

The impact of education organizes Chapter 6. The new financial strength of the most popular Maliks, or workshop-owners, is primarily used to provide higher education for the younger generation. This generation has now entered Kumartuli with their degrees in art and business from colleges and universities. The Internet becomes an important tool; a degree in art becomes an asset in securing contracts with clients. The divide in Kumartuli is now between

---

8 সর্বজনীন, *a.* good for all, universally good; universal; public, common (Samsad Bengali–English Dictionary 2000: 990). Also written সার্বজনীন, sārbajanin (ibid.: 1007).

those who have education and those who don't. At the same time, the project of turning Kumartuli into a multi storied heritage centre is the current culmination of commodifying caste.

Finally, in Chapter 7 I return to the overall approach to a caste-based community in the twenty-first century. During the past hundred years, Kumartuli as a site has changed little, but the Kumars have. Starting out in some cases as newly settled artisans from Nadia (and later East Bengal), the Kumars are now artists and businessmen and women actively engaged in a globalized world. We have followed the Kumars as they talk about their life and work, from informal know-how concerning clay-modelling using artistic and innovative capabilities, to formalized know-how concerning art and business in a global market. Based on these insights I argue for a new understanding of modernity that goes beyond narratives of European Enlightenment, capitalism, rationalism and so on, as the possible genealogies of various modernities should not be part of its definition. It is a modernity through which caste has been converted into an advantage through its commodification in order to legitimate control of the market.

As I have noted above, the general outline of this book is historical. I begin with the beginning of Kumartuli in the seventeenth and eighteenth centuries, and end with the present situation, where education in a globalized world is a major topic. Along the way, there are chapters on the introduction of new murti styles in the 1920s, Partition in 1947 and economic reforms and political unrest in the 1960s and 1970s. Cutting across this chronological structure is the use of a number of cases connected to each chapter – cases that centre on the various topics mentioned. Thus, Chapter 3 is not only about changes in the profession that take place in the first half of the twentieth century; more importantly it is about the role of innovation and the artistic aspects of the profession until the present. The chapter that makes Partition the major topic is also about caste affiliations and belonging, as social organization within Kumartuli is based on notions of adibari. This affects how the place is organized even today. When I discuss economics with cases mainly dating thirty to forty years back, I also draw the argument as far back as the nineteenth century with its economic realities. Education as an asset in contemporary Kumartuli is generally about the kind of modernity that the younger generation express with reference to knowledge. Again, I return to older, emic perspectives on knowledge.

Ethnographically speaking, the histories of Kumartuli as told by the Kumars are thus about the individual artists, social structure, economic features and knowledge. What prevents this book from being a proper work in the tradition of the likes of Malinowski and Radcliff-Brown is a chapter on religion. While the entire book is about the making of the clay deities that unite most Bengali

Hindus, the absence among Kumars of religious sentiments beyond what is common among Kolkatans is striking. The Kumars might house a few more pujas than most Kolkata Hindus, but that is due to the availability of murtis, not because they are 'more religious'. Thus, religious affiliations and practices among the Maliks are not given a separate chapter but treated when necessary within the framework of the other chapters. Moreover, I do not pretend to present a total portrait or image of the Kumars of Kumartuli's world; this is rather an attempt to make a representative number of Kumars answer the question: 'Who are you and what do you do for a living?'

Chapter 2

THE CIVILIZED POTTERS
AND THEIR NEIGHBOURHOOD

Kumartuli is both a neighbourhood in its own right and, in this book, a field-work site. As a place, Kumartuli is a combined residential and commercial neighbourhood. All the protagonists of this book work here, and some also have their homes here. In this chapter, I present Kumartuli as the site of research, both physically and through the Kumars working there and their oral histories. Going back to *sei samay* 'those days', of the contemporary Kumars' precursors is a long journey. The main aim of this chapter– after presenting the site, the people and their work – is to bring together some of the many histories of the Kumars: their group's origin, the beginning of the Kumbhakars' work as image makers, their establishment in Kolkata and Kumartuli and their first 150 years of making murtis for the Kolkata pujas. It is difficult, if not to say outright impossible, to exactly pinpoint the timespan covered by this section; however the stories will end roughly with the Kumars who started to work as fulltime murti makers in Kolkata in the early decades of the twentieth century.

And the beginning? Where to begin is always difficult to decide when one sets out to describe the historical lines of development giving rise to the contemporary conditions of a society. There is always a new 'before', an earlier incident leading up to something relevant to the present-day situation; not to forget the competitive element of being able to date something earlier than others, the 'idol of origins' (Bloch 1954 [1952]). The Kumars themselves operate with several beginnings. They have their creation stories concerning the very first Kumar and the beginning of pottery as an occupation. Then there are the stories concerning the beginning of their work as image-makers and the creation of Kumartuli as the hub of clay murti making.

I have approached the beginning by introducing several departures concerning the history of the Kumars of Kumartuli. I begin with stories of the emergence of Kumars, and then move on to the establishment of Kolkata and her Kumartuli. The lives of the first Kumartuli Kumars are briefly described before I outline the contemporary world of the Kumars.

The first part deals mainly with the contemporary Kumars' own rendering of their history. It starts with stories of the first Kumar, one mythical, and one more in tune with naturalistic explanations. Then I return to their way of life in the early days, as potters and seasonal image makers. What becomes evident in many of these narratives is how the Kumars use these histories to represent themselves today. They combine a conception of historical developments with a conception and self-representation of who they are today, as these are their own histories, presented and created by them. Thus, they use their option of emphasising what they feel is important.

Another problem in finding the beginning is the fact that Kumartuli has witnessed several waves of immigration. To name one group as the original dwellers is highly problematic. Within greater Bengal there has always been great mobility of people (Sanyal 1981). Political changes and changing natural conditions, as when rivers alter their course, have resulted in repeated changes in the demographic pattern of the area. Thus, in present day Kumartuli there live people from two main waves of immigration. The oldest is the Nadia Kumars, who came to Kolkata first as seasonal workers at the time when Durga Puja started to gain momentum among the rich and noble between the 1750s and the 1850s. The newcomers are the Bangladeshi Kumars who came around the time of Independence in 1947, as a result of Partition and the creation of a Muslim-dominated East Pakistan. They are, however, both Rudrapals with an origin story in common.

The implication of this is that the elders among the Nadia Kumars have lived their whole lives in Kumartuli, as their fathers and grandfathers did, while the elders among the Bangladeshi Kumars remember when they immigrated to Kolkata. Thus, when it comes to the old days of Kumartuli, which also will be presented in this chapter, it is mainly the West-Bangali (*edhesi*, of this land) Kumars who have any stories to tell.

The second part concerns the establishment of Kolkata and Kumartuli, where the Bengali landlords built their new palaces, and the origin and development of the Durga Puja. This twin development paved the ground for the foundation of Kumartuli as the place of clay image makers. This part is largely based on historical sources and secondary literature in which the Kumars are non-existent. With these limitations in focus, let me start with an overview of the site, of Kumartuli as a business area and a working place and a neighbourhood.

The First Kumar

While people making pottery have existed since neolithic times in Bengal, the history of the potters as a jati is uncertain (Varma 1970). In general, the

Kumbhakars constitute a big group of families and clans found more or less all over northern, eastern and central India. Puranic scriptures often refer to the origin of the group as the offspring of an illegitimate relationship. In the *Brahmavaivartta Purana* it is written that the Kumbhakar is born of a Vaisya woman and a Brahman father, the *Parasara Sanhita* says the father is a Malakar (gardener) and the mother a Chamar (leather worker caste), while the *Parasara Padhati* makes the father a Pattikar (weaver of silk cloth) and the mother a Tili (oil presser) (Risley 1891b: 518). Sir Monier Williams in his *Sanskrit Dictionary* describes the Kumbhakars as the offspring of a Kshatriya woman and Brahman man. Such descriptions, which try to reconcile Brahmanical theory with its four varnas with the great number of jatis, are very common in scriptures and among Orientalists from the nineteenth century and earlier, but they are not part of the Kumars' perception.

Of Rudraksha and the forefather of Bengali Kumbhakars

Turning back to Kolkata, the outlook concerning the origin of the jati is thus quite different. All contemporary Kumartuli Kumbhakars, be it from East or West Bengal, have Pal as their surname. This is an abbreviation of their proper name, or title, Rudrapal, and the Rudrapals have their own origin history – a history some elder Kumars know well, but of which most have only a faint concept. Those who know the story of Shiva's creation of the Kumbhakars tell it like this:

> **Gour:** It is a story [...] that when *Mahadeb* (Shiva) married *Sati* (Durga) [...] I do not know whether this is true or not, but this is the story [...]. From one of the beads of the garland of rudraksha he [Mahadeb] used to wear, he created this caste of Rudrapals. This story [...] I have listened to [...] I do not know whether [...] So, from rudraksha, seed used in prayer beads, he created this *caste* to make all the ingredients like an un-shaped pot and other kitchen utensils as we usually use in our pujas [...] Do you know? Earlier everything was made of clay, these utensils.
>
> These Kumars are almost a thousand year-old caste. Other castes have a [...] Nowadays they are getting clay pots or clay images almost everywhere under the earth so [...].
>
> I do not know whether these stories are true or false, but I have heard from my ancestors that Shiva created Rudrapals from rudraksha and he gave the boon that whatever they [the Kumars] would try to create, it should be created by them. Maybe these things are true, but I have never read the *Purana*s [...].

Potters used to work on the *cakra*, the wheel, and the cakra was then given us by Narayan (Vishnu). On his finger you see a cakra, a discus (weapon, metal ring with a sharp edge) – that is the cakra he gave us. He gave us his cakra in order for us to use it as our [potter's] cakra.

Through this story, the Kumbhakars confirm their importance in the world at large, as without them no puja or marriage can take place, not even that of Mahadeb, the Great God. The family based on marriage between man and woman is one of the most important constituents of any society, and it is within this context that the origin myth of the Kumbhakars should be understood. Their importance as the provider of the necessary utensils for any occasion that requires a puja is emphasized, and pujas as the practical aspect of a religion or moral law (*dharma*) are a signifier of a civilized society.

History is one of Niranjan's passions, a passion he feels few care about these days. The other Kumars and people in general do not much care to listen to his stories or to discuss them. He is regularly visited by journalists and academics as the storyteller of Kumartuli, but then mainly for short periods. My visit provided him with a listener who shared his interest. He repeatedly mentioned that at his age, 86, he no longer had any friends left who shared his interests and with whom he could discuss such matters. When Niranjan talks, it is with frequent digressions and without references to dates. Instead, time is established with reference to certain persons or well known incidents. This is a common narrative style among all the senior Maliks. When Niranjan from West Bengal narrates the story of rudraksha he tells it slightly differently:

Niranjan: When Shiva and Durga were married [...] Durga means the daughter of Giriraja, he is Himalaya [Giri=mountain, raja=king], King of the Mountain [...] In our marriages we need *ghat*;[1] in Hindu culture we use these kinds of small clay pots. Then there were no one to make these clay pots. Nobody at that time used to do the Kumars' job.

I [...] on my own, with my own reading have created one history, which is my own history. But let me first finish this topic first, and then I will explain that one [below].

So then Mahadeb from his Rudra [...] Like you can see these beads [showing beads from a necklace hanging on the wall], though these are made of sandal. So Mahadeb has one bead named Rudra. Mahadeb used to wear these kinds of beads around his neck. He threw one of

---

1 घट, ritual pot; little clay, earthen or metal pitcher or pot; symbol of purity and blessings from God. *Mangal ghat*: blessings from God, the place where God is residing.

those beads from his neck on the ground and created the Kumbhakar. So we are the Rudrapal. In Bengal there are so many other castes that use Pal as their title, but Kumbhakar are the Rudrapals. We are Rudrapals as we are created from rudraksha.

It is an old story [*golpa*]. It is our old history, just as we have a story of Ramayana. Yes, there must be some truth in it. Who created the story of Ramayana? It was Valmiki. [...] So this is the story of the origin of the Kumbhakar *sambrodaj*, community. This is the puranic story, just as the Ramayana is a puranic story.

Among Bengalis in general, Rudra is a recognized name for Shiva as the destroyer, and when the Kumbhkars use their full title, it evokes a relation to him and their ancestor whom he created and to whom he gave the title Rudrapal. It is common among jatis to trace their origin back to a divine creation, at least among those belonging to the higher half of the hierarchy. Take for instance the large oil-pressing and trading caste of Tilis (or Telis), which is also among the Nabasakha castes. There are several stories concerning the creation of the first Tili, all of which follow the same pattern of divine creation. One is ascribed to Shiva, and it goes as follows. Just when Shiva had finished his bath, he decided to rub himself with oil and not wood ashes as he generally used. Since he did not have any oil at hand, he created a man named Rupnarayan Teli or Manohar Pal from the sweat of his arm and instigated the man to make an oil-mill (*ghani*) (Risley 1891b: 306). The first Tanti (weaver caste) was also created from the sweat of Shiva, this time while he was dancing (Risley 1891b: 295). Again it is Shiva who needs someone to do him a service, to provide him with something he needs, that catalyses the creation.

As pointed out earlier, the story describing the creation of the first Kumbhakar from Shiva's rudraksha is shared by the two major groups in Kumartuli. Moreover, it is or, more correctly was, shared by probably all Bengali Kumbhakars. Also potters elsewhere in India have rather similar creation stories. In *The Tribes and Castes of the Central Provinces of India* we encounter a story which also relates to Shiva's marriage, this time however the parentage is leads back to a Brahman and not the rudraksha:

The caste themselves have a legend of the usual Brahmanical type: 'In the Kritayuga [or *satyuga*, the era of truth when man is governed by gods], when Maheshwar (Siva) intended to marry the daughter of Hemvanta, the Devas and Asuras [gods and demons] assembled at Kailas (Heaven). Then a question arose as to who should furnish the vessels required for the ceremony, and one Kulalaka, a Brahman, was ordered to make them. Then Kulalaka stood before the assembly with folded hands, and prayed that materials might be given to him for making the pots. So Vishnu gave his Sudarsana (discus) to be used as a wheel, and the mountain of Mandara was fixed as a pivot beneath it to hold it up. The scraper was Adi Kurma the tortoise, and a rain-cloud was used for the water-tub. So Kulalaka made the pots and gave them to Maheshwar for his marriage, and ever since his descendants have been known as Kumbhakar or maker of water-jars.' (Russell 1916: 4)

Most potters in Bengal, and all of the Kumartuli potters, have Rudrapal as their titles in memory of their creator. However, emphasis and awareness of this relation between their jati and Shiva is uncommon among the Kumbhakars. While some elders can tell the story, most have only a faint knowledge that there exists a connection. A consequence is that most Kumbhakars do not use the reference to Shiva, Rudra, in their surname. Instead they only use Pal and that is a surname they share with many jatis.

Elders like Gour are highly aware of this change, but even though he is part of the generation that started to use only Pal as a surname, he is unable to give an explanation as to why this has happened, other than that people no longer know their origin history. Another explanation could be dissolution of the caste system, since with Pal as their only title it is not possible for anyone to deduce their jati-background from the name alone. However, as active and proud Kumars, as members of the Kumbhakar jati – a jati that is not only shudra, but sat shudra – there is little about the Kumars to support such a desire among the Kumartuli Kumbhakars in general. Nevertheless, adding to Gour's explanation of communal amnesia, a more market-sensitive attitude to business might have played a part in the rejection of 'Rudra' in the surname. Making the name short and common was probably something that the business-minded Rudrapals found useful. Although they live daily with the gods through their work, they are running a business, a business where they want to be approached like regular businessmen without the involvement of the gods. They make thakur murtis, but they are part of this world of economic transactions. This corresponds to Gour's son's explanation. He emphasizes that it is easier and something more common, which places him within the community at large to a greater extent. It makes him more part of Bengal than the title Rudrapal does. Again, this is not said with reference to the caste hierarchy, which did not suppress the Kumbhakars, but to a more modern outlook on his jati's place in society.

A religious role for Rudrapal, the ancestor of all the members of the jati, is nonexistent in today's Kumartuli. This may have always been the situation, but according to Risley, some groups of Kumars from mainly Orissa, the Uria Kumars, worshiped Rudrapal as a patron saint. Risley continues:

[Rudrapal's] image is placed between the images of Radha and Krishna in the Bhagwat gadi, or room set apart for the reading of the sacred books of the Vaishnava sect, and on the *Sukla Sasti*, the sixth day of the new moon of the month of Aghrán, fried paddy, plantains, cocoanuts, and similar offerings are presented to him. A Brahman recites mantras, or mystic invocations, and receives as his perquisite the articles offered to Rudra Pál. This festival is called Ohran Sasti. (Risley 1891a: 523)

Other groups among the Bengali Kumars are also known to have worshiped their group's ancestor (ibid.). Correspondingly, in the state of Maharashtra the Kumars are known to worship Saint *Gora Kumbhar*, seen locally as the great saint of the Kumbhakar community (Bhanu et al. 2004: 1179). One might thus suggest that the tradition of worshiping Rudrapal used to be a more common feature also among Bengali Kumbhakars. There exist no available historical or ethnographical materials that might substantiate such a hypothesis. and it remains a speculation.

Burning jungle and the first pottery

One of Kumartuli's best known local storytellers, Niranjan, who told the latter story of the Rudrapals' creation from the rudraksha above, says he does not believe in it, even as he says there must be some truth there. As an alternative he tells another story about the origin of the Kumars, a story which he says he has figured out himself. The naturalistic history differs in many ways from the story of rudraksha, but there is a common feature – the equation between civilization and the potter. The self-representation and self-understanding of the potter's place in society is an important feature.

Niranjan's story starts thousands of years ago, when the humans' ancestors still lived in the jungle:

Niranjan: Let me tell one thing which is absolutely of my own thinking. On this earth there were no human beings at the very beginning. Human beings came much later. Of all the different types of creatures (*prani*) you find in this world (*prithibi*), the human beings are the latecomers.

Humans used to eat *kaca* (uncooked) meat. I have made my own logical thinking about the time when humans used to eat raw meat after hunting. Occasionally there were fires in the forests. Then, naturally, people ran away from that forest. In such fires some human beings along with other animals usually died. Then again, the survivors returned to their forest [...] when the situation became normal in the forest after burning, the fire naturally stopped when there was

no longer anything to burn in the forest. But there also may have been
some rain there that stopped the fire.

So when the humans, the inhabitants of the forest, returned they got
baked, *jhalasana*, meat and baked clay (*para mati*). When we eat meat
now, it is baked or roasted. And humans found it tasty, so they started
to eat that baked meat. And they also noticed that in some places the
soil had become hard. It did not melt in water. Then they started to use
that kind of soil and that was the time when clay pots were made the
first time. This is my own thinking, my own theory.

There is a separation between the time of eating raw food and cooked food,
which coincides with the beginning of using clay to make pots and other utensils. The fire that made people turn away from raw meat marks the beginning
of civilization in the narrative of Niranjan. As with the story of Rudraksha
this also marks the origin of the first potter.

Niranjan: At the very beginning, humans started to make clay pots.
Humans from that period started to use clay for utensils and they noticed
that burned clay pots do not melt in water. They are my ancestors.

I am perhaps going backwards, but this is my personal thinking. What
happened after that? They also had a shortage of food, because the animals started to become aware of their activities – so humans started to
eat vegetables. They started eating vegetables, and in this way they were
growing towards civilization. This is world history [...] this is not particularly about India, England, America. They had many groups. They
produced wheat only to serve their own purpose and the purpose of
their group. And the rest of the seeds they usually preserved with the
help of one person. They had some grain reserves [...] a granary for it.
Whenever they needed, they went to that person and had their seeds such
as wheat, rice and others [...] lentils. And the other vegetables, leaves and
fruit they did not store, because they did not have the knowledge about
how to store in a cold storage then [...] there were no cold stores at that
time. And they also had their leader, head, who was there to take care of
them. Then after 200 or 400 years [...] this is my story [...].

Geir: Yes, your story [...].

Niranjan: You can examine my statements to see it is my history or not.

The early leader was then dead and in his place was his child or
grandson. Human beings cannot live very long and in his place there
was his son or another person. Then these people [leaders] refused to
share the rest of the seeds with the entire community.

In South India there are some places where they make salt and they supply it to the whole of India. In those early days it was this policy of give and take (*binimay pratha*). For example, I give you rice and you give me anything I need. So those people became very rich and they suppressed the other community members, so thus started *jamidari* [private control of land]. It is the first jamidari. And these people became rich, but those who became labourers did not know anything. They thought 'we can get food through working' – so it is nice in that way. I think we had only clay pots in those early years.

Niranjan adds that this story is the same for all potters all over the world, it is the creation of both pottery and potters as such. References to a purely profane common human past combined with an evolutionary pre-understanding point towards a modern mindset. With this story, Niranjan places the Kumars of Kumartuli within a great tradition of artisans, linking them to every potter in the world. At the same time, the making of pottery originates from the same event that functions as a catalyst for civilization.

As both one of the oldest Kumars of the area and the person whom everyone refers to when it comes to knowledge about the past, his stories are as authoritative as it can get among the Kumars. Perhaps this view unlocks the answer to why the older puranic story has lost momentum, as well as explaining the decline of the use of 'Rudra' in the title. As most Kumars today have some formal education, similar origin stories, now framed as being scientific, are commonly shared.

Both histories of the origin of the Kumars either concern every potter in the world or are (or were) shared by all the members of the Kumbhakar jati of Greater Bengal. This makes at least the historically more common rudraksha story part of a shared identity; even if it's contemporary standing in Kumartuli is weak.

Most striking in both stories of origin is how they connect the emergence of the first potter with the emergence of civilization itself, or with major institutions such as religious rituals at large or marriage. Through these stories, even as they are retreating in the collective memory of the Kumbhakars, their self-representation as a crucial element in any society emerges. Without potters we would still live like animals in the jungle, without rituals and families providing a structure and direction to our lives.

Behind the Potter's Wheel

The history of unbaked clay images is difficult to trace and only limited work has been devoted to the theme. Most important in this respect is still the formative work *The Indian Technique of Clay Modelling* by K. M. Varma (1970). According to his research, archaeological findings in India at large date the production of unbaked clay images as far back as the first century CE (Varma 1970: 188). Concerning literary sources, the first to mention unbaked clay images is probably the Korean Buddhist pilgrim Huei-ch'ao, who visited India in 726 CE (Varma 1970: 225–26). Still, based on old *Agama* texts he argues that their origin can go back to as early as the eighth to ninth centuries BCE (Varma 1970: 245). In a Bengali context, the question of the origin of the use of unbaked clay images in worship has usually been investigated with reference to Durga Puja. Bhavadeva Bhatta, who lived in the eleventh century CE, is usually cited as the first to mention worship of a Durga image made of clay, but the actual practice of making clay images might very well be much older, and Varma argues that literary references take us back at least to the sixth century (Varma 1970: 218–21).

At least in Bengal, it seems rather certain that the production of clay images did not become a widespread practice before the time of Krishnachandra. Consequently, making clay murtis was not an important source of income or part of the regular work for any jati before the mid-eighteenth century. While it slowly became an important auxiliary occupation for some Kumbhakar families from the mid-eighteenth century onwards, murti production gradually turned into a fulltime occupation from the period around 1900.

Life and work in the days before Krishnachandra among the Kumbhakars of Nadia and elsewhere in Bengal mainly revolved around making earthenwares on the *chak* or the potter's wheel. In every larger village there was at least one family of potters that produced clay vessels and utilities for a variety of uses. In the cities there were small neighbourhoods of potters, like Ghurni and Palpara in Krishnanagar (Robinson 1983: 175) and Kumartuli in Gobindapur (which were moved after 1757 to the Sutanuti-area in North Kolkata). The potters worshiped their wheel in the month of *Jyaistha* (May–June). During the *chakrapuja* or wheel-worship, a clay image of Shiva was placed near the wheel, where other tools were also collected. The gods Indra, Agni and Brahma were also worshiped (Risley 1881: 522–23; Saraswati and Behura 1966: 185). In the month of Baishakh (April–May), the wheel was given a complete rest, culminating with a worship of Bishwakarma. Even as they regard Shiva as their creator and give him great importance, they were seen as Vaishnavas. Vaishnavism gained great popularity in Bengal due to the saint Chaitanya (1485–1535) who created a movement in which vernacular poetic language was used to celebrate Radha and Krishna (Sengupta 2001).

As village artisans, they had a monopoly on production of the pottery that the villagers needed. The diversity of earthen articles made by the Kumbhakars was great. There were water vessels to cooking pots of various designs and uses that had to be made. Many kinds of eating plates and drinking cups were also made of clay. And for worship the Kumbhakars' products were also a necessity, like the small *ghat* [pot], which is a symbol of God itself and the *shanka*, which is an ersatz of the conch shell. The main tool was the *chaka* 'a circular table of baked clay weighted along the rim, revolving rapidly on a pivot cut from the heart of a tamarind tree' (Risley 1891: 524). While the neck and shoulders of round vessels were made by the Kumar with the wheel, the body was fashioned by hand, often by the *Kumari* or woman potter. The earthenware was not glazed, but occasionally painted. Occasionally the village potter holds *cakaran*,[2] or a grant of land given in lieu of salary, on the condition that he supplies the village community or the *jamidar* with all the vessels needed for the festivals they observe (Risley 1891: 525). The earthen utensils were destroyed when a person of the household died or on other prescribed occasions, a practice that gave fresh impetus to the trade (Mukharji 1974 [1888]: 283).

While image worship has existed for at least two thousand years, the construction of images has not been a job for the Kumbhakar for such a long period. During the last centuries the worship of unbaked clay images appears to have been especially popular in Bengal and the neighbouring states of Assam, Bihar and Orissa (Robinson 1983: 74); but the practice has recently become more widespread with, for instance, the worship of clay images of Ganesha in Maharashtra. It is difficult to trace the beginning of this tradition, but it is seen as a continuation of an ancient tradition (Varma 1970: 221). Some of the potters made crude images for their customers. Supposedly, these were hollow clay models. The price was calculated on the same basis as was that of pots, the price being set as the amount of rice the vessel could hold (Goldblatt 1979: 48). Later on, the use of straw brought about significant changes in the technique (Varma 1970: 220), making more elaborate designs and larger sizes possible. Image making became important as a sideline for the potters after the puja celebrations became more popular in rural areas and small towns of Nadia because of the influence of Maharaja Krishnachandra in the mid-eighteenth century. While Krishnachandra made the Kumbhakars make the clay images for his pujas, the subsequent growth of clay image worship also gave new sidelines to other groups. In Krishnanagar, and later in Kolkata, a carpenter often made the wooden frame (*takta* and *kathama*), while the painters painted the image and the gardener decorated it. Moreover, in other parts of Bengal, different jatis than the Kumbhakar were given the job of making the actual clay images. Thus, in Bishnupur (Bankura District), the

---

2 চাকরান in Bengali.

images are mainly made by people from the carpenter, Suttradhar or Cuttor, jati (Östör 2004 [1980]: 58).

The Nadia Kumars, especially those from the city of Krishnanagar, were also famous for their ability to make small-scale clay models of different characters or groups of people. The clay models were exhibited abroad at least from 1851, when they could be seen at *The Great Exhibition of the Works of Industry of all Nations* in London (Mukharji 1974 [1888]: 59). From that exhibition on, the figures are said to have 'acquired great celebrity, and they have repeatedly gained models and certificates' (ibid.). Such models could depict people from various castes and tribes or be a miniature scene illustrating Durga Puja. The making of such dolls occurred probably around the same time and within communities who started to make the deities for the rajas. According to T. N. Mukharji, a high ranking Bengali civil servant and art expert of the late nineteenth and early twentieth centuries (Childers 2004), the making of such models actually originated from the making of idols for worship (Mukharji 1974 [1888]: 62).

Only a minority of Nadia potters devoted time to image making in the households of affluent Nadia landlords. They entered into a hereditary patron–client relationship with the house that hired them to make images. The artists worked and ate in the family home for as long as it took to make the image, and were often given grants of tax-free land for their services (Robinson 1983: 78). The patronage was typically extended when the landlords left for Kolkata and established their homes there. Thus many of the Kumars started their seasonal migration to the colonial city. And as the market for images started to expand in the growing city of Kolkata by the end of the eighteenth century, other potters also migrated to take advantage of the new opportunities there (Goldblatt 1979: 49).

The Development of Kumartuli – the Story without Kumars

Kumartuli as the home of the murti makers is a result of the convergence of two developments: first, the creation and growth of the autumnal Durga Puja as a festival arranged by the jamidars ('landowner, revenue collector') around Bengal; second, the development of colonial Kolkata as the new place of residence for the Hindu landlords (Deb 1990). The newly settled landlords brought with them Durga Puja from the districts to Kolkata, where it soon became an important institution. When they arranged their pujas in the city, they brought with them the Kumars whom they had employed earlier in their rural homes. While this general outline is undisputed, information concerning both the origin of Durga Puja as the autumnal festival that we know today and the foundation of Kolkata's Kumartuli is uncertain and contradictory. While the pre-colonial history of the villages that became the capital of British India is also hard to trace, that of British Kolkata is rather well documented. Thus, I start the story of the development of Kumartuli with a history of the Kolkata that attracted so many rich landlords and babus.

Kolkata

On a slight eminence at the eastern side of the river Hooghly, or Ganga as I will call the river hereafter, there existed three villages: Sutanuti, Kalikata and Gobindapur. The main village in terms of inhabitants was Gobindapur, while Sutanuti was a marketplace, mainly for cotton. Kalikata was probably the smallest one; perhaps there was a yearly or seasonal market there. All three villages belonged to an administrative area named the Twenty-four *Parganas* or the Twenty-four Divisions. The villages were under control of the Muslim ruler, the Nawab (Nair 1990). Tax collection was controlled by jamidars, of which many were Hindus.

The actual age of the villages is uncertain, but their existence is attested to around 1550 when one family of Sens and four families of Basaks, all merchants from the weaver caste, arrived in Gobindapur from the upriver port of Satgaon. Satgaon was along with Chittagong one of the two major ports of Bengal when the Portuguese arrived around 1518 (Nair 1986, Losty 1990: 11). The two families moved due to the gradual silting up of the river and because the Gobindapur villages were situated at a place that could still be easily reached from the Bay of Bengal (Losty 1990: 11). Due to this, Sutanutee was developing as an important new market for cotton under the control of the Seths and Basaks. Moreover, almost directly opposite on the other bank of the river, the temporary town of Betor had been established to service the traders during the season. Later, in 1557, the Portuguese received permission from the Mughal Emperor Akbar to found a settlement at the town of Hooghly (*Hugli*) further up the river (Losty 1990: 11). Thus, Betor lost its importance, became largely abandoned and the trade was transferred to Sutanuti. Hooghly was later captured by Akbar's successor Shah Jahan, who disliked both the presence of infidels and the Portuguese inability to fulfil their part of the bargain to halt piracy, in 1632.[3] This ended all serious Portuguese economic activity in Bengal, except piracy.

Further south of the Sens' and Basaks' new home resided the Sabarna Chowdhuries, who were the jamidars of the area. Thus, the elevation along

---

3 The Portuguese were supposed to keep the eastern seas free of renegade Portuguese and Arakanese pirates. When Hoogly fell after a three-month siege, all its Christian survivors were moved to Agra as slaves (Losty 1990: 11).

the Ganga, with marshes and salt lakes on three sides, was a thriving market and port, joining upstream and inland Bengal with the world at large more than a hundred years before the British made it their main foothold in Bengal.

The Sens, the Basaks and the Sabarna Chowdhuries all had their adibaris, ancestral homes, further up the river. Although it is hard to find any indications of how large either Sutanuti or Gobindapur were around 1690, the existence of residing Kumbhakars is highly probable. Gobindapur must have been a rather large residential village, with both the nearby market(s) and the Kalighat temple, which as the most important in Bengal attracted pilgrims (Losty 1990: 16). The Kumbhakars' products were needed for both domestic and ritual use. It is difficult to establish from where the pre-1757 Kumbhakars came, but one of the contemporary Kumars suggests that they, as the Nadia Kumars, came from the Rarh region (between the western plateau and highlands and the Ganga delta), perhaps Birbhum.

While the Portuguese trade still flourished in Hooghly, the British established their first trading post in India in 1612, thirteen years after the first English East India Company was founded. In 1651 they managed to establish themselves in the Gangetic delta at the old trading post of their Portuguese enemies, Hooghly. From here they competed with the Dutch to control European trade with Bengal (Losty 1990). There was much conflict with the Nawab and after the Bay War (Nair 1986: 324) in the 1680s, the Englishmen were forced to quit their trade. After the Mughals defeated them at Hooghly in 1686, a group of Company men, including the chief of the trading post Cossimbazar, Job Charnock, fled and encamped at Sutanuti. From here he tried to come to terms with the Mughals, but in vain. Charnock left to continue the fight, and returned a second time to the Gobindapur villages in 1687. He stayed for a year, but was unable to resume the trade and fled south to Fort George in Madras (now Chennai).

When Ibrahim Khan became Emperor Aurangzeb's Nawab of Bengal in 1689, the Company was invited to resume their trade. Job Charnock, after thirty years in Bengal and three former attempts to establish a secure settlement, found Sutanuti to be the best choice since it was only possible to attack it from the river side. Charnock and his men reached the village and the ruins of his former buildings on the 24th of August 1690, and started the establishment of a permanent trading post for the English East India Company. At the time of the British arrival in the three villages, the Sens and Basaks still controlled the Sutanuti market (Nair 1986: 337, Losty 1990: 15).

The name 'Kolkata', or 'Calcutta' as the English called it, is probably not derived from the village name 'Kalikata', but from *khal* meaning 'canal' and *katta* to emphasize that it was natural, since at that time the three villages were connected by small canals (Nair 1986). The modern name is derived from

Persian 'Kalkata', but the words have Bengali origins. The name 'Calcutta' for this area is found in the English East India Company's records several times from 1688 onwards (Nair 1986: 57). However, the Company as well as Charnock referred mainly to the new area of settlement as 'Sutanuti' and the settlement itself as 'Fort William'. From 1704 onwards, the name 'Calcutta' is commonly used (Nair 1986: 26).

Thus, it was among the Gobindapur villages that Agent Charnock established his new trading post. Some of the buildings from his former stays were restored and a few new thatched huts with mud walls constructed. While the East India Company was given permission to trade custom-free in Bengal, it was not allowed to construct brick buildings. The local jamidars approved the Company's presence, since they expected better revenues. What later became British Calcutta was thus established long before the arrival of European settlers as an important market and residential area. The British, after securing the tax rights in 1698, turned the villages into an administrative centre – a European trade bastion with Fort William in its centre and a 'City of palaces'. Due to its location on the navigable Hooghly and the safety provided by British, it turned into, to phrase Ulf Hannerz, an *urban swirl*, a metropolis of high cultural complexity, a place of 'unusually lively cultural production' (1992: 174). It attracted people from all over Bengal and the rest of India, as well as from China and Europe. Gobindapur with its adjoining markets was and is a meeting place, a crossing point of flows that reach most parts of the world. In the context of this book, the fact that Kolkata under the British turned into both an administrative and military centre and a cultural and economical meeting place is interesting. It is exactly these factors that constitute the major structural conditions that made it possible for the Kumars to make Kumartuli into what it is today – a global marketplace for the traditional jati-based occupation of making murtis.

The prospects for trade and other kinds of occupations attracted large groups of Indians to the city. The British were completely dependent on intermediaries to run their trade operations. Another group of people who moved into Kolkata came as a result of instability and military threats in the rest of Bengal. Initially this meant the peril from raiding Maratha warriors.

The Battle of Plassey in 1757, in which they conquered the local Nawab, proved to be an important watershed in the history of the British presence in Bengal and India, whereby they secured political and military control of large parts of Bengal. As the British settlement grew, Calcutta attracted a growing number of local associates and workers. These were mainly Hindus, and as their wealth grew along with the city, the development of the Bengali pujas hit a new, fast-moving track. At this point, Kolkata was firmly established as a British stronghold with a large group of resident Hindu rajas and babus.

Kumartuli before and after Durga hits town

Kumartuli's history is difficult to trace and several contradictory notes on it exist. Little is written about the Kumars and Kumartuli in documents from British India, since the Kumars did not partake in any business or occupation that catered for the British population in a major way. They made their products mainly of clay purchased and used almost solely by the indigenous population. In comparison, other occupation groups are often mentioned, like carpenters, smiths, weavers and sweepers, due to their use and importance for the colonial masters. Thus, in the gazetteers, statistics, correspondence, etc. the Kumars and Kumartuli are rarely mentioned.

When it comes to Durga Puja, there is much more information. In paintings and writings, foreigners and locals alike have described the puja and thus presented us with knowledge concerning the early days. Although there are several competing stories concerning the origin of the autumnal Durga Puja as the direct predecessor of today's puja, there is consensus among most commentators that it was a festival popularized by Raja Krishnachandra of Nadia (1710–1782). The Raja was granted his title of Maharaja of Nadia in 1728 and he established his capital at Krishnanagar, where a former ruler had built a palace. As part of his religious duties, the Raja arranged pujas at the palace and ordered his subjects to arrange pujas. It is known that he frequently gave orders to his subjects to perform Kali Puja or face harsh penalties. Consequently, Krishnanagar was famous for Kali puja being performed in more than ten thousand homes (Ward 1811: 191; Robinson 1983: 177). Besides popularizing the autumnal Durga Puja and increasing the number of Kali Pujas, Raja Krishnachandra is also named as the founder of several other pujas.

In the context of Kolkata, it was Raja Nabakrishna Deb at Sababajar Rajbari in North Kolkata who, inspired by Krishnachandra, brought it to the city in 1757. It should be mentioned that some families of Kolkata, like the Sabarna Chowdhuries of Barisha, probably arranged their own Durga Puja from 1610. Still, it is hard to place this puja in the genealogy of the contemporary practice. Thus, Durga Puja as we know it came to Kolkata in 1757. The images were made by Kumars and brought to the city from Krishnanagar; and this is the beginning of the Kumartuli of the image-makers whose relatives still live and work there.

Concerning Kumartuli, the most important indicator of their historical existence in written records is the name of their neighbourhood, Kumartuli. The primary units of old Calcutta were *paras* or localities (Nair 1990: 20). These were organized around caste, professions or migrants from a given village. Smaller than the paras are the *tolas* of professional groups. A small tola was naturally given the name *tuli*, which is its diminutive form. Kumartuli is such a locality, at the same time as it was used by the colonial administration to designate a larger *thana* (literally police station, around which the unit was organized). *Kumar* means potter, and as tuli indicates a small neighbourhood or locality, Kumartuli means the Neighbourhood of Potters. The name figures in the earliest list of thanas, an important administrative unit after the Battle of Plassey in 1757. The list is from 1785, and here Kumartuli is included (Nair 1990: 15). While many of the thanas refer to villages that were incorporated into the British-controlled area in 1717, those thanas that were situated within the three villages the British first came to control in 1698 are given names according to bazaars, ponds or residents. Later, in 1888, the thanas were recorded under twenty-five police stations, which were turned into administrative wards under the Calcutta Municipal Act of 1899. Here we again find Kumartuli as one of the thanas (Nair 1990: 15–16). During the eighteenth century some of the most famous Bengalis 'lived here: Nandaram Sen and Gobindaram Mitra, "Black Zamindars" or Deputies to the English Collectors, and Banamali Sarkar' (Nair 1990: 16). It was a Hindu area, and until 1911 Kumartuli was the thana with the highest concentration of Hindus, numbering 95 per cent.

However, it seems evident that it existed before Durga Puja became a known and widely celebrated festival in Kolkata. Moreover, it is realistic to believe that Kumars had their own neighbourhood in the area that existed before the British established Kolkata. Since the area that became Kolkata was populated before the British settled there permanently in 1690, it is highly likely that the earlier villages included some Kumbhakars. Potters existed in every large Bengali village.

According to some, there existed a Kumartuli in the village of Gobindapur before it is mentioned as a thana in Sutanuti. Gobindapur was situated where today's Fort William is. After the Battle of Plassey (1757), the Company wanted a better fort that could withstand attacks. The Old Fort William, which was easily captured by Siraj-ud-Daulah in 1756, was replaced by a new fort at Gobindapur. By way of compensation, the old inhabitants were given land in Sutanuti (Banerjea 2005: 24); thus the location of Kumartuli was shifted to its present area. There might already have existed Kumars in Sutanuti: according to the journal *The Bengal Consultations* from 1707, Kumars occupied 75 acres of land in Sutanuti.[4] The Kumars are said to have arrived from Krishnanagar in South Bengal, in search of a better livelihood in the thriving and prosperous village of Gobindapur.

---

4 http://www.indiaprofile.com/art-crafts/claymodelling.htm

Another version of Kumartuli's origin is given by Sumanta Banerjee (1989). He notes that the first labouring class to settle in Kolkata were the artisans, and among them were the Kumars. Further he writes: [5]

> Kumortuli, in north Calcutta, [...] is one of the oldest settlements. Gobindaram Mitra, who was the dewan to the zamindar of Calcutta and was known as the 'black zamindar' because of the undisputed power he wielded over the indigenous inhabitants in the mid-eighteenth century, built a number of temples, for which purpose he imported clay-modellers from the nearby village of Banshbeḍey. They came by boat and settled down in Kumartuli. Soon after this, clay modellers began to arrive from Nabadwip, Krishnanagar and Shantipur – old towns of fame which were well known for this particular art. Leading among the first settlers were Madhusudan Pal, Kangalicharan Pal, Kashinath Pal, Haripada Pal and Annadacharan Pal. (Banerjee 1989: 31)

According to this description it seems that in the 1750s there already existed a Kumartuli, but that the resident Kumars where not capable of providing the clay-modelling needed for a temple. Perhaps the old Kumars only made pots and utensils, while the immigrant Kumars made sacral artefacts and images?

The rich Hindu noblemen recreated Durga Puja in extravagant forms to confirm their position, and thus started the Durga Puja tradition that turned into the present day pujas that constitute the main or sole source of income of the Kumartuli Kumars. Kolkata housed more babus and rich people than anywhere else in Bengal. Consequently, the number of Durga Pujas arranged here was quite large. This might be the reason why there probably did not exist any community pujas here in the nineteenth century. There is a small reference to a *baroari* (public) puja in Behala, which was within the borders of the city at that time; in 1840, however it seems to be one single occasion (*The Calcutta Courier* 1840 in Banerjee 2004: 46). However, in the early twentieth century, individual initiative to arrange Durga Puja had declined profoundly. And in 1910, a new puja tradition was initiated, the *Sarbajanin*[6] *Durgutsab*. Whether it was the Indian National Congress or the Sanatan Dharmotsahini Sabha that organized the first Sarbajanin puja is not important. The fact remain that, in the early twentieth century, Durga Puja had moved out of the courtyards and into the streets. Pujas were arranged by local committees, whether based on

---

5 Banerjee's reference: Bireshwar Bandyopadhyay. 'Kolkatar Kumortuli'. *Purasree* (in Bengali), 23 October 1978.

6 সর্বজনীন a. good for all, universally good; universal; public, common.

a common residential area, groups of businessmen, political or humanitarian organizations or any other constellation of people who felt the urge to arrange a local puja. The Sarbajanin puja are based on the all-inclusiveness of the baroari puja, but are more expansive than the strictly local baroari (Banerjee 2004: 49). At a time in history marked by growing nationalism, the open pujas were a good and suitable opportunity for anti-colonial work.

The present day Bengali Durga Puja tradition goes back to the rich peoples' quest to imitate aristocratic religious festivals of bygone days (Banerjee 2004: 43). They sought social prestige rather than to maintain a link to the common people like that between the rajas or jamidars and their tenants (ibid.). While the *nouveau riche*, the babus, opened their houses for every class, there was no guarantee of full participation by local residents, as for example at Savabazar Rajbari, which entertained the public free for twelve days, but restricted entry during the three most important nights. Then the British were invited over for 'some sherry, champagne, brandy [and] biscuit' (Shripanto 2003 in Banerjee 2004: 44).

As Durga Puja turned more and more into 'business entertainment' (Chaliha and Gupta 1990: 332), the common people experienced that their space was shrinking. This paved the way for pujas arranged by 'common' people. It started in the districts, or to be more precise, in Guptipara (Hooghly), where twelve Brahman friends had been denied access to a household puja. Consequently, they decided to institute their own puja. The occasion is mentioned in the journal *The Friend of India* in May 1820:

> A new species of Pooja has been introduced into Bengal within the last thirty years, called Barowaree [...] About thirty years ago, at Gooptipara, near Santipoora [...] a number of Brahman formed an association for the celebration of a Pooja independently [...] They elected twelve men as a committee from which the circumstance takes its name, and solicited subscriptions in all the surrounding villages. (Binoy Gosh 1978: 279–80 in Banerjee)

A plaque at Bindeshwaritala shrine dates the event to 1168 SAKA or 1761, while *The Friend of India* dates it to 1790. According to Binoy Ghosh, a list of articles used during the second puja in Guptipara found at a private residence (of the Mukhopadhyays) indicates that the first year have been 1759–60 (Banerjee 2004: 93). However, this was the beginning of the community pujas totally open to local residents and common people. It is said that 'Durga Puja went democratic years before the country did' (Banerjee 2004: 45).

The puja was financed through collecting subscriptions in the area. Later, in some areas, this practice turned into something more resembling extortion.

Wealthier people had to travel incognito; females would suffer abuse if they did not pay, as well as threats. A common way of punishing those who did not want to contribute was to leave a Durga murti their house, forcing the victim to hold a puja and spend many times more money than the collectors would take (Banerjee 2004: 48).

The community-based pujas, which are the common form of pujas in Kolkata today, were initiated in 1910 (Chaliha and Gupta 1990: 332, Banerjee 2004). There is some discrepancy concerning the place and moti-vation. Banerjee writes that it took place in Sanatan Basu Ghat Road in Bhowanipur, south Kolkata, and was organized by Sanatan Dharmotsahini Sabha (2003: 49). Chaliha and Gupta write that it was held at Balaram Basu Ghat and was organized by the Indian National Congress as a nationalist forum in religious guise (1990: 332). Nevertheless, others soon followed and similar pujas were organized in south Kolkata in Ramdhan Mitra Lane and Sikdar Bagan; in the north came Simla Byayam and Bagbazar Sarbajanin (ibid.). The latter was first arranged in 1919. Thus started the Sarbajanin Durga Pujas – the pujas for everyone – in Kolkata.

However, the people of Kolkata appreciated the new form of Durga Puja. Its popularity grew rapidly, as did the number of pujas. With the 'democrati-zation' of the puja in Kolkata, the number of pujas increased (Goldblatt 1979, Banerjee 2004). For the Kumars of Kumartuli, this meant more work. While some families from Nadia already had settled there, the custom of seasonal travel to Kumartuli in order to make murtis ended around the time of the first Sarbajanin pujas. Now the Kumars moved their families to Kumartuli and became regular residents. Moreover, they got an entirely new market to cater for, that of the bazaar.

Another change took place after Indian Independence in 1947. From the early 1960s on, individuals from a different background started to design the images, as well as more spectacular pandals. These individuals, many of whom were Art College educated, became increasingly popular among the more prestigious 'theme pujas'. Thus, people from outside Kumartuli were able to earn more money on Durga puja than most Kumars. Only, in the 1990s did the Kumars start to challenge the outsiders as designers of theme pujas.

There have been waves of Kumars from various parts of Bengal settling in the area from the time before and after the British settled among the three villages. In order to deepen our understanding of life as it used to be in the early days, we have to return to the stories told in present-day Kumartuli. And as mentioned above, the only accessible stories today are those of the Kumbhakars who originated from Nadia district. They are the forefathers of the first Kumars who made the production of thakur murtis an important part of their profession, and as the communal pujas became popular in Kolkata a hundred years ago, also their main source of income. In short, the stories of the Nadia Kumars are the stories of the murti makers of Kumartuli, the kind of Kumars that Kumartuli is today identified with.

Life and Work as Seasonal Image-Makers of Kumartuli

The murti makers from Nadia came to Kumartuli on a seasonal basis until after Independence. The stories that live on concern travel by boat from Nadia to Kolkata, the kind of work they did and the people for whom they worked, and the general social conditions at that time. As these stories are retold by Kumars of today, they must be seen as the contemporary representations of the past that they actually are, while at the same time as narratives containing parts of historical realities first told by those who experienced them.

It should be noted that it proved difficult to find people who were able (and/or willing) to share with me stories from the times before they were born. While they are comfortable talking about histories from their own lives and times, on which they are all experts, bygone days are not a field they are willing to easily discuss. Few seem to have any interest in the histories of Kumartuli. Even as I made my quest for people who could tell me about sei samay, those days, of their forefathers, only one man can be listed as the main informant in this respect. Many others provided small glimpses into the history, but most of them referred to Niranjan as the person who knew about such things.

According to Niranjan the story of this tuli goes like this:

Niranjan: Now I shall talk about Kumartuli. Before, it used to be a jungle. And there used to be many dacoits (*dakat*) here. The Chitpur road is named after Chitteswari Mandir, which is a temple of Goddess Kali. Here we have another Kali temple; this temple belonged to Raghu Dacoit. His full name is Raghu Mitra. This Kali temple belongs to Abhay Mitra.[7] Abhay Mitra was also a dacoit, but later he became rich. On which road did you come?

Geir: On Chitpur road where there is a big, red temple (*lal mandir*).

Niranjan: This temple has a history. This red temple used to have one pagoda. And it was higher than the Monument [Saheed Minar, earlier named Ochterlony Monument]. But it was all gone in a storm.

Geir: Was it the Nine Jewel Temple (*nabaratna mandir*)?

---

7 In Bengal many dacoits worshipped Kali, something to which the term ডাকাতে কালী, *ḍākāte kāli*, testifies. *Ḍākāte Kāli* is Kali as worshipped by dacoits.

Niranjan: Yes, it used to be the Nine Jewel Temple. And this temple belonged to Gobindram Mitra [?-1766]. [...] Earlier there was a Kumartuli here, but we were not. There were no makers of thakur murtis in Kumartuli then, they used to make clay pots.

We are from North Bengal, Nadia district, Krishnanagar village. My adibari is in Krishnanagar. My grandfather came here. Have you seen the old houses with big pillars? Decorations like that on the top of the pillars were done by my grandfather and he also used to make murtis. Since then we have been here.

You know why Kumartuli is situated here? Because earlier there used to be people from South Bengal, from Burduman, Bankura, Birbhum – they are what we call *raṛh*, because of its soil.

My forefathers used to make clay pots, but not here. Here were those people [potters] from South Bengal, that's why it is called Kumartuli.

According to Niranjan, Kumartuli was first settled by potters from southern Bengal. Then, with the need of artisans who had mastered the craft of making images, Kumars from Krishnanagar were brought in. The narrative emphasizes their group's connection to the more respected process of image making. As with all such origin stories, there is a break between a before with little refinement and a new time which coincides with the immigration of the Krishnanagar Kumars. Here the contrast is between two different groups of Kumbhakars, but the structure of the narratives is the same, with stress on the advancement they (the narrator's group) represent. Niranjan continues:

Niranjan: Then your countrymen (the British) came here; some of our people helped them; they got titles like 'raja' and became rich. The Sobhabazar rajbari-people became rich because of the British. Raja Rajbollo [...] there is also a street named after him. Have you seen this temple (pointing)? Very rich people used to live there, since it was the Saraswati river there [Ganga]. I can't remember the place, I will tell you later.

People there [at other places outside Kolkata] became very rich because the only transport at that time was by boat, no train, cars – and they lived by the river [...] so they became very rich. Later those rich people came to this Kolkata and started living here with other rich people who became rich through betraying their own countrymen. Those who were in Gobindapur [...] there, there were some people who had the jamidari (tax right for farm land) for these three villages – they sold it to the British for 1600 rupees.

The British had their own soldiers, so the *rajas* (noblemen) became more secure here. So that is why they came here. Some of these people started Durga Puja. Durga Puja then was the most beautiful occasion. These rich people wanted to manifest their richness. Durga Puja was their only way to show their richness.

While the Bengali autumnal Durga Puja dates back to the early years of the seventeenth century, as mentioned above it gained momentum after Raja Nabakrishna Deb arranged his famous Durga Puja in 1757, celebrating the British victory over the Nawab. He belonged to the growing group of landowners or petty kinglets who moved from their capital towns into British Calcutta in order to seek protection during the seventeenth century.

Sundip, a soft-spoken and still active resident Malik in his eighties, tells about the beginning of Kumartuli differently:

Sundip: Kumartuli existed from the time of the British Raj, for almost 300 years. It was after the British came here, then Kumartuli [...] All the artists say they have lived here for 300 years, after the British came here; they made this Calcutta, then this side of the river was cleared. Earlier there was some jungle and so on here; then it was cleared. When the people of the village asked the Sahibs what they were doing, what they would do when they had cut down the jungle, the Sahibs replied in Bengali 'Kal Kata', we cleared it yesterday; they did not know Bengali very well, so that is how the city got its name.

Kolkata's etymology, as explained by Sundip, is a popular one in Bengal. The more well-read Niranjan says it is not true (interview 22/02/07). Nair also confirms this in the most thorough study of the city's etymology (1986), where he says it is the natural canals that gave the city its name. Niranjan is perhaps not a typical storyteller of Kumartuli, as he has read a lot and actively comments on discussions that go on in newspapers or within academia.

Niranjan continues his story about Kumartuli, talking about the Krishnanagar Kumars' seasonal work in Kolkata. Niranjan's grandfather was the first in his family line who came to Kumartuli and Kolkata from Krishnanagar and as he tells it:

Niranjan: As my ancestors were Kumars, they used to make clay pots. We have one phrase in Sanskrit 'Khumba karuti (kore) kumbha kar' – those who make the pots are the Kumbhakar. Sanskrit is our old language, India's old language. My ancestors, fourteen–fifteen generations ago, used to make clay pots. Back then in Krishnanagar they also used to make little clay models which were world famous. Have you seen the boats (*nauka*) carrying raw materials [for the image making, a common sight on the Ganga next to Kumartuli]? Have you observed those boats? Krishnanagar clay-modellers made little models of that type of boat [...] including models of the two-inch-tall men who are picking up the sail and working in the boats, the men who are rowing the boat. It looks like the original; they were so good in making models. Those two-inch clay models look like real-life persons.

My village is in Krishnanagar. There it is a river that goes to Mayapur in Nabadwop. And then from Mayapur it was easy to come to Kolkata. It was on the day of *Rathyatra* (a chariot festival held in the last part of the month of *ashar*, in early July), people from Krishnanagar came to Kolkata, they stayed here for work for a few months and left after Kali Puja (*Kartik Amavasya*, October/November). [...] In Maniktolla there were storehouses for wood, frame-wood from Sunderi trees from the Sunderban. We used to get bamboo from Shalkia. Raw materials like wood, bamboo, straw and clay were easy to get here. The expenses for raw materials were very low here, because of the river.

According to three original maps from the first half of the nineteenth century exhibited at Victoria Memorial, there existed a place at Maniktolla also called Kumartuli. No other reference than Nirjanjan's are made to this area with reference to the Kumars. Whether it was a place where the Kumars had storehouses, as Niranjan suggests, or perhaps at some time a place where Kumars also made murtis, is impossible to deduce from my material. It should also be added that the location of Kumartuli by the river is seen as a necessity by every commentator upon Kumartuli, insiders and outsiders alike.

Niranjan: Generally there was a ritual in connection with them coming there on the day of *Rath* or the birthday of Krishna – *Janmastumi*. Then the first thing they had to do was to cut a piece of bamboo or other wood like *goran, sunduri* – and give it to the man of the house in which they will build the Durga murti. And initially one has to worship that piece of wood at the house [this worship is also common today, but now the Brahman or someone else arranging the puja takes care of obtaining the bamboo piece]. And then after 3-4-7 days, Kumars started working there.

In those days, Kumars used to work in the houses of rajas and jamidars. Usually they did not make the murtis here in Kumartuli. And the place of the house where one makes the murti is called a thakur dalan.

There is one ritual [...] that they believed in. It was not like that in all houses. Kumars used to start working on the same day, but there

were some special days like *Janmastumi* and *Radhastumi*. To start making a murti, we do not have any formal rituals as artists. We think of
God and ask for his blessings. No formal rituals. In India we have lots
of gods and goddesses and we believe each of them to be the same.
I believe in all gods. This is Jesus [points at a ten-centimetre tall statue
of crucified Jesus on the wall besides the bed], I have read the Bible
and the Koran – and I have also read the Veda.

As Niranjan says, the Kumars used to make the images at people's houses
as there was no practice of making ready-made images for an open market at that time. Another aspect of their work in earlier days emerges when
Niranjan, on a separate occasion, starts to talk about his diet. He lists what he
usually has for breakfast, lunch and dinner. He is an old man and like many
Bengalis in their old age, he eats a more or less vegetarian diet. In addition, as
a believer in the philosophy of Gandhi, he says that he wants to live a modest
life – something he has tried to do throughout his life, most times out of sheer
necessity. In his own words:

> **Niranjan:** My breakfast is so simple with some *muri* [puffed rice], one
> banana and some curd. But a rich man would never like to dine with
> such simple food; he would very much like to dine with various types
> of food. This simple food is also very good for my health. I prefer
> vegetables. I have stopped eating meat and eggs, but as any Bengali
> man I like fish – I eat fish thrice a week. I used to eat meat, but then
> I stopped when I felt like it. This is the situation.

He takes a small pause, smiles, then continues to talk about how they took
their food while working in the houses of the rich in the old days.

> **Niranjan:** If they were proper people, with good background, like
> Brahmans, we would accept their food and water. Then we would take
> the food they presented. It would be part of our payment. But if there
> were other people, we would make our own food and bring our own
> water. This is how it used to be, today it is all different.

As mentioned earlier, the Kumbakars belong to the clean Sudras and the
Nabashaka group, which means their position in the local hierarchy was relatively high. Only when they came to the house of people of a really good
ritual standing, like Brahmans, did they accept the food and water presented;
otherwise they made their own preparations. This is the only statement that
refers to a time when the pure–impure distinction that informs a hierarchy is
given to me by any of the informants without me asking specific questions.

Niranjan goes on telling about the kind of work his grandfather did around the 1850s.

Niranjan: My grandfather used to decorate the great palaces of the rajas. One can get those designs in two types, one of cement, the other from burning soil (*mati purie*). Have you seen B. K. Pal's Dispensary? You can see my grandfather's work there. B. K. Pal's name is Batakrishna Pal.[8] He used to sell German medicines. Now, these days, they also have a shop in Rajabajar. Sir Harishanik Pal was their forefather, it was he who got the title Sir.

My paternal grandfather had his home here, but not in this house. Now we have two new houses of our own by the airport. We rented the ground floor of the building situated opposite this building for forty-five years. This house used to be my workshop.

Nimai, an active Malik and head of the West Bengali Kumars' organization, narrates the beginning of Kumartuli as follows:

Nimai: It was 300 years back when Job Charnock came to Kolkata. Then they came here to the ghat, on the Ganga. They first came here. Then the potters here only worked on the wheel. And first Raja Krishnachandra [Roy of Krishnanagar], he brought an artist from Krishnanagar to make a thakur for his house, for Durga Puja, and to worship the goddess Durga, it was the first and then the puja started. At first it was one puja then *aste-aste*, slowly, it became more. *Bhadralok* artisans came from Nadia [district], [the town of] Krishnanagar. They came here to Kumartuli to work. The people came here from Shantipur, Ranaghat and Krishnanagar, almost all the people came here and made their settlement here, started Kumartuli.

Nimai uses the term *bhadralok* artisans to describe the group of potters who came from Krishnanagar. 'Bhadralok' means the gentle people or a gentleman, and is the name used for the educated elite starting from the mid-nineteenth century. As does Niranjan, Nimai marks the coming of Krishnanagar potters as the arrival of higher class of potters in Kolkata.

---

8 Also known as Butto Kristo Paul in old style spelling, the well-known nineteenth-century owner of pharmacies and the Edward's Tonic, a cure for malaria and fevers of all kind (Das 2007). His grand family home was and still is in Sobabajar, North Kolkata. His family came originally from Howrah (ibid.)

Sundip's story of the beginning of murti making in Kumartuli is slightly different from Nimai's. Still, he emphasizes that potters from Krishnanagar were brought into Kolkata in order to make the images.

> **Sundip:** At that time, they did not make murtis here; they were working with the potter's wheel. Then slowly we started to make murtis, and that was work done by people from Nadia [like himself]. Raja Nabakrishna [Deb, 1733–97], and different others, started to do pujas with potters from Nadia. Earlier there was not too much idol-making here, there were a lot of people who worked on the wheel, they made the pots, vessels, et cetera, but not the idols. The Raja Nabakrishna and some other people, the big people, they wanted to do some pujas, then they brought these artists from Nadia.

Here both the names of Raja Krishnachandra and Raja Nabokrishna have surfaced as originators of Durga Puja. As mentioned above, Krishnachandra lived in Krishnanagar and it is thus perhaps natural that he is credited as the main promoter of the festival (Hardgrave 2004, Chaliha and Gupta 1990: 331), and the one who introduced and popularized the worship of clay Durga murtis. Nabokrishna of the Shobhabajar, in North Kolkata, is said to be the founder of the family puja and the one who first really started to use it to enhance his business interests just after the Battle of Plassey in 1757 (Chaliha and Gupta 1990: 332). Durga Puja, although it has a history in the Kolkata area that predates Krishnachandra by more than 150 years, can thus in the form we witness it today be traced back to him and to Krishnanagar. At the same time, it gained momentum a few years later in Kolkata with Nabokrishna, who probably was influenced by Krishnachandra to such an extent that he invited Krishnanagar Kumars to create Durga murtis for his royal house's thakur dalan: an indication that even after the Battle of Plassey, Kolkata was still not the undisputed centre of Bengal.

Niranjan proudly says that the Krishnanagar Kumars came here to make murtis, since the Kumars already living here were not skilled enough to make good murtis. Krishnanagar Kumars are specialists in making murtis.

> **Geir:** Did your people use to make murtis in Krishnanagar before coming to Kumartuli?
>
> **Niranjan:** Yes, we have been doing it for a long time.
>
> **Geir:** It is an ancient tradition?
>
> **Niranjan:** Yes, *onek din*, long time.
>
> **Geir:** When did you Krishnanagar Kumars settle here permanently?

Niranjan: When we started to get a lot of work, work of idol-making and house-decoration.

Geir: Was it 100 years ago, 150 years ago [...]?

Niranjan: It is hard to say in which year they settled down. But it was in the time of the British, when they came and started to rule Kolkata. Perhaps after five years.

While Krishnanagar Kumars might have settled in Kumartuli in small numbers throughout the entire period, it was only later that most of those who engaged in murti making settled permanently.

Geir: At that time they only spent a few months here and then went back to their village?

Nimai: Yes, only a few months and then back to the village. It was a seasonal job.

Geir: When did it stop being a seasonal job and start being a full time job?

Nimai: I am not sure, it was in my father's time, it was 80 to 85 years back when he started to do a full time job.

Niranjan, Nimai and Sundip tell about how Kumartuli existed as a place for potters who worked on the wheel, making pots and utensils for a whole range of requirements. It was with the beginning of Durga Puja that potters skilled in making murtis, statues, became a necessity in order to make better Durga statues. The Kumars from Nadia District already had a reputation as skilled murti makers, and given their relatively easy access to Kolkata, they became the preferred choice. Thus started the seasonal work in connection with Durga Puja. The Nadia Kumars came in early July and stayed for three to four months. It is difficult to interpret what Niranjan means when he says that the Kumars settled five years after the British came, but to date incidents in this way is not unique to him. One should instead emphasize the fact that the Krishnanagar Kumars came only shortly after the British. Still, he seems to indicate the fact that only after the British came did Kolkata turn into a place that attracted rich Hindus and thus made it an important place for making images for residential pujas.

The Potters' History and Their Society

It seems probable that the Krishnanagar Kumars started their seasonal work in Kolkata in small numbers, following the popularity given to Durga Puja with clay murtis created on commission from Krishnachandra, and introduced to Kolkata by, at least, Nabokrishna.

The actual Durga murtis also looked different earlier. It was only with the entrepreneurship of a single Kumar in the 1920s, Gopeshwar Pal, that this tradition was broken. This disjuncture with tradition is the topic of the next chapter. However, there is a common understanding among Kumars that there existed few variations concerning the appearance of the murtis before Gopeshwar broke the rules. In the old rajbaris, royal houses, that still arrange Durga Puja they use actual moulds, said to be part of a line of copies, that guarantee that the murti's appearance has not changed since the first pujas 200–250 years ago. There exist a few engravings and paintings made by Europeans depicting Durga Puja from the nineteenth century. Perhaps the oldest is Balthazar Solvyns' 'The Durgah Pooja', probably made in 1809 (Hardgrave 2004). These support the position that there was little variation in the style of Durga images until the first half of the twentieth century.

Since the stories about the time before the communal pujas are few, it is hard to emphasize any trends or aspects. Still, I would like to point to a few important themes that emerge from the stories, beyond the actual historical developments concerning seasonal work, immigration, and so forth.

First there is a tendency among the Kumars to contextualize themselves within the historical narrative of British Kolkata. There is an awareness that Durga Puja, as we know it, was created by the nobles, the *nouveaux riches* Hindus that came to prominence due to their collaboration with agents from the East India Company. It was they who created a demand for qualified artisans from Nadia district to make their thakur murtis for the 'new' Durga Puja.

Another interesting aspect is the fact that no one in Kumartuli would say that their adibari, their ancestral home, is in Kumartuli – they are either from Nadia or East Bengal. This adds to the flavour of Kumartuli as not primarily a residential neighbourhood, but as a place of work. While it probably was a residential area for ordinary potters when the Nadia Kumars came for seasonal work, since their arrival it has primarily been a workplace for most of the Kumars. Even today, most Kumars have a family home outside Kumartuli, although they sleep within their workshops during heavy periods of work.

For all the Kumars working and/or residing in Kumartuli today their jati's former life as potters making pots and other utensils is a life that existed somewhere else. For people from both Nadia and Bangladesh, Kumartuli of Kolkata has always been a place for making murtis.

Most important in these stories from the old days is the emphasis given to the role of the potter in society. From their importance in the marriage of Mahadeb, to their abilities as image-makers required by the rich for their celebration of the most important religious festival of the Bengalis, potters are given an integral role in society. The potter and civilization (as a complex society controlled by certain laws) seem to go hand in hand. The narratives of the Kumars present an important insight into their self-understanding, as they use them to represent themselves in history. Whereas in the 'official' history of Kumartuli presented in the first part the Kumars are hardly given a place in any history of Kolkata or Durga Puja, in the Kumars' own stories they are carriers of civilization.

Contemporary Kumartuli Realities

Kumartuli is situated in North Kolkata, in the middle of the old indigenous part of the colonial city. This part of the city is what was called Black Town. With its narrow lanes and Bengali-style houses and palaces it was seen as almost a separate town. At present it is the more run-down part of the city, as southern Kolkata and various suburbs have attracted those who can afford them. North Kolkata is seen as more conservative, as the last resort of the Bhadralok, the Bengali gentleman. In contrast to central and south Kolkata, there are no new shopping malls here. As is Kumartuli, North Kolkata is often stereotyped by Kolkata inhabitants as belonging to a slightly different time (Figure 2.1).

The neighbourhood lies west of Rabindra Sarani, commonly referred to by its old name, Chitpur Road, and the railroad that runs along the River Hoogly, which is always called Ganga in the vernacular. To the north is Bag Bazaar;

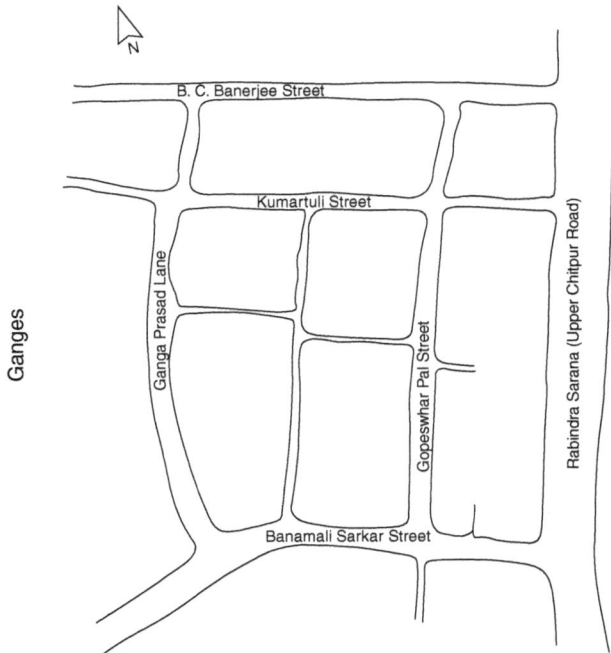

Figure 2.1 Map of Kumartuli.

while to the south is Soba Bazaar and Sonagachi, the major red light district of Kolkata. The place is just where the weekly cotton-market village of Sutanuti was for at least 200 years before the British finalized the establishment of their new Bengali trade post in 1690. Encircled by multi storied concrete buildings on three sides and the river ghats on the fourth is the collection of seemingly dilapidated workshops and low buildings, scattered among a few temples, a royal palace and a couple of lost commercial buildings reaching for the sky, that make up Kumartuli. The cluster of mainly workshops, residential buildings and small shops is approximately 150 metres wide and 200 metres long, but there are clay workshops also outside this core area. Kumartuli lies within Wards 8 and 9 of the 141 wards that make up the total jurisdictional area of Kolkata Municipal Corporation. There is an 'official' entrance to the neighbourhood on the Chitpur road, with a signboard and a small office that charges money from those who want to take photographs of the Kumars (Figure 2.2).

One will never miss it when one enters Kumartuli. Clay statues in various stages of completion fill the workshops and line the narrow alleyways. It is a slum, it is a residential area, but most importantly it is a business area, with buildings constructed for the needs of the ongoing work.

The buildings are a combination of *kaca* and *paka*, which in this context means buildings made (a) by 'traditional' and 'crude' materials such as mud,

Figure 2.2 The 'official' entrance to Kumartuli. Photo by author.

clay tiles and bamboo and (b) cement and brick, respectively. Modern *kaca* buildings also consist of plastic and metal plates. All the houses and workshops have electricity, but only a few have water. Water is available from communal pumps. A couple of the 'main' roads are *paka* (asphalt), but most of the narrow lanes are *kaca*. The drainage system is also locally called *kaca* now.

The sizes and shapes of the workshops vary greatly. Some are rather narrow in width, around three metres, but extend backwards to a depth of ten to fifteen metres. Yet again, others have a wider frontage, but are shallower. Heightwise, there is also a great variation, since the roof height is very important because this governs the height of the images a Malik can make. The shops are constructed using a great variety of materials for a single workshop. The main supports might be bamboo poles, while the walls are sections of woven mats, tin, bricks or other available materials. The floors are of mud, while the roofs are mainly of clay tiles. A separate room in the larger workshops or a corner in the smaller ones is used as an office. This area is furnished with a couple of plastic chairs, sometimes a wooden bench, and a desk. The walls in the office are covered by calendars and pictures of images made in that workshop. This is where negotiations between the Malik and customers usually take place, as well as the more formal and recorded interviews I carried out in the workshops (Figure 2.3).

It is difficult to give a definite number of workshops, as the term is rather elusive in the context of Kumartuli. While a few families have several workshops within the neighbourhood, others work mainly in the street. The latter usually have their residence in Kumartuli, but no exclusive building to make the images. Still, they are all Maliks working on their own in the business of making murtis for sale. According to my own survey there are around 180 workshops engaged mainly in murti making in Kumartuli. Around a quarter are run by East Bengalis, who spatially dominate the southwestern parts of the area.

Numbers and classes

Kumartuli is a mixed residential and occupational area. Less than half of the people connected to the area as residents or through their occupation are Kumars from a family running a murti workshop. There exist several other workshops specializing in decorations of various types used by the Kumars, and cottage industries like making the plastic sheets used to wrap cakes. Another large group consists of those who work as full-time or seasonal workers in the Maliks' workshops.

This study is, however, limited to the Kumars running their own workshops, or members of their family. Around 2,500 people live and/or work in Kumartuli. Among those, about 180 are Kumars with a workshop of their

Figure 2.3 One of the larger workshops. Photo by author.

own. It is people from this group, together with their families, that constitute the study's main informants.

The streets of Kumartuli are lined with various workshops, of which a majority naturally consist of image making ones. Other workshops are mainly those engaged in the production of decorations used to adorn the images. In addition there are a few tea shops and a number of residential buildings that are usually situated behind the workshops. Turning to the image makers, they constitute several different classes. When it comes to the Maliks, there is a difference between those running a single workshop and those who run a small-scale art industry with a number of workshops and storehouses within and outside Kumartuli. While they are all dependent on loans in advance of the pujas to finance the construction work, the latter often have a chance of acquiring a surplus that they can reinvest in the business, their children's education and so on. In terms of lifestyle these Kumars belong to Kolkata's middle class. While a majority of the East Bengali Kumars belongs to this class, only a minority of the West Bengalis does. A majority of the Kumars does not live in Kumartuli, but has houses elsewhere in Kolkata. All Maliks are dependent on wage labourers. There is a small group of female Maliks in Kumartuli. Among those whom I was able to identify, they entered the business either when their fathers died without having a son or son-in-law to continue the business, or when their husbands passed away before any male children were old enough to work as a Malik. The stories of these women do not differ substantially from those of the men; they all say they are respected by their male counterparts. On the other hand, one of them expressed her frustration at having to work full-time in order to support her family. She would have preferred to stay at home taking care of her children as a regular housewife.

The wage labourers that every Malik utilizes are either migratory or live in the vicinity. While the migratory workers live in Kumartuli during periods of work and have ten-hour working days, the local workers have eight-hour working days. The former are given food and lodging as compensation for their longer working days. The migratory working force constitutes a majority of around 70 per cent of the wage labourers. Generally, two types of work are available for them. They can work on a temporary basis for a number of work-shops and be paid by the day; or they get more or less permanent employment from a single Malik for a given period, often the whole season, and receive a fixed payment. Among the group of semi-permanent workers there is also a group of apprentices who are learning the trade.

The people – Maliks, Kumars and Kumbhakars

The Maliks as well as their wage labourers place their 'original' home, adibari, in either Bangladesh or in Nadia District in West Bengal. Thus, the notion of adibari links the jati to either West or East Bengal. The various histories of immigrations to Kumartuli will be discussed in subsequent chapters; still it is important to note this divide as an important social feature within the neighbourhood, which divides the Kumbhakar population into two groups. The Maliks have organized themselves into two samitis (associations) dominated by East Bengalis and West Bengalis respectively. The hereditary occupation that the contemporary Kumars have more or less actively chosen to pursue is only one aspect of their identity, and equally important is their experience of being connected to a geographical area. I will also use the terms East and West Kumars when it is necessary to distinguish between the two groups. In Bengali there are several terms that distinguish between those East and West of which bangal and ghoti respectively is most common. It should be noted that the term for East Bengalis, bangal, is mainly used as a derogatory term.

Regarding jati affiliation, most of the people engaged in the clay production are Kumbhakars, but there are a small minority of people from other jatis as well. The latter work as Kumars, but they are not Kumars. The profession of image production has for more than a decade attracted people from other jatis; and they have been accorded the possibility of establishing themselves both as wage labourers and Maliks. Thus, the common portrayal of a jati enjoying an occupational monopoly is not entirely correct. At present there are several Maliks from other jatis, like Brahmans and weavers. Every Malik and labourer is aware of his or her jati affiliation. As for the Kumbhakar majority, they are potters, Kumars or Kumbhakars. It is they who make the unbaked clay thakur murtis, while their forefathers used to work at the potter's wheel making pottery, and with their foremothers they made clay putuls (dolls and miniatures). The caste knowledge seldom extends further than this jati awareness. Knowledge of *sreni* and *gotra* (two kinds of sub-groups, often used interchangeably) is lacking among the great majority. Most have a rudimentary knowledge of the jati's creation history. Still, as I will discuss later, the jati affiliation is used as an asset. During the last decades a growing number of non-Kumbhakar artists from outside Kumartuli have started as designers and makers of images. Often they have an education from an art college and their work is highly popular among the larger and wealthier puja arrangers. As a competitive move, the Kumbhakars often emphasize their jati affiliation as a guarantee of their artistic abilities, claiming 'they have it in their blood'. The purchase of an image from Kumartuli is thus advocated as a purchase of an image with a genealogy going back to the 'old' history of the Bengali people.

Most of the people working in Kumartuli are Hindus; as for those engaged in image making, everyone is a Hindu or at least born one. People with another religion, which in practice means Muslims, are not hired at any level in the actual clay work. Kumars belongs to mainstream Bengali Hinduism.

The pujas and / as the Maliks' work

There is a Bengali saying *baro mas tero parban* – twelve months, thirteen festivals – and it speaks for the popularity of festive occasions among the Bengalis. To paraphrase the Sanskrit poet Kalidasa, it is tempting to add that 'Bengalis are, by their very nature, fond of festivals'[9] (Sharma 1978: 3); many Bengalis will approve of or proclaim such an essentialistic statement. And there are more profane and secular festivals than thirteen. For the Kumars it is the various pujas where images are required which organize their work.

9 The actual line reads (when translated): Men are, by their very nature, fond of festivals.

The pujas are themselves organized by the Bengali calendar, and dates are provided in the almanacs (*ponjika*, or *ponji* as it is colloquially called). The dates of the pujas are not fixed, but are determined by calculations done by the almanac-makers who use the Bengali version of the composite lunar–solar calendar used throughout South Asia. For Durga Puja, it is the movement of the moon that marks out the beginning. The Bengali calendar is a super-imposition of a solar year of twelve months upon the cycle of lunar months (Nicholas 2003: 13). This necessitates some adjustments, since the solar months are slightly shorter than the lunar ones. The New Year's Day or *Pohela Boishakh* always falls on the same day, but every third year an extra month (*malamas*) is introduced to bring the two cycles together again.

The exact dates of the various pujas differ from year to year and are determined by astrologers. Take Durga Puja: the first day of the puja proper was in 2013 on the 12th of October, in 2014 on the 2nd of October; while in 2015 it falls on the 21st of October. As all the pujas take place at roughly the same time every year, a list of the most important pujas for the image makers looks like this:

Bengali months	Seasons	Gregorian months	Festivals important for the Kumars
Baishakh – বৈশাখ	Grishma summer	April–May	Ganesh puja
Jyaishtha – জ্যৈষ্ঠ		May–June	
Asar – আষাঢ়	Barsha rainy	June–July	Rathyatra (images of Subhadra, Jaggannath and Balaram)
Sraban – শ্রাবণ		July–August	Manasa puja
Bhadra – ভাদ্র	Sarat autumn	August–September	Biswakarma puja
Ashwin – আশ্বিন		September–October	Durga puja
Kartik – কার্তিক	Hemanta harvest, dewy	October–November	Kali puja; Laki (Lakshmi) puja; Karttikey puja; Jagaddhatri puja
Agrahayan – অগ্রহায়ণ		November–December	
Paush – পৌষ	Sit winter	December–January	
Magh – মাঘ		January–February	Saraswati puja
Phalgun – ফাল্গুন	Basanta spring	February–March	Gopal/Krishna puja
Caitra – চৈত্র		March–April	Annapurna/Basanti puja

The different pujas can be divided into categories according to where the actual puja generally takes place, for example temple worship or domestic worship. The Kumars construct images with an intentionally limited lifespan since most of them are immersed in the Ganga when the puja is finished. Thus, one will seldom find an image made by a Kumar in a temple. Their main venues are public and domestic pujas at places like makeshift pandals, private shrine rooms, the thakur dalan of mansions or permanent pandals (a contradiction in terms, but still used locally). Images for domestic use are usually much smaller than the ones designed for public appreciation.

Of all the pujas that the Kumars make images for, Durga Puja is the single most important. In 2006, the number of Durga images made within the neighbourhood is said to have reached a stunning 12,300. A further introduction to what Durga Puja is all about is thus necessary.

Durga Puja: the worship of goddess Durga. The day preceding the ten days of Durga Puja, on *Mahalaya*, men crowd the sides of the River Ganga. They face the sun, chant mantras and offer purifying water and respect to their forefathers. The radio is broadcasting *Mahishasuramardini* (an old religious radio program), recitations and songs. It is the day of the new moon preceding the puja. There can be no doubt – Durga Puja is about to start. While scripturally, the puja is said to begin on the first day of the waxing moon of the Bengali month of *ASwin*, the action takes place from the sixth to the tenth day.

While the history of the first Durga Pujas of Bengal is lost, it is commonly accepted among scholars that the custom started among the landowning families in the early seventeenth century (Banerjee 2004, Blurton 2006). Moreover, Durga has been known in the Indian subcontinent for nearly 2,000 years, and depictions of her as the killer of Mahisha, the demon in the guise/cover of a buffalo, date back at least to the Kushan period of the first centuries CE in the Mathura area of northern India (ibid.). In Bengal one finds terracotta and stone plaque representations of Durga killing the buffalo Mahisha dating back to between the third and sixth centuries CE, a period seen as a stage in the iconographic standardization (ibid.). The first scripturally elaborated source is the *Devi Mahatmya* from the fifth to the sixth centuries. It contains several stories about the Goddess, including the two stories that are invoked in Bengal during the puja. One is that of Durga as the killer of the Mahisha, the other is her departure from her husband Shiva's home in the Himalayas and the return to her family home.

Her visit is celebrated as the annual homecoming of Durga to her family home, escaping for a few days from her wild and unpredictable husband Shiva, and of Durga as the killer of the Mahisha. These two major elements might seem contradictory. One centres around the pacific and the family, the other around the martial and cosmic.

As the goddess of victory, we see her has triumphing over the forces of cosmic disintegration. While many regional traditions exist, there is a core narrative which is common in Bengal (Blurton 2006). According to Blurton (2006: 30–37) and Banerjee (2004) it goes as follows.

Ages ago, the demons made the gods grant them favours, through building up merit by practising intensive yogic exercises. Their austerities brought the demons so many favours that in the end they could rule the world. Deities tried to conquer the demons, but without success. Ever higher forms of divine beings tried to defeat them, only to suffer their entire armies being completely annihilated by the demons. It became evident that no being in the divine hierarchy could face the demons. The combined fear, agony and anger of the greatest gods coalesced in an epiphany of frightening and brilliant light – and the goddess Durga was born. The great gods each armed the ten-handed Durga with one of their weapons. From Shiva she got the trident, from Vishnu a discus, from Vayu a bow and quiver, from Agni a mace, from Mahakaal a falchion, from Yama a shield or magic staff, from Varuna Nagpash – a missile which spouts poisonous snakes. From Indra she received an elephant goad and a bell, while Visvakarma, the god of craftsmen such as the Kumars, gave Durga an axe. Himalaya, the god of the mountains, gave her a lion for her mount, and, thus, she was ready for the battle with the demon chief Mahisha. Durga's battle cry unleashed cyclones in the sea and landslides in the mountains. Initially Mahisha laughed at the appearance of Durga and, when she asked to meet him in battle, he sent his armies of demons against her, which her lion killed with ease. Then he finally appeared on the battlefield himself and soon they were raging through the universe.

It is a battle for the ages. Mahisha continually changes shape, becoming a lion, an elephant, et cetera, in his attempt to destroy Durga. She besieges all the manifestations of the Mahisha, beheading the lion and cutting off the trunk of the elephant. Then Mahisha becomes a buffalo again and as he rages across creation, Durga raises a cup of intoxicating alcohol to her lips, stares with blood-shot eyes at Mahisha and says: 'Roar as you please, you foolish beast. When I destroy you, the gods will make more noise in celebration'. The buffalo speeds towards her, neck craned and horns pointed, but Durga leaps onto the creature and beheads him with one blow. Mahisha tries to escape out of the creature's body, whereupon Durga, almost nonchalantly, pierces him with her trident; the contest for cosmic sovereignty is concluded. And this is the moment that is captured in the images worshipped during every Durga Puja.

As the beloved daughter returning to her family, she is envisaged as pacific and maternal. She is thought of as the daughter of the presiding deities of the Himalaya, Himavant and Menaka. Durga is also known as Parvati, the daughter of the mountain. Like so many other women, especially in past centuries, she has been married young and moved to the residence of her older and dissolute husband Shiva. Shiva, lord of the mountain Kailash, is both frightening and exciting. He is a drug-crazed and lazy madman, who makes Durga suffer in his palace, where she has to cohabit with Shiva's second wife Ganga. Her parents are horrified by her situation, but only once a year is the family united. This takes place during Durga Puja, when the goddess is honoured as the killer of Mahisha. As Durga Puja is the major festival in Bengal, this is also the time when Bengalis return to their family homes in order to celebrate. Like Durga they unite with family and friends, enjoying the days away from school or work of their Puja Holiday.

The joyful emotion engendered by her return to Bengal and the related unhappy end of her visit, combined with the victory over Mahisha constitutes the important and symmetrical parts of the whole puja (Blurton 2006: 39). Little happens during the first five days of the puja, but on the sixth, on the evening of *Sashti*, the rituals start to take place. Durga is brought to life, given her weapons; her mirrored reflection is given a bath. And she is worshipped and admired, until the last day, *Bisharjan*, the day of immersion, when the drumbeats carry a mournful sound. Women apply vermillion, the mark of a married woman, to Durga's forehead, stroke her gently with betel leaves, feed her sweets and pan and touch her feet as they plead with her to come back the next year (Banerjee 2004). In the afternoon or evening she is carried to the river followed by people from the given community. Again the drummers are central; they lead the profession, drumming as though in a trance, followed by young boys and men dancing with abandon within the sad procession. The goddess and her children are carried on lorries lighted by powerful lamps powered by diesel generators and equipped with hi-tech sound systems. Other members of the community, women and children, men and elders, might also get a place on a lorry. They shout and sing, waving to the onlookers on the pavements. The noise of the puja, with the drummers and the recorded music, is a nod towards the noise the gods will make as they celebrate the conquest of the Mahisha. It is as integral a part of the ritual as the whispering of mantras done by the Brahmans.

Finally, they reach a ghat on the Ganga. There some male members of the group carry Durga and her children on poles on their shoulders. Turning around a few times, they descend the steps down to the river. There she is immersed together with her children. Durga has returned to her husband at Mount Kailash. Another group of people swims towards the immersed images, dragging them to another ghat in order to recycle whatever they can, like reselling the frames to the Kumars.

Dramatically divergent stories of the goddess cover many human experiences and the myths' presence can be felt in many aspects of human life (Blurton 2006: 41). It is not difficult to relate to the underlying themes of

Durga Puja, and this is perhaps an indication of the reason why it still remains enormously popular.

Durgotsab: the Festival of Durga. People from the highest to lowest strata of society, from every jati, from every religion, are welcome to celebrate Bengal's great festival. And it seems that just about everyone turns up at this festival: walking with friends and relatives from pandal to pandal through the streets lined with hawkers; judging the murtis, the pandals, the ambience; eating snacks and taking a ride in a Ferris wheel; dressed in new clothes, looking forward to the big puja dinner at home. At this dinner, the better-off get a taste of every traditional Bengali dish that is so time-consuming to make that they rarely eat it on regular days, at least not in such quantities and such variety. There is giving and getting of gifts, mainly new clothes, but perhaps the long desired mobile phone suddenly becomes more than a dream?

Most of today's pujas are Sarbajanin durgutsab, that is, a puja arranged by a committee for the local community. Some (smaller) committees depend on subscriptions in order to collect money for the arrangement, but most depend on sponsors and renting out of space to various vendors. Thus, creating an impressive puja is important both to attract big sponsors and to demand a high price from vendors. There are theme pujas with pandals resembling anything from Harry Potter's school Hogwarts to an Egyptian pyramid, from a celestial wagon to the robbers' cave that Ali Baba discovered. Fantastic decorations may be made of buttons or kitchen utensils. It is an occasion for meeting the neighbours at the local pandal; talking about the new shop next door, last year's events and the joys of the local puja.

Among the other important pujas, in terms of the income they generate, are the Kali, Laki and Bishwakarma pujas. The latter is also the Kumars' 'own' puja, as Bishwakarma is the god of artisans and other craftsmen. This one-day puja is mostly performed in factories, garages and workshops where any kind of tool is used. On the day of Bishwakarma Puja, professional drivers of taxis, buses, trucks and so on also decorate their vehicles. Historically any undertaking of religious art should be preceded with a Bishwakarma puja. While the use of small, temporary shrines and clay images has been customary for a long time, artisans in the past performed the puja upon the tools. For the potters this meant a puja held upon the potter's wheel. Ganesh puja was not commonly celebrated on a large scale in Kolkata, but its popularity has gradually increased during the last decades.

When a puja approaches, a committee or family that wants to arrange one has to go to a Kumar in order to purchase an image. This can be done in two ways. Either they go from a couple of weeks up to several months in advance to a Kumar and place an order. Such commissions are common for the larger pujas where images in a specific style are desired. The style and size is then decided through discussions with the Malik, who often himself suggests a certain look. The other way is to visit the Kumars shortly before the puja to purchase a readymade image. Kumars prepare a large number of such rather similar looking images for the open market. Customers wander around to see the style of the different Kumars and ask for prices. Commissioned images are usually of a better quality than the readymade and thus more expensive.

Constructing an unbaked clay murti

For the numerous pujas the Kumars construct images of various gods and goddesses from unbaked clay. Their work is based on an oral tradition and regional custom, thus the Kumar have been labelled 'traditional' or 'folk' artists, distinguished from 'classical' Indian artists, who follow textual injunctions like that of the *Silpa Sastra* (Robinson 1983: 10). While the work of the Kumartuli Kumars bears strong regional (Bengali) characteristics, it often maintains many of the conventions of the classical, scriptural tradition.[10] This is especially so when the Kumars make murtis in the (traditional) bangla style. While the bangla style was the only style of murti until the 1930s, at present there are many styles, as discussed in Chapter 5.

The unbaked clay images, also called *terracruda* (raw earth), are typical for Bengal. Other materials than clay are becoming common as export sales to other states and countries grow. Some also get commissions to make profane murtis of everything from historical figures like Mahatma Gandhi to movie-figures like Spiderman (Figure 2.4). Some of the Maliks running small workshops make figures or dolls (putuls) for decorative purposes. Still, with a great and growing number of pujas celebrated in Bengal, the main market lies within the manufacturing of images of deities, *thakurer* murti. It is the pujas that count for almost all of the Kumars' work.

The unbaked clay images are referred to as *Sudhu*[11] (only) or *kaca*[12] (raw) *matir* (clay) murtis and are thus distinguished from baked clay (terracotta) images called *paka* or *pora mati*. The construction of all the various clay murtis follows a similar procedure. Only images smaller than two or three feet in

---

10 Scriptural conventions often emphasize the rules of measurement concerning the iconographical proportions. Other important aspects concern the various qualities like fearful, passionate, malignant or tranquil that the images should possess, hand gestures or *mudras*, attributes like multiple hands holding various objects, dress and ornaments, postures, colours and choice of materials (Robinson 1983).

11 শুধ in Bengali.

12 কাঁচা in Bengali.

Figure 2.4 Secular fibreglass image and sacred-to-be clay images. Photo by author.

height are made with moulds, the rest are largely modelled by hand. When the design and size are chosen, the construction can be divided into four stages (for a comprehensive description of the process see Robinson 1983 and Varma 1970): a) construction of the framework, b) straw binding of the figures, c) application of clay and d) painting and decoration.

Framework: According to the form and size, a wooden platform is made of intersecting planks of hard wood nailed or bolted together. This foundation is called *takta*,[13] which literally translates as 'a piece of board', but it also denotes a throne. Mango wood used to be the preferred material (Robinson 1983: 79), but now any kind of hard wood is used. On this base, vertical bamboo rods are inserted into drilled holes. The framework is called *kathama*,[14] from *katha* meaning wood. It is set to hold the image in place. The images may be made directly on the bamboo poles or raised on a frame of spliced bamboo tied together. The framework is usually reinforced with wooden poles angled to support the finished murti. Most images also have a semi-circular backdrop known as *cali*,

13 তক্তা in Bengali.
14 কাঠাম in Bengali.

from *cala*[15] which means 'shelf', 'roof' or 'thatched roof of a house'. The *cali* can also support the images, but is sometimes detachable in order to make it possible to manoeuvre larger images into confined spaces. The *cali* is usually made of strips of bamboo tied firmly together, though sometimes plywood is used. This is then covered with clay and straw; or a piece of cloth is stretched tightly over it and tied on the back, making it a *markin* cali, where *markin*[16] denotes a coarse white fabric or unbleached muslin (oddly enough, *markin* also connotes the USA or an American) (Figures 2.5 and 2.6).

Straw-binding: When the frame has been completed, the process of straw-binding starts. This is an important part of the work, since the straw body determines much of the final appearance, as it provides the basic shape and most of the volume of the figure. The process is vernacularly called *ghor-bata*. Paddy straw is most common, but also *ulu*[17] grass is used. The straw is tied into bundles with a string and these are then used to compose the overall shape of the figure. The straw figure is attached to the framework. It is made without head, fingers or toes (Figures 2.7 and 2.8).

Clay: There are several kinds of clay used in the making of the images. The clay itself is applied in two layers, a process known as *do mati* (two layers of clay). For the first layer one uses *entela mati*; this is a rather sticky clay and is applied roughly over the straw-body. After the application of the first layer, the murti is left to dry. The second layer is then applied, sandy clay called *balu mati*, which is watered down and filtered through a cloth to make a smooth finish. Anatomical details are made at this stage, often using a stick to make details such as beauty lines around the neck and navel. The idols might then be left to slowly dry thoroughly in the sun or in the workshop. If the clay dries too fast, it cracks. To partly prevent and mend this, water (or extremely watery clay) is applied (*phata jorano*). Sometimes it is necessary to strengthen and/or mend the image; this is then done with pieces of cloth that are dipped in watery clay and put on the image.

At the same time, the face, fingers, toes and other details are made of clay from moulds or by hand. The face is usually made from a mould (*chanc theke mukh banano*). The clay used for the face is a mixture of the two types of clay used on the body. The mould, made of plaster of Paris and both baked and unbaked clay, is dusted with fine ash before the clay is pressed into every cavity. Then a kneaded mixture of entela mati and husks or jute fiber is used to form

---

15 চালা in Bengali.
16 মার্কিন in Bengali.
17 উল, a kind of reedy grass.

Figure 2.5 Making a wooden frame. Photo by Prodyut Pal.

Figure 2.6 Frames. Photo by Prodyut Pal.

Figure 2.7 Straw-binding. Photo by Prodyut Pal.

Figure 2.8 Headless straw Durga. Photo by Prodyut Pal.

Figure 2.9 Applying clay. Photo by Prodyut Pal.

the back of the head. After the face is removed from the mould, the features are refined using a brush or a small stick. Then the head and the fingers are fastened to the body, with clay and/or pieces of cloth. The murti is now ready to be painted and decorated (Figures 2.9 and 2.10).

Décor: Air-brushes are today common tools to apply paint, but regular brushes are used to paint the finer details like the three eyes and beauty lines. First a foundation colour is applied; usually this is white. While there used to be relatively strict codes concerning the colours, like green skin on Mahisha and yellow on Durga, this is not so anymore. The paint is often blended with a mixture of soap and glue to give a shiny, oily surface. To provide a glowing effect a varnish, a kind of oil, is applied. This is also seen as resembling mild perspiration, in itself a mark of beauty. There is no special sequence to the painting process after the foundation is finished. The eyes are made by a senior artist, since this is a special moment in the process when the image is brought to life. The quality of the eyes is also important for the Kumars. Often it is stated that the Malik himself does this job, preferably at a time when he gets peace enough to concentrate properly. While this might be the ideal, other

Figure 2.10 Clay Durga. Photo by Prodyut Pal.

artisans than the Malik also paint the eyes, even at times of the day when Kumartuli is as busy as it gets.

The ornamentation consists of a crown, jewellery of various kinds and a breastplate. These are mainly made of pith (*sola*) and tinsel (*daka*). Occasionally real jewellery is used. The females commonly wear a sari, while the males wear a dhoti and shawl. Other kinds of costumes are also used according to the style of the image. The type of fabric depends on what the customer wants to pay. The hair is made of jute (Figures 2.11 and 2.12).

In the end

So when the image is finished, it is time to get it transported to the place where it will be the centre of a puja. The images are carried out by hand or on simple carts from the narrow alleyways into the larger streets where they commonly are placed on a lorry.

Only occasionally does the Kumar travel to see images they have made installed in the pandal, if it is not a local or especially famous puja. All they can do is hope that their image will be given a prize in the many contests that

Figure 2.11 Making decorations. Photo by Prodyut Pal.

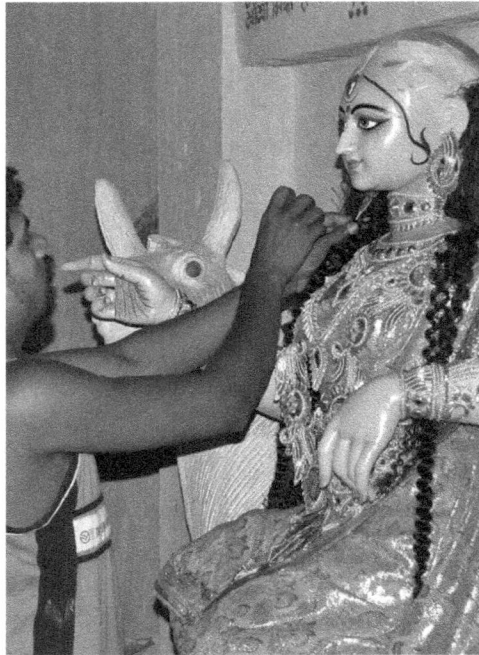

Figure 2.12 Ornaments and hair. Photo by Prodyut Pal.

take place during Durga Puja. Such contests are arranged by a number of groups ranging from newspapers to large multinational corporations. To collect a prize for the work means an enhanced reputation. And as a Kumar's reputation together with his artistic abilities is his main asset in the market, such prizes result in more customers the following year.

Chapter 3

BIRTH OF TRADITION, COMING OF MODERNITY

The gradual change of Kumartuli from an artisans' neighbourhood into a hub of clay-modelling artists took place through much of the twentieth century. After the pujas moved from the palaces and courtyards into the streets, in a slow process which lasted until Independence in 1947, the Kumars started to work fulltime in Kumartuli, mainly with the community based pujas, the sarbajanin durgutsabs. This paved the way for Kumartuli's most famous son, Gopeshwar Pal (1896–1952). His eminence as a sculptor made it possible for him to travel to England for the International Exhibition in 1924–25, followed by Italy where he attended a sculpting course. Later, the committee of the Kumartuli Sarbajanin Durgutsab in 1935 asked him to create its Durga pratima, image. He accepted the proposal and introduced what is described by contemporary Kumars as a dramatic stylistic change in the tradition of modelling for the Bengali Durga Puja.

The 1935 Kumartuli Sarbajanin with Gopeshwar's groundbreaking image is analysed as a key event in establishing a modernity in Kumartuli when it comes to the Maliks' attitude towards their profession. Starting with Gopeshwar, this chapter will describe and analyse the Kumars' relationship both to their artistic work in general and to individual innovations in the making of images. The beginning of this line of modernity in Kumartuli also witnessed the birth of the most senior inhabitants and workers of today. And some of the most senior Kumars tell about their ambivalent relationship to the break with tradition.

Gopeshwar Pal – an Artist?

The development of the image from the beginning of today's Durga Puja in the early seventeenth century is difficult to trace. A few old paintings dating from after its popularization in the last part of the eighteenth century, as well as oral tradition, provide some clues.

Figure 3.1 *Ekchala thakur* at the *thakurdalan* of Sababajar Rajbari, 2006.
Photo by author.

Originally it was *ekchala*[1] or single-framed (see Figure 3.1), which means that the images were placed within a shared structure, a style contemporary Kumars call *bangla* (Bengali). Durga stands solemnly with one of her hands holding the trident which ends in the chest of Mahisha with his green skin colour. Her mount is a lion, an animal not indigenous to Bengal. It does not resemble a lion at all, since the modellers at that time did not know what a lion looked like, but more like a horse. The ancient face (*pracın mukh*) of Durga is round in shape like a betel leaf (*pan*), with stretched eyes (*tana chok*) formed like bamboo leaves, the nose is pointed like a parrot's beak and the skin colour is yellow (see Figure 3.2).

The Durga Puja at Sababajar Rajbari, one of Kolkata's old palaces, provides a glimpse of how pujas were organized before the time of Gopeshwar. This puja was first celebrated in 1757, three months after the Battle of Plassey. It is widely acknowledged as having been initiated by Raja Nabakrishna Deb

---

1 চাল [cāla] n. a thatched roof or covering, a thatch (ঘরের চাল, নৌকার চাল); a circular canvas of mat containing paintings of heavenly scenes placed at the back of an idol (usu. চালচিত্র) (Samsad Bengali–English Dictionary 2000: 355).

Figure 3.2 The face of Durga: round in shape, yellow, with bamboo-leaf eyes and a parrot beak nose. Sababajar Rajbari, 2006. Photo by author.

as a celebration of the British victory at Plassey, with Robert Clive as the guest of honour. The heirs of Nabakrishna Deb deny this, stating it as a 'baseless legend spread'. Nevertheless, the thakur, god, is said to be moulded as it was 250 years ago, using the same moulds for the faces. While this is a highly debatable claim, as moulds do not last that long; the stylistic appearance, including form and colour, have probably not been changed, as these coincide with the scriptural rules that the Kumars used to follow (Robinson 1983). That this image represents the traditional style is a shared understanding among the Kumars, as well as being supported by older paintings and engravings of Durga Puja (Robinson 1984, Varma 1970). As a tradition, the Durga Puja is still celebrated in the palace's worship hall, and its images are of the ekchala bangla style. When Durga Puja was in the hands of the rajas (like Nabakrishna) and the babus of Kolkata, the Nadia modellers made their seasonal travel to the city to make the Durga images. The form changed little. It was through the use of costly material for clothing and precious metal and stones in the orna-ments, in addition to the ostentatious distribution of sweets, food, cloth and other gifts that the organizers showed off their economic power.

   With the decline of the palace pujas and the growing popularity of sarbaja-nin puja this was all set to change. The market for images grew, making ready-made murtis a popular choice; the pujas became politicized as a venue for the fight for self-rule and later independence (see Chapter 4), as well as being democratized in terms of being arranged by people from almost all classes. While this started early in the nineteenth century, it did not become a common feature before the early decades of the twentieth. As a result of the growing demand for images, the Nadia clay modellers started to settle in Kumartuli. Gopeshwar Pal was one of the persons from Nadia who travelled to Kolkata in search of a fulltime job there. The workshop he established is named after him and is today run by Byomkesh. He is not a direct successor of Gopeshwar, as his only child, a son, never had any children. Byomkesh is related to Gopeshwar through his sister Jamuna, who was married to Gopeshwar's son Siddeshwar. The story of Gopeshwar is vague and there exist many versions, especially concerning how he was appreciated in England. With the help of Byomkesh, various articles (some collected by the latter) and a book about arts and artists from Krishnanagar (Chakraborty 1985), the story can be told as follows.

Gopeshwar was born in 1896 (Ghose 1981: 46) as the youngest of Binodbhiari and Kusumkumari's three sons. Binod was himself a potter of Krishnanagar but he died when Gopeshwar was just a child, an event that threw the family into poverty. It was his maternal grandfather Paranchandra who became his first teacher in the profession as a potter: Here he probably also learned the craft of clay doll making, which the Krishnanagar potters were famous for. Besides Paranchandra (1826–1924), his two maternal uncles Satishchandra and Kshitishchandra were important teachers, together with the famous Krishnanagar artist Jadunath Pal (Chakraborty 1985).

His maternal uncle Satishchandra's daughter Krishnabala was married to Ramnrisingha, whose father was the idol-maker of Panchakot rajbari ('palace') (Chakraborty 1985), a job which guaranteed a high status and a far better payment than common potter's work. Ramnrisingha brought the young Gopeshwar to the palace, where he got a job and learnt the craft of image-making. While he was working for Ramnrisingha's father he also learnt painting from an unnamed foreigner (ibid.). Gradually he became well known in Nabadwip, Krishnanagar and Ranigunj for his artistic abilities. Already an image of this person as a special individual emerges through the narrated fact that he learnt painting and became famous while still a young man.

At this point the history of Gopeshwar becomes a little hazy. On one hand it is said that in 1910, at the age of 24, he left his native Krishnanagar and travelled to Kolkata with just ten *annas* in his pocket (Roy 2005). For a few years he took various jobs in the city, and in the end had saved enough money to buy a small house. He worked as an image maker and was soon developed a reputation as a fast and excellent artist. Another, perhaps more convincing, story has it that Gopeshwar made regular journeys to Kolkata in order to work as a portrait and architecture painter (Chakraborty 1985). Many others worked as painters in this way, but the others often had a formal education from abroad (ibid.). Even before he went abroad, Gopeshwar seems to have chosen a rather unpredictable path of life. This choice of breaking with his jati's occupation, in which he had been successful, points towards an individualism often described as both modern (Gaonkar 2001, Narayan Rao et al. 2003, Chekuri 2007), as well as typically non-Indian (by Dumont 1980: 184–85, also Dirks 1992, Mines 1994).

What is certain is that in 1924 his life took a new turn. Byomkesh says that in that year Gopeshwar found an advertisement for the British Empire Exhibition, a colonial exhibition to be held at Wembley, London in 1924–25 (Knight and Sabey 1984). What made the journey possible is uncertain. Byomkesh says he just applied together with the renowned dancer Udayshankar and they were selected to go. A recent newspaper article states that it was Percy Brown,[2] then principal of Government Art College (in the period 1909–1927), who selected Gopeshwar to represent India at the exhibition in Wembley, due to his extraordinary skill of sculpting the likeness of any person in a matter of minutes (Roy 2005). Yet another story claims that the contemporary Bengali Governor Lord Carmichael[3] saw Gopeshwar's work in Krishnanagar during an exhibition there in 1915. The Lord was very impressed and almost ten years later he suggested that Gopeshwar should be sent as one of the representatives of Bengali artisans to England in 1924. The fact remains that he left for England that year, a journey that his family did not support.

In England he showed his talent as a clay artist in various ways. Byomkesh says he made a horse's head in forty-five seconds. King George V and other members of the British royalty are said to have visited the exhibition (Roy 2005). And among all the artists from colonial countries, it was Gopeshwar who stole the show, by making a statue of the Duke of Connaught in a very short time, impressing the royal family immensely (ibid.). Moreover, it is claimed that Gopeshwar was placed in a room with glass walls so that all the spectators could see him work (Chakraborty 1985).

Due to the reputation he reportedly gained in England, Gopeshwar was asked to embark on a tour around the world to exhibit his talent. Gopeshwar turned the offer down and decided to go to Italy, where he attended a sculpting course (Roy 2005). It was some members of the Exhibitions Committee who helped him accomplish this (Chakraborty 1985). There he learned to make sculptures of stone and bronze.

When he came back to Bengal, Gopeshwar made two decisions: to establish a workshop in Kolkata's Kumartuli, not in Krishnanagar, and to work with stone and bronze, not clay. In Kolkata, he was able to get support from the rail company owner Sir Rajendranarayana Mukherjee. Sir Rajendranarayana

---

2 Best known as the author of *Indian Architecture* (1942–1943).
3 Governor from 1912 to 1917.

approached some foreigners who were able to help Gopeshwar, providing him with, according to Byomkesh 'some important instruments' or machinery to continue working with bronze and stone (also Chakraborty 1985). As part of his production he later made one eight-foot five-inch statue of Rajendranarayana which was placed in the Victoria Memorial.[4]

Gopeshwar's reputation as an eminent sculptor grew in Kolkata, and in 1932–33 he was requested to make the Durga idol for the Kumartuli Sarbajanin Puja. As he also had adequate knowledge of working with clay, he accepted the offer of again working with clay. While the ekchala (single frame) Durga was the rule, Gopeshwar seized the opportunity of launching the trend of representing the deities as separate idols.

Thus, Gopeshwar abandoned the ekchala image and separated Durga and her children (Agnihotri 2001, Banerjee 2004). In addition, he wanted to capture the action of Durga killing Mahisha and, thus, did away with the iconic representations of the figures. He designed Durga as a battle-hungry goddess with her trident raised to kill Mahisha as he was pursued by the lion, while Mahisha 'had rippling muscles to accentuate the glory of Durga's victory over him' (Banerjee 2004: 49). When Jagadish Pal, who was to do the actual sculpting work, was told how to proceed, he quit, feigning illness. Gopeshwar had to make the image himself. The style is said to be based on western or Greek traditions of sculpting (Agnihotri 2001). This claim is not substantiated, as other, indigenous sources of inspiration could have been influential as well. The fact that Gopeshwar went to Europe does not imply that everything he did was based on European traditions. According to Byomkesh, Gopeshwar left no papers that could reveal his sources of inspiration. Most probably, he found inspiration in both Indian as well as European practices. Further, it is said that Gopeshwar made the image as a still picture from a 'western' theatre scene, with the image frozen in action (ibid.). Again, this might be the case, but at present no one can authenticate such an interpretation. Western theatre traditions were indeed popular in Kolkata from the 1850s onwards, but so were many indigenous forms (Heierstad 2001).

The new form of Durga was appreciated by the people, but the pundits (priests) were annoyed and initially refused to worship the image (Agnihotri 2001). However, the favour granted by the people made the style widespread. This was the first *art-er pratima* (literary art image), and the beginning of a new era. And for eight consecutive years, the now famous Gopeshwar made the

---

4 The statue is at present displayed in the garden of the Victoria Memorial. According to Professor C. Panda, secretary and curator at the Victoria Memorial, they do not have any additional works of Gopeshwar (personal communication).

images for the Kumartuli Sarbajanin Puja. On 9 January 1952 Gopeshwar died. But his reputation lives on among the other Kumartuli image-makers, and in a street of the neighbourhood that carries his name – Gopeshwar Pal Street.

In a newspaper interview the senior master Malik Mohanbanshi of Kumartuli is asked about what he thinks about all the different and new styles of Durga. While he is not very loquacious, he soon mentions Gopeshwar in a short lecture on images:

> The great divide between 'then' and 'now' [...] came with 'art-er pra-tima'. I can't give you the date, but Gopeshwar Pal first sculpted art-er pratima. That started everything. For Mohanbanshi, there are only two kinds of pratimas, 'ekchala and art'. Earlier, there would be one structure supporting the deities. Gopeshwar made the first free-standing figures, or 'art-er thakur'. This freed the imagination, for the artists and puja organisers, and eventually led to the current innovation of 'theme pujas'. (*The Telegraph* 28 September 2006)

While artisan craftsmanship could always be divided into excellent work and not so excellent, the invention of art-er pratimas opened up the making of images to purely artistic challenges and possibilities. Even as there are several limitations involved when making the Durga pratimas, artistic freedom, excellence and innovation became important and appreciated by, at least, the common people after Gopeshwar's 1935 pratima. With the break with the Durga image tradition, the imagination is set free. Moreover, it becomes an important asset in securing well-paid commissions for making images for the larger pujas.

The sculptures of Durga Puja are first and foremost sacral objects that serve as a dwelling for the gods during the puja. The statues are worshiped and given baths and food. It is taken for granted that the images are 'infused with the presence or life or power of those deities' (Davis 1999: 6) they depict. In short, to most of the participants, the pratimas of Durga Puja are animated beings.

Walter Benjamin (1985 [1968]: 224) made a distinction between art works of either cult or exhibition value, which can be used to illuminate the ambivalent relations most Kumars have to the images. Roughly speaking, the distinction is between religious and secular works of art, according to how they are approached, used and esteemed in a given context. Intuitively one would place Durga images within the cult value category, as they are works of art made for and used in religious ceremonies. This goes for many or most Indian images. Richard H. Davis, professor of religious studies, writes about old, recovered statues that are turned into objects of worship by people of the locality where they have been found (1997). Others, like scholars and British colonists, see the object as a historical and artistic artefact that belongs in a museum or an exhibition place (ibid.). This is then portrayed as two worlds colliding, and in many Indian museums or heritage sites today, one can see placards announcing that veneration is not allowed. For the pratimas this distinction should be seen as a continuum and not simply two colliding views: An image during Durga Puja is given both a cult and an exhibition value by artists, organizers and spectators alike. There is no clearcut distinction between these two values. This was the case both before and after Gopeshwar. In earlier times the appearance of the image was standardized, but in size and adornments the rajas competed to impress the public. With the decline of the rajas' pujas in the first part of the nineteenth century, the exhibition value of the image was small. After Gopeshwar this changed again, but now it was the communities together with the Maliks who demanded images that broke stylistically with tradition, and thus attracted attention. The responsibility for the Maliks thus changed, from using the same old moulds year after year, leaving the dressing-up part to the desires of the raja's household; to becoming the ones who decided on what changes were to be made and which innovations were to be implemented. Gopeshwar broke with the traditional approach to the process of making murtis and in the process, identified the 'traditional' style as such. The appearance of Durga was no longer unilaterally prescribed; she could be depicted in various ways. The sense that something called 'tradition' exists, and that it is not 'natural' is an important hallmark of modernity (Miller 1994). Historical depth and development are brought to the surface of peoples' views of society and its practices, with the sensation of presentness that the creation of 'tradition' presents. Gopeshwar's helpers' and the Brahman pundits' outrage showcase the unnaturalness experienced with a different Durga. Was Gopeshwar's 1935 rendition of Durga, Durga at all? Was it blasphemous to both make the image and worship it? The Brahmans, at least, acted as if it was. The new image placed all the other images in relief; it was now possible to compare and see what was the, until then, accepted style of Durga, her children and the Mahisha. And due to the positive response from the public at large, this new approach gained tremendous momentum over the following decades.

The exhibition value given to an image by the participants, e.g., organizers and spectators, is based on several features. According to the Kumars, few outsiders are able to appreciate the quality of the work; instead the outsiders usually pay attention to the innovative aspects. And there are limitations on what kinds of innovation the participants will accept. Too much 'innovation' when it comes to the image and the pandal is said to not provide a feeling of devotion. It is impossible to pinpoint when the exhibition value dominates in a way that is disliked among the Maliks. Not only is there great variation in individual preferences, but also many markers are used when discussing such a topic. There is a continuum from cult to exhibition value concerning how people approach the image. While a Kumar might see exhibition value in the quality of how the face is moulded, its proportion and the painting of the eyes, common people will primarily see a regular animated image of worship. When commoners are faced with something they experience as new and/or grand, they start to acknowledge the exhibition value. If the image of the god, thakur, is made and placed within a solemn environment, as most thakurs are, they also get a devotional sensation. If, however, the pandal and the image are turned into what they call a 'theme park', then there is mainly exhibition value left. And this is a view that both the image makers and the participants share. To the Kumars, the ideal image should display both maximum exhibition and cult value at the same time.

The Gopeshwar style of art-er pratimas turned out to be a regular crowd-puller. Attracting many visitors is an important aspect for many puja organizers. Organizing a Durga Puja is a costly affair; traditionally the expenses were covered by collecting subscriptions. But as the collection became more and more a nuisance and the need for even more money increased, sponsorship became widespread from the beginning of the twentieth century (Goldblatt 1979, Banerjee 2004). In order to attract sponsors, the organizers need to draw a huge crowd. The biggest pujas are multimillion rupee events, with major national (Tata) and international (Pepsi) companies as sponsors. Here the devotional aspects are hard to see, it is mainly about exhibition. Such pujas are few, and to most people just part of the general entertainment. The great bulk of pujas are smaller, attracting primarily local sponsors, and are seen as devotional. To return to the continuum between cult and exhibition, cult can be said to represent devotion or aspiring to bring forward a sensation of devotion, while exhibition is also about business or the financial aspects of arranging a puja. And the financial aspects are important to all organizers.

To the Kumars, especially the seniormost, there is a pronounced ambivalence between the devotional and financial aspects of the pratima. Most of them say they prefer the traditional pratima described above, since it gives them a proper feeling of devotion. On the other side, the market demands more groundbreaking pratimas. And the Kumars are in no financial position to refuse all such requests, since the payoff and reputation granted by theme images are substantially higher than that of readymade ones. Then there is the third aspect, the artistic challenge. At least some of the Kumars find satisfaction in making pratimas that combine both the devotional and the innovative.

According to the Kumars of today, Gopeshwar was the main or sole creator of the art-er pratima. They experience his break with the ekchala Durga as a caesura in their history. Art image is the Kumars' term, describing all styles that differ from what is perceived as tradition. As this term suggests, Gopeshwar was the first maker of an 'art Durga', and was also the first artist. From then onwards the Maliks could use their faculty of imagination; imitations of past murtis were not the only approach. The Maliks were given, in their own eyes, the possibility of creating art. Gopeswhar makes the rest approach their work and think about it in a new way. From the Maliks' point of view, after Gopeshwar created the new Durga of the 1935 Kumartuli Sarbajanin Durgutsab, creating art images became a possibility. Individual innovative and artistic abilities became an asset; the former style became 'old' and 'traditional'. In short, Gopeswhar makes other Kumars modern as he makes them see their work and themselves as on the other side of a caesura.

In the following, we will return to Kumartuli and the stories of the present day Kumars. From their recollections of Gopeshwar to their appreciation of various pratimas, their relations to *tradition as a modern experience* will be elucidated.

'We Used to Listen to These People's Names'

Most of the elderly of today's Kumartuli were born here, except those who arrived from East Bengal after Partition. They were born when Gopeshwar was at the height of his fame. Their lives started when their fathers and mothers started to settle permanently in Kumartuli and art-er pratimas became the preferred choice of the customers. The name and legacy of Gopeshwar is still alive in Kumartuli today. And stories of his abilities as an artist are often told. The following information about Gopeshwar and his peers is typical; the narrative style of referring to the memory of famous Kumars occurs in most discussion. Nimai and Gour provide good examples of how the past is recalled, and the similarities in the discourse of most Kumars suggest that their memories, of especially Gopeshwar, are collectively shared. In the narratives of contemporary Kumars Gopeshwar is a defining moment.

Nimai owns a small workshop in Gopeshwar Pal Street, a narrow lane that hardly has space for a motorcycle. His ancestral home is in Shantipur in Nadia and his family has worked in Kumartuli for five generations. He is among the most reputed Kumars and possesses a central position in the Kumartuli Mritshilpa Sangskriti Samiti, the association for (primarily) the West Bengal Kumars – a position he holds partly due to the fact that he is among the few senior Kumars with a college education. He aspired to be a doctor, but was asked to join his father in the workshop before he could pursue his dream. Recently he told his youngest son to quit his education in order to learn the trade properly, so that he could take over the business after him.

It is out of season and he is alone in the workshop. While I start my interview with him speaking Bengali, I soon realize that he understands English. Thus, I start to ask most of the questions in English, while he replies in Bengali. I begin to ask about the time when his family settled permanently.

Nimai: The making of images, pratimas, was a seasonal job. Only a few months here and then back to the village.

Geir: When did it stop being a seasonal job and start being a full time job?

Nimai: I am not sure, it was in my father's time, it was 80 to 85 years back when we started to do a full time job.

Geir: Did your father tell you any histories about the first pujas and its images?

Nimai: It was the ekchala Durga […] Netaji Subhas Bose came here to celebrate one festival, Durga Puja […] Gopeshwar Pal was the first artist who tried to make the separation from this ekchala, he made many chalas. 80 to 85 years back, Gopeshwar Pal created the first separation. We [the samiti, assoication] have some souvenirs with the written history of Kumartuli, I can give you that [it turned out that they did not have any leaflets left]. Gopeshwar Pal was a big artist, and he went to England, and when he came back he could make a total face within seven minutes. It was the face of *Rani* (Queen) Elizabeth.

Geir: How much time do you need to make a face?

Nimai: Two days […] ha ha.

In the old days of the first pujas it was ekchala – full stop. Nimai can tell about the rajas and babus who first started the tradition; he is well informed. When it comes to the pujas and images as such, they were ekchala. And while ekchala images are still regularly made, it is the end of the total dominance of that form which Nimai emphasizes. When thinking of bygone days, it is the name of Gopeshwar he recollects and presents. While Gopeshwar did not get any education in England, as he was present as part of the Exhibition, it is said that he made sculptures of the faces of a few celebrities there (as narrated above).

Gour, who in his early twenties came to Kumartuli from East Bengal after Partition, soon learned about the legend of Gopeshwar. In his eighties and too sick to work in Kumartuli, he has time to talk about old days while sitting cross-legged on a charpoy in his room. As one of the few East Bengalis, he comes from a family who were primarily making pratimas before they came to Kolkata. When he talks about bygone days and the story of his family, the reference to Gopeshwar is never far away.

> **Gour:** Yes, we have actually always done the work of making pratimas. My paternal grandfather used to work with the [potter's] wheel but it was too hard work – so the main work was to make idols in others' homes. In those days, there was no such market of images. Then we started living here [in Kumartuli after Partition] and gradually we are in the state of – what you are observing now [among the big and successful Kumars].
>
> We have heard about N.C. Pal [Nitai Chandra Pal] – he was still living that day, but Gopeshwar Pal was no more [in fact Gour arrived in Kumartuli before he died, but he was probably not working and living here anymore]. […] They were big artists. They have raised the name of Kumartuli.
>
> Yes, there were many others, but these people were famous. Gopeshwar Pal went to *bilat*[5] (a western country), he made a statue of *George the Fifth* within fifteen minutes. […] Such was his power (*ksamata*). His ancestral home (*adibari*) was in Krishnanagar. And N.C. Pal was also one of the great artists of India.
>
> We used to listen to these people's names. And I have seen N.C. Pal – his house was there. But his sons were not able to continue the glory of his work. Mani Pal is the nephew of Gopeshwar Pal. Mani Pal is also a great artist. After his [Mani's] death, perhaps Gopeshwar Pal's sons are working now [Byomkesh is now running the workshop, His sister Jamuna was married to Siddeshwar, who was Gopeshwar's only son]. Gopeshwar Pal was the greatest artist we ever came to know about – there is still much of his handiwork in Kolkata – like in Dalhousie, in Rupbani (Hatibagan). […] He is the best. Before we came – Gopeshwar Pal used to make the idol of 'Kumartuli Sarbajanin Durgutsab'. Once the idol was burnt – within one night he had created it again!

The fact that Gour mentions Gopeshwar when asked about his family's background and their arrival in Kolkata is typical for a successful artist like himself. An 'outsider' from East Bengal, he nevertheless places himself within a genealogy back to the master craftsman from Nadia. Thus, he places his family within the historical development that predates their arrival. The

---

5 বিলাত [bilāta] n. England or Europe and also America; (loos.) a western country overseas (Samsad Bengali–English Dictionary 2000: 767).

heritage of Gopeshwar belongs to all the modern Kumars, be it from the Kumbhakar jati or others. He is a common forefather in terms of working as an image maker, and is incorporated by most individuals in their rendition of their family's history. Such genealogies cannot be called mythical or invented, as they are not told to explain actual (biological) ancestry. Moreover, Gour, as a successful Kumar, places himself within the history of famous Kumars. As do most East Bengali Kumars, Gour talks about himself within a tradition of the Krishnanagar image-makers, something that the people from Krishnanagar regularly argue against (as discussed in Chapter 6).

Stories of Gopeshwar's success in London and his ability to work extremely fast are a common source of pride for the Kumars. It tastes of international success and an increase of the artisans' status. He is seen as the one who raised the name of Kumartuli in the eyes of everyone outside. The descriptions by Nimai and Gour are not unusual, they are typical. Gopeshwar is a personified turning point, a redefining moment for the Kumars. As Mohanbanshi says, Gopeshwar defines the transition between 'then' and 'now', between traditional thakurs and artistic work.

And 'now' is the time after Gopeshwar, the era of today's Kumars. Making pratimas is 'now' a fulltime profession; artistic innovation provides reputation and improved profit. When the pujas were in the hands of the aristocracy, the Kumars went to their places to make the pratimas. There was a patron–client relationship that, as will be discussed in Chapter 7, could last for generations. With sarbajanin durgutsab the puja took place in temporary temples, pandals, in the streets. The Kumars had to make most of the pratimas in their own workshops and transport them to the pandals when they were finished. Most of the readymade murtis for sale to the various committees shortly before the actual puja are more or less made on an assembly line basis; they are rarely of the traditional style. Murtis ordered a long time in advance for the larger and/or richer pujas are the most innovative. Here the Malik and the committee members discuss the style and size, as innovative or especially well-crafted murtis are what the committees desire. These specially ordered murtis are the ones which provide a high income and a good reputation. But does the new way of providing high quality innovative art murtis imply that the Maliks' relation to the work is different than that of their forefathers? This remains to be investigated in the following.

The change from being an artisan to being an artist is seen in the change of descriptive terms that starts after Gopeshwar. The self-descriptive term that the Kumars use is *shilpi*, which denotes both an artist and an artisan. Their work is *shilpa*, which can denote everything from a work of art, a craft, a handicraft, arts and crafts, a technical art to an industry. But when they describe the transition from traditional to modern pratimas they incorporate the English word 'art', as in art-er pratima [-er marks the genitive case]. The traditional is Bengali; it's the ekchala with the old face (*pracin mukh*). Another later example is the change from naming the workshop a *karkhana* (workshop proper) to referring to it as a *studio*. Again, an English word is used to emphasize this change. While most Maliks still refer to their work-cum-exhibition-space as a karkhana, a small minority would insist that it is a studio. Some also use the term *studio* in the shop's name, while there has been and is no practice of using the word *karkhana* in this way. The word *studio* is connected to the workplace and exhibition room of an artist proper. Thus, there has been a need to communicate a difference between traditional and contemporary styles and practices: a need that resulted in the incorporation of English words into the vernacular, which is not uncommon in Kolkata or elsewhere in Bengal and India (e.g., Agnihotri and Khanna 1997).

In the work of image making, the change of style represented by Gopeshwar defines a moment when tradition is seen in the making. How to make an image in terms of style is not given anymore, it has to be continuously reinvented. The growth of pujas in the decades before independence (Goldblatt 1981) probably made the competition to attract subscribers, sponsors and other participants tougher. In order to survive or even gain popularity, they followed the Kumartuli Sarbajanin Puja which gained increased popularity with Gopeshwar's images.

The old style of making images was not sufficient; what the Kumars had learned about style did not matter anymore. A break or caesura emerges, and the past becomes separated from the present. This break actually creates the 'traditional style' in the sense that the sensation of a 'before' and 'now' in the practice of image making became evident only in Gopeshwar's wake. Thus, the important impact made by Gopeshwar does not depend on whether he was modern or not, but on the fact that his innovations created a new market and an environment where innovative forms and individual styles became an asset. The activities of Kumartuli's most famous son made the other Kumars see themselves and approach their work differently.

The introduction of an innovative approach to image making is reflected in the Maliks' relationship to their work, through stories concerning their own or their family members' individual abilities to create innovative and artistic images. It is also visible in the ambivalent feeling many have towards 'art images'.

'I Have to Accept My Father First, Only Then Can I Accept My Son'

The introduction of the new approach to the making of pratimas for Durga Puja gained prominence fast. This was mainly due to the customers' demand for artistic idols which incorporated an exhibition value. The image makers did not embrace the new style without objections. When they talk about styles of image making, the ambivalence towards the art images becomes evident. The elders feel a strong attachment to the old style. There is definitely an ambivalent feeling towards artistic freedom, which, according to most seniors, should not imply a total rejection of tradition. Interesting in this aspect is the juxtaposition of a conceived tradition as what used to be, and the present as the period that started with Gopeshwar.

Let us return to Nimai and his views concerning the changes in the making of the idol and his emphasis as an artist on its face and eyes.

Geir: The making of the images has changed [...].

Nimai: Yes, they [the images] have been become modern (*adhunik*).

Geir: In which ways?

Nimai: At present it has a touch of Hindi films; they look more like regular persons. It has become a business. Earlier it was a tradition, an old tradition, of the face of the idol, but today the customers want something else, like the face of Hindi films [...]. So, that is the change.

Geir: How do you feel about it?

Nimai: No, I do not like this. As an *artist* [using the English word], I like the old ways. I love the old tradition. Of course it is good to create a new thing, but not by the destruction of the old. I have to accept my father first, only then can I accept my son.

Nimai, reputed among his colleagues as an innovative image maker with a style of his own, does not like art-er pratimas which completely break with tradition. When Durga's face is modelled like that of an ordinary person, it loses its devotional aspects and turns into business, according to him. Innovation must be in touch with tradition; this is the source, the father. The sensation that there existed a valuable tradition in earlier times is clearly voiced.

Geir: But the process of making [...].

Nimai: Change; there has been a lot of development.

Geir: In which ways?

Nimai: Good finishing and good colours [...] because now we use compressors and spray machines. These days the finish is very good. Now people can apply colour to three idols in one day, earlier one man could only paint one idol in a day. We expend a lot of effort on the painting now, and the finishing is very good with the modern accessories.

Geir: But is this the only thing that has changed?

Nimai: No, the type of the work has also changed. At present, when we work with the thakur, we work on different themes. But earlier we used to make only one type of murti. Now humans are growing more sensitive (*sugrahi*) [sic] [...] so the taste has changed.

Again, previously there was only one type, a statement which all the Kumars I talked to agreed with. Whenever I spent time with them in the workshops and they had made a bangla image they commented upon it: 'This is the traditional style'; 'This is how we made them before.' As mentioned in the previous chapter, the little evidence concerning the style of pre-Gopeshwar murtis corroborates such a view (Robinson 1984, Varma 1970). The similarities were more striking; they had all the same round face with bamboo leaf-eyes and a pointed nose. And Durga, her children and Mahisha were all placed under the same chala, structure. The scriptural prescriptions concerning style were to a large extent reproduced in the murtis of those days (Robinson 1984).

Sundip, one of the oldest Kumars, with his ancestral home in Nadia district, adds to this picture:

Geir: I would also like to know more about the process of making idols and its changes. In which ways has the making of idols changed?

Sundip: Before we made many *debi* pratimas (goddess images), all with the traditional face. Now we make many works with Ganesh, the size has also changed, many want bigger images now[...]. Earlier it was the traditional face of goddess Durga, and then the concept was changed. The face became human-like, more like people's, like man, not gods. At present there are again some people who prefer the traditional faces.

Geir: What kind of pratimas do you like?

Sundip: I like the traditional faces best, but I am a professional and must make what the customers want. We are professionals so we have to make what the customers want, but I personally like the traditional face because it is godlier and creates a type of devotion in my heart [...] in everybody's heart and that is not present in the face of today's god which has a more human-like face.

After Gopeshwar there are several varieties of the pratimas, some mention two, others three. According to Nimai, there are at present three types of

Durga's face. The face is the most important part of the image and is usually made by the senior Kumar himself or herself. Nimai explains:

Nimai: Yes, yes. If I want to create something new, I have to put my entire mind on that thing, otherwise I cannot [do it]. It has to be very peaceful, especially when I make the eyes (*chokkhu dan*). We have some special type of work [commissioned], some type of idols which we send abroad […] when we make the face of the idol, any idol, then there should be no one else but me, so I can concentrate on my work.

Geir: The face is the most important part?

Nimai: Yes, 100 per cent. Everybody just looks at the face first, then at the body proportions, then if the fingers are OK. But first at the face, then the rest.

Geir: What is a perfect face (*thikthak mukh*)?

Nimai: My mind will tell me while working. It is all in the proportions between the eyes and various parts. The proportion of its nose, eyes and mouth should be perfect. There are three types of faces, one is old, the second is a mix and the third is like film. And the proportions are four, four, four, three, three and six, six, and this is the general way. If the head is of 16 fingers, then the proportion will be 4:4:4:4 [using his fingers to illustrate]. Two of the eyes will be 3:3. The cheeks will be 6:6. But for different types, there are different ways. Then the eyes and nose are different, they will be changed. And in the old, the eyes are big and old, the bamboo leaf-eyes.

There are three types of face. Prachin (old) face, *dobhasi* face, which means Bengali plus modern face and *chabi ana* face, when the face is like a film star.

The face is different according to different idols, Such as – Durga and Kali have two totally different faces. The face also depends on the height of the idols.

Nimai mentions several times that the eyes are the most important part of the face. And eyes that are formed like bamboo leaves look, according to his taste, good. The painting of the eyes is the final touch, called *chokkhu dan* (gift of the eye).

It is, ideally, done by a senior artist as a ceremony bringing her to life. Aware of this, I continue and ask Nimai if he gets a sensation of the pratima becoming alive:

Nimai: Yes, when I do the eye, then I feel that life is there. Then my mind is fully concentrated. If I cannot concentrate properly, than I just cannot paint the eyes. When I do any big work, good work [...] frequently in the middle of the night when there are no people, no sounds, just a calm and quiet situation [...] then you can do things perfectly.

Night time in Kumartuli is, if not totally silent; relatively quiet, with few people in the streets or trucks passing by on the nearby roads. Still, most of the time the eyes are painted during the day as regular work; this is especially so for the readymade images.

The perception of the quality of work is important for most Kumars. It is in their work that they invest their pride. And after Gopeshwar, innovations became an important asset in order to win respect and new customers; it has become an important economic incentive.

'The age of reproduction'

Gour is proud of his family's work to refine the making of pratimas. Here, the artistic drive is visible, together with the competitive situation created with the introduction of community pujas.

> **Gour:** Many of my works are in the collection of every artist – photos, *Nataraj* [another name for art-er pratima, free-style images] and many other works – I have discovered many new forms of art work (*shilpi kaj*).
>
> The hair they now use for the idol [...] earlier its quality was not very good. We [Gour and his brothers] and our father used to think about how we can make it better. Then we discovered a totally new thing. We coloured those jute fibres and tried it [...] and then we put oil in it and then passed a comb through the jute in order to arrange it. But now you can see this type of hair everywhere [...] people were able to duplicate it. Now thousands of people are using this method in order to earn an income. Now you can buy it everywhere.
>
> But how they managed to copy the formula, I do not know. So we left the work of making hair. Of course it was hard work. But if you ask anybody the name of the inventor [...] they cannot tell you. They will not tell you – even if they know the name. This is jealousy.
>
> Earlier it was ornaments made of spongewood. The labourers usually delayed the delivery of the ornaments. Their work was also not very satisfactory for us – so we decided to do it on our own. We, together with our father, discovered the pattern of ornaments made of *jari* [golden or silver thread]. Our new invention made everyone suspicious. It became so popular that my father had to pay attention to only making ornaments in order to satisfy the demands of the customers.

There was no other artist who could make the ornaments like my father Gora Chand Pal. Then people started to respect Gora Chand Pal. They felt that it was quite impossible for them to stop this man as he was such a brilliant person. He was an inventor.

And then this style of ornament was also copied by others. Then we stopped making ornaments. It is quite tough to continue with all the new discoveries. After the discovery, the thing becomes the possession of every-body, then it is quite impossible to continue with it as solely your possession.

And nobody will remember your name as a discoverer. Though they do remember your name as a discoverer, they will never mention it to anybody. Inventors are always left in darkness.

The competitive environment in Kumartuli is hard. Although the commissions grow steadily, so does the number of modellers. To emulate Gopeshwar in terms of making innovative art images is central in the competition to attract customers from the big, prestigious and better financed pujas – emulate, in the sense of creating something new that the participants like and want more of. If a prestigious puja committee is your client, then smaller pujas also want to be a client – the competitive environment is almost as hard between the puja organizers who depend on sponsors as it is between the Kumars.

While mentioning one's own or one's family's 'discoveries' is rare among those I talked to, since it is actually few who can claim to have made such 'discoveries', emphasizing one's workshop's good workmanship is common. This is usually done with reference to which big pujas they have made pratimas for. And it is hard to verify claims of 'discoveries', as Gour mentions, due to the competitive environment of Kumartuli. However, since many of the big clients want pioneering pratimas, the financial situation of a family is a good proof of innovative capabilities. Thus, Gour can demonstrate that his three sons have been given higher education; they have one of the biggest work-shops in Kumartuli and two minor ones within the neighbourhood, as well as a big family house for their extended family in one of Kolkata's northern suburbs, only a thirty-minute bus ride away from the workshop. This proves the success of the family in the business and, consequently, demonstrates the abilities of the clay-working members to meet the demand of the market, a demand that is satisfied by high quality and innovative pratimas.

The competitive situation is connected to innovation in clay modelling. Gour starts to explain, as his wife brings us some tea and biscuits that some younger woman of the household has made:

Gour: There are many pictures in our old albums. You can have a look at them in order to know the variety of our work. Now we do not get the right price, and we do not want to do the hard work of inventing new patterns. If you visit our workshop, you can have a look at those old albums.

I had already spent some time in their workshop and was familiar with the albums and the 'old' work. More interesting is his statement that they, his family, do not want to do the hard work of invention. Here there surfaces, as described later, Gour's lack of faith in the new generations of his family. He continues:

> **Gour:** Some days back there were some journalists from a newspaper – they wanted to take some of the old photos for their newspaper. Everyone knows my work […] all over India. They have seen my work, but they have not met me. But everything is suppressed. You need the help of the media in order to get publicity. Now it is the media who always give publicity to any Kumar, but they have never tried to know the genuine artists [*prakrt shilpi*].

The prakrt shilpi, genuine artist, is an intriguing concept. *Prakrt* denotes 'genuine, true, real, pure' and so on and carries a connotation of naturalness and of not being artificial, as it has its etymological root in *prakrti* 'nature'. Using this word, Gour makes a division between genuine artists and those who are not genuine. He thus advocates a view in which there are not only different styles of images, but also different kinds of artists. He elaborates:

> **Gour:** Now anyone can win first prize. But I know who really is a real artist. Such as Sanatan Rudra Pal – do you think he knows the work? [Before I can answer, he continues] No. Only one person is a real artist in their family and that is Rakhal Pal. But Rakhal Pal has five brothers, and those five brothers have their own children who are working in Kumartuli, but none of them is an artist aside from Rakhal Pal. Such as Mohanbanshi Rudra Pal [cited above…]. He has two sons – one is Sanatan Rudra Pal, another is Pradip Pal. Sanatan Pal is not an artist; he even does not know how to bind the straw [laughing resignedly]. Rakhal Pal also has his two sons. One of them is involved in this business, though he cannot do anything without the help of labourers. Nepal Pal is someone doing original work. He is an original artist. His original work has now been duplicated by his nephew […] such as my father and I had invented.

He uses the term 'genuine artist' not in the sense of something that is inborn and inherited across generations. It is an individual characteristic which has to be earned. There are two aspects connected to being a real and proper artist according to Gour. That of knowing the entire process of making the image, including binding the straw; and the aspect of innovative qualities. Before the times of art images, the latter had no importance in the making of murtis. The need to constantly create new images increases the pressure on the Maliks. The hostile environment that this creates engages Gour emotionally as he continues:

Gour: My own work (different types of faces of Durga) has been stolen by my own labourers. They were bribed by some other artists.

Gour's wife [sitting on another bed in the room, occasionally making small remarks, breaks in]: The tea is getting cold […].

Gour: [briskly] I shall not drink it.

One year my labourers were bribed and they stole thirty faces of Durga, Laxmi, Swaraswati, Kartik and all were duplicated [the moulds used to make the faces had been stolen, not the actual faces]. Ramesh Babu, the famous artist, his work was also stolen by someone. Almost all the artists use the faces created by Ramesh Babu. It is a painful event for me that none of these 200 artists have their originality. Every artist should have his own trend or pattern. They may try to duplicate my work, but it will never be like my own work. Nepal Pal also has his different pattern, which is quite impossible to duplicate [100 per cent].

As for me, I always have tried follow my father's pattern and to invent something new from it. Then I tried to follow the beauties, those who look beautiful among girls. Durga must be a beautiful woman. Beauty has no end. Beauty has variety – which I always tried to portray on Durga – this is my only desire. Those faces have been duplicated by others. After the immersion they used to break the face [remove it from the statue] as they were given money in order to do so. Many of them were often arrested.

For Gour, Durga does not need her 'old face' to be godly. Instead, she should be as beautiful as possible. And he does not aspire after the *aloksundar*, superhuman or unearthly beauty, but regular *loksundar*, human and earthly beauty. The scriptures are clear concerning what constitutes *aloksundar*, a concept that was reproduced in the non-scriptural practice of pre-Gopeshwar image-makers and the stylistically similar representations of Durga produced earlier. The art images break with this practice and the concept of beauty as an attribute of Durga changes accordingly. While many Maliks have, and do copy, the faces of movie heroines and heroes in order to make a face that the public accepts as beautiful, others, like Gour, also look for beauty in the streets. Whereas the beauty of the old Durgas had a definite look, the beauty of the new Durgas has 'no end' and 'variety'. As Gour despises duplication of others' work and takes pride in innovation, his sole desire is to make beautiful Durga images. The Maliks' capabilities of making 'discoveries' emphasize individualistic achievements, witnessed for instance in the end of patron–client relationships that had lasted for generations on the question of who should make a puja's image. To this we can add that even the representations of Durga have become individualistic. For many committees there is no satisfaction in showcasing a Durga that looks like that of the neighbours.

> **Gour:** Now is the age of reproduction (*ekhan nakaler yug*[6]). I cannot find out even one of them who is creating something new or is trying to create it.
>
> Have you heard about Alok Sen? He is also a man of copying [a hypocrite]. But he is reputed enough and has passed out from Art College. He even does not know how to bind the straw. In our Government Art College they never teach how to bind the straw (laughing). But there should be a department for straw binding.

The making of traditional pratimas was based on re-creating the former years' images. At the Sobabajar Rajbari they say that the face is similar to that made for the first puja in 1757; the same moulds have been used every year and new moulds are made similar to those they replace. While there were variations in the size and the actual appearance, all the images were made according to iconographical injunctions, they are standardized in a way which strongly resembles scriptural sources (Robinson 1981). This is so, although the knowledge of the Kumars was orally transmitted. With the reuse of moulds it was rather similar to a mechanical reproduction on a very small scale. However, with the emphasis now on innovation, according to Gour, the age of hypocrisy and copying has begun. This is a sign of the importance placed on creating something new, an image that carries the 'signature' of the maker. While making the annual reproduction of the image was the traditional job of the Malik, copying began to be seen as deceit and doubledealing when innovative work became appreciated and requested.

Innovation is not an easy job; it places more responsibility on the Malik since 'tradition' no longer provides the mould for the statues. Before I turn

---

6 The word used for imitation is *nakal* (নকল), which also translates to imitation, mimicry, a copy, a transcript, and the act of copying from another's script etc. by adopting unfair means. Thus, there is a connotation of something illicit to the word, as in reproduction (*nakal*) by stealing (*cori*) moulds, concepts or ideas.

to an elaboration of the modernistic turn in Kumartuli, an example of the innovative process and the artist's situation in the 'new' trade is presented in order to contextualize the artistic craft of making 'discoveries'.

Innovation and pride

Innovative abilities are an important source of pride, and many Kumars talk about their capacity to make something new. It is an important part of the image maker's self-understanding and is usually central when Kumars narrate their life-stories.

Gour and his family are renowned for their work as innovative image makers. His narrative of their capabilities is more pronounced than among most others. At the same time it is typical. The phase of most innovation in the family's work took place just after Partition and lasted until the 1970s. An important feature is the emphasis on the active process of creating something new; a new sort of reflexivity is, I argue, evident in his discourse about their approach to image making.

Gour: We had to think a lot in order to create new idols. Such as – how was the fight between Durga and Mahishasur? We used to think about these things. My father had some friends from whom he used to learn about the proper mythology of Durga. [...] from different *sloks* of *Chandipath*, Puran. [...] how it is described in mythology; from those sources we used to sort out the stories. How was Durga created? Who gave her the different weapons? What are the names of the various weapons?

All these stories were known by my father from different Brahmans. He was eager to know the details. He was really a discoverer. I listened to these stories from my father. I do not have any academic education or background. For me it is impossible to go through the books in order to know the truthfulness of these stories.

From these stories we usually invented different models. [...] As for instance, now people usually get killed with a revolver, before it was with a cannonball, with a sword [...] earlier, kings used to use swords. [...] I have designed Durga as a common Bengali girl, wearing a white sari with a red border – with no ornaments. I have made her *Bhairabi*[7] [female counterpart of Shiva as Bhairaba], wearing a tiger-skin. I also have created her like a queen. I have created her as a beggar – and also as a queen.

---

7 Sanskrit *Bhairava*, meaning the terrible or frightful, is a manifestation of Shiva. *Daksha Yajna* is a central story of Bhairava. According to this story, Sati kills herself on her father Daksha's sacrificial fire after he insults her husband and herself. Maddened with anger Shiva tramples around the world carrying the corpse of his wife. His actions threaten the

I have also made Mahishasur like a king, and sometimes he had only the bark of a tree as his dress. And sometimes I made that Mahisha look like British people. We were oppressed and turned into victims by the British.

Earlier Mahisha was coloured green, but we gave him the colour of human beings. According to the *Puranas* they were blackish, but not everybody is black. Maybe the king was black, but the soldiers were not black, as it is quite unnatural. We also made the Mahisha as a Briton. We made the hair reddish. Now you often use red colour [henna] in your hair, which we were the first who dared to give to Mother Durga.

Then it was the golden era of Uttam–Suchitra [Uttam Kumar and Suchitra Sen] in Bengali films. And great heroines like Suchitra Sen would dress their hair in a rounded mass (a bun). It was the trend. And from the downy fibre of jute we used to make a big bun. Now almost everyone has short hair. We also made Durga like the film star Hema Malini [one of the greatest Hindi film heroines].

We have made the face like that of a human being. We always tried to make the face beautiful. Beauty is the truth. In the *Puranas*, Durga has her pure golden-coloured skin, but we also changed it into human skin colour.

The meaning of *asur* (demon) is the one who is a tyrant. The British were also tyrannical. So we made the Mahisha look like them [...] we showed that the white-coloured Mahisha was hanged by Durga with the help of a snake. That carries a sense you can easily understand. We made many discoveries and now they are only using the old methods [that we invented]. We made idols like the sculptures of Ajanta.

Once I was making an idol – Durga was looking like a Bengali girl and the Mahisha like a British man. The Mahisha was just getting out of his disguise as the buffalo and trying to throw the buffalo at Durga. So in the structure, the dead body of the buffalo was held by the Mahisha in his hands. Suddenly, a group of foreigners with one interpreter [guide] entered my workshop. They became surprised by the structure – because it seemed quite impossible to make a structure

---

world and Vishnu intervenes by throwing his discus at Shiva. The discus hits Sati's corpse, which is slashed into fragments that fall to earth. These places, thus, turn into a *pithasthana* or a place sanctified by the fall where the very essence of divine energy can be worshipped (Chatterji 2006:16). One of the more famous such spots is at the well-known Kalighat temple in Kolkata.

in which a buffalo was held by only two hands. Then they asked if we became artists after learning engineering. Because that type of structure can be made only by engineers. Then the guide told them that these people are only artists, but they have their own brains – though they have never achieved any degree from any college. And they were surprised by our *art* [in English] work.

The pride concerning the artistic and innovative achievements is clearly expressed. The sources of inspiration are old scriptures, but not those containing manuals of how Durga should look. They search for inspiration in other stories than those of *Devi Mahatmya*. They make the pratimas with reference to popular culture like movies, to history and the local beauties. Innovation becomes equal to creating art. Art is something new, something that is not a copy or a regular production of an old style Durga. There is a continual urge to outdo earlier works and an awareness of one's own position. Gour's story is a reflection upon his own and his family's approach to image making. He is constantly aware of what they have achieved, or, at least, of what he feels should be acknowledged by others as his achievements.

Individual members of the family are mentioned as innovators. And the individualistic aspects are important. With innovation the individual is placed in the forefront.

When Modernity Settled in Kumartuli

After the introduction of Sarbajanin Durga Puja, the request for images became large enough to support a settled community of clay modellers. A new and larger group of clients emerged, which requested readymade images delivered to their temporary pandals. Thus, the process of work changed. And shortly after the introduction of sarbajanin durgutsab, Gopeshwar did the unthinkable; he changed the form of Durga. Gopeshwar was not responsible for all the changes in idolmaking, but he was the catalyst. According to the stories, he departed from the ekchala pratima and placed Durga and her four children under five separate frames, pacchala. Moreover, he also departed from the iconic depiction of Durga, creating her in such a way that the action of killing Mahishasur became evident in what has been described as a Western theatre style. The puja at which this image was 'staged' created a big controversy; it is said to be the first exhibition of an art-er pratima. And the people loved it. A new market opened up, emphasising innovative images in the organizers' quest for sponsors. Thus, the approach to the process of image making changed. The public wanted the Kumar to turn into an artist like Gopeshwar.

Consequently, many Kumars made their own 'discoveries' concerning everything from hairstyle to colourization, in order to being able to continue their work. Artistic freedom is both a source of pride – and, as described earlier, sorrow. This brings us to a discussion of the modernistic turn in Kumartuli.

In retrospect, many contemporary Kumars state that after Gopeshwar, exhibition value became requested in addition to cult value by the clients, in a totally different manner than before. This changed most Kumars' approach to their work and themselves – a change which can be analysed as a modernistic turn. Gopeshwar can thus be said to, if not exactly facilitate, then exemplify an alternative route to modernity through his break with traditional model making. This specific example of 'individuation of tradition' (Errington and Gewertz 1996) is a signifier that modernity is approaching, a time when reputation is fragile and the past does not provide all the answers (Miller 1994: 321–22).

Gopeshwar's annexation of a new approach to modelling is his way of practising the modern. As an entrepreneur, as Kumartuli's equivalent of Fredrik Barth's 'tomato man' (1967: 171), Gopeshwar simultaneously utilizes his newly appropriated knowledge of Italian sculpting in the conservative setting of modelling Durga images, and creates a new way of relating to the work that the Kumartuli Kumars have to accept in order to survive financially. Through his travels, he is able to bring a new set of ideas to Kumartuli and Kolkata concerning what an image can look like. He opens up a space that breaks most of the boundaries concerning how Durga can be modelled. Now it becomes the responsibility of individual Kumars to go out into the streets and cinema halls and seek inspiration in order to create something 'new'. And it is all done within the generations-old market of sarbajanin durgutsab, the capitalistic heir to former days' patronage.

Thus, there are certain aspects of Kumartuli that are important indicators for an emerging modernity. Sarbajanin durgutsab democratizes the arrangement of pujas as it slowly makes it acceptable and common for ordinary people to arrange their own puja. The market for pratimas for sarbajanin durgutsab replaces the patronage relationship between Kumar and client. Gopeshwar, with his impulses from abroad, changed the common understanding concerning how an image could look. These factors combined created a market for innovative images. Kumartuli had already been turned into a bazaar for (mainly) readymade religious statues. To cater for the high-end market with commissioned images, the Kumars had to reinvent themselves as innovative artists. Some make pure exhibition images, while most of the time they attempt to make devotional ones with a distinct style that is experienced as innovative by the organizers and the public.

During the twentieth century, Kumartuli and the life of the Kumars changed dramatically. But how can these changes be said to be related to an attitude of critical self-reflectivity and questioning of the present with reference to image-making? The answer to this question can be said to constitute the modernity test (Miller 1994, Gaonkar 2001), as these are perhaps the most important markers of modernity, irrespective of whether one sees it as only a Western born phenomenon or not (Gaonkar 2001, Narayan Rao et.al 2003 and 2007).

While the changes brought forward by the introduction of sarbajanin durgutsab and Gopeshwar's individual treatment of the tradition were significant, it was the changes they brought forward among the general Kumars of Kumartuli that are important. The introduction of a market for ready-made images caused the Kumars to settle in Kumartuli and establish their workshops there. They were still modelling as they always had done, but in larger quantities and not only for commission. After Gopeshwar, the market demanded annual innovations. Thus, the Kumars went from making Durga images to imagining and inventing images. The world of possible inspirations and references grew dramatically. As mentioned above, this is seen among the Kumars as the break between then and now, between making traditional ekchala images to creating works of art, art-er pratimas, in a market largely controlled by the clients demand.

The senior Kumars are ambivalent towards the new images for Durga Puja. In their eyes, the images are becoming less devotional as a result of the clients' demand for more innovative designs. The breach or disjuncture in the approach to design has enforced/necessitated a new reflexivity in connection with their work as Maliks. They have to both relate to tradition and to present designs in a completely new way. The exhibition value of the images as part of sarbajanin durgutsab has made the Kumars artists, as makers of artistic Durga images.

After Gopeshwar forged his innovative pratima, the rest of the Kumars became forged into a new approach to modelling. This new approach creates the necessary disjuncture that makes reflection possible, in a way that is typical for modernity, as it is 'forged with a sense of struggle and fragility, a sense that it could be otherwise and a constant fear that it is otherwise' (Miller 1994: 321–22). The reflection is born out of the new approach, which marks the end of the natural and a priori conception of how Durga should be made. The way of the past becomes tradition. It could still have been like it was in the time of standard ekchala pratimas, but they have invested too much time in the process of making names as innovative artists to really want the old days back. Which style will be appreciated each year is impossible to say in advance; there is a feeling that coincidence, and not genuine artistic capabilities, decides who will be famous and receive the media's attention. The struggle is constant, people copy others' discoveries. Reputation is fragile, the media and committees do not know how to see the difference between the genuine and duplicates. The past represents to many Maliks an ideal, while they all work within and reproduce the present constant quest for conceptualizing an image that makes the news as an innovative piece of work. Stealing moulds and making copies cannot have been a practice of pre-1935 Kumartuli, as the various moulds looked quite similar for the readymades and belonged to the rajas.

However, not every break from traditional practices is a turn towards modernity. While the market mode of supplying images according to the clients' demands is an important basis in the modernistic turn, the emphasis on innovation is the main signifier of an emerging modernity. It necessitates the need to go outside what has become tradition, to search for inspiration 'elsewhere' and to compete on the level of the ability of imagination. In short, it forces the Kumars to connect with the present, be it in hairdressing styles or contemporary popular renderings of history.

Thus, the Kumar as artist, as the maker of nontraditional pratimas, is in the context of Kumartuli a 'figure of modernity' (Gaonkar 2001: 3), in the same way as Dipesh Chakrabarty's Kolkata man engaged in *adda*, 'long, informal and unrigorous conversations' (2001: 124). The activity of adda in a few decades before and after 1950 promotes democratic speech, literary cosmopolitanism, enlarged ethical mentality and discursive self-fashioning. At the same time it traditionally offers no space for women, results in neglecting work and domestic responsibilities and is oral, thus going against modernistic work ethics and bourgeois domesticity. But in total, adda serves as a dwelling for the constant 'struggle to make a capitalist modernity comfortable for oneself, to find a sense of community in it' (ibid.: 123). The Malik as artist and artisan, in opposition to the Malik as only an artisan, is also an important part of this struggle with the introduction of a modernity that has come to affect the work of clay-modelling. When the patron–client relationship became less relevant, individual Kumars had to promote their work and themselves in a way that attracted customers in the new market. The first person to do so, to fashion himself as an artist, was Gopeshwar. He utilized the new possibilities in the space of agency created by the sarbajanin durgutsab. While the traditional image was made using a given household's special mould to shape the face of Durga in the same way as it always had been, the new one demanded a new mould every year. The individual Kumar had to spend time investigating how to create a Durga that would be appreciated by the committees and the audience. He had to mould with reference to prevailing fashion (the hair in a bun) and popular culture (heroes and heroines), contemporary events (also post-colonial demonizing of the British) and so on. He had to seek inspiration from tradition, from the scriptures as well as from Bollywood and Hollywood movies.

When the Kumar artisan threw away the moulds, he turned into an artist. This was not done without regret, as there was a sense of decline in the devotional value of the images and of denial of heritage. Increased exposure to the market not only provided opportunities for the innovative Kumars, it also reduced their ability to plan their future. To sum up, modernity had reached Kumartuli.

While Gopeshwar probably gathered inspiration from his travels abroad, whatever he saw was something that could easily have been seen in colonial Kolkata. His sculpting course in Italy might also have given him courage to approach the image making back home in a different way. Many modernities can be said to have existed in nineteenth and early twentieth century Kolkata, many of them indigenous, others Western.

Still, there is in a sense the birth of a new modernity that takes place in the Kumartuli of 1935. The breach that took place, which created a concept of tradition, provided historical depth to the image making and forced the Maliks to take an active stance in the reinvention of annual Durgas, were a result of changes in their own approach to the work. They saw the new opportunities in the market after Gopeshwar and utilized them; thus they reinvented themselves as self-proclaimed artists with innovative capabilities. They did not copy changes in other art markets, they just came to understand that what Gopeshwar had done due to artistic desires could be utilized by them also in the business. Individual capabilities combining craftsmanship and innovation distinguished the real and proper artist from the ordinary ones. Being a child of a reputed Malik no longer guarantees success or even work; each Malik has to contribute. The search for newness continues today, with young Maliks seeking new sources of inspiration by attending regular art colleges and thus in a sense formalizing their position as artists in a European way, and not based solely on caste affiliation. As historical awareness and a sense of tradition occurred in pre-colonial India with the 'invention' of a new way of writing, and can be described as an early indigenous modernity (Narayan Rao et. al. 2003), a similar break took place in Kumartuli after 1935. The incident of Gopeshwar's image and its response created a rather abrupt break from within, through which the past way of working became pronounced in the actual image. This is not merely an alternative modernity, a reconceptualization of a western modernity. One should look beyond the genealogy usually attached to modernity and see the new Kumartuli that emerges as the place of Kumars representing a new modernity as inspiration and influences probably came from several sources, foreign as well as indigenous.

Later, since the early 1970s onwards, the newspapers pay more and more attention to the surprising new styles, as if they had started to emerge that very year. Thus, when people talk about the Harry Potter theme puja of 2007 and its like, they often do it with reference to the 1990s globalization of the Indian media world. In this way, they hide the fact that this kind of creation has a much longer history. Whether the inspiration is from abroad or simply outside the scripturally based style does not signify a great difference. From the birth of art images until the present, inspiration has been sought everywhere. And Durga can appear as both a beggar and a queen. On every annual homecoming of Durga, she manifests herself in continually new forms. There is an evident progression as she changes style and outlook, a progression that did not exist (in the same degree) earlier. While she does not age as we do, she changes style as many of us do. In the hands of the artist Malik, she has entered time as it slowly progresses through history, a time that was more secluded before 1935, at least in the descriptions provided by outsiders (Goldblatt 1997, Robinson 1983, Banerjee 2004). This change is marked in the language as well as in the stories of the past and the work-process.

With modernity settling and the creation of tradition in Kumartuli, it is time to approach the impact of immigration from East Bengal to Kumartuli, an event that more firmly established a competitive mood in the locality. Then I will continue with the impact of economic changes and education and globalization, as they forge the life of the Kumars into new stages of capitalist modernity, and a new way to approach the process of making pratimas.

Chapter 4

ANCESTRAL HOMES – EAST VERSUS WEST

Following Independence, the Partition of India made a significant impact on Kumartuli with the immigration of East Bengali Kumars. Politics at large, on the national and state levels, influenced the Kumars. Partition reshaped the fabric of Kumartuli and created new lines of conflict and hostility. In the historizing narratives of the Kumars, and especially among the East Bengalis, Partition is a moment that recurs in many conversations: a moment which shaped and to a certain extent still shapes who they are today, for they came as Bengalis but were received as Bangals, the second rate and unrefined East Bengalis. The narratives of the East Kumars mainly concern the animosity expressed by the West Kumars rather than sectarian strife between Hindus and Muslims preceding and during the Kumars' migration.

For those who lived at that time, the hostility towards the East Bengalis was inscribed on the images themselves, with the introduction of an East Bengali style in Kolkata as the most visible evidence. Perceptions concerning artisanal quality and work ethics also became important in the fight concerning who the proper Kumars were. Testimonies of Partition are also visible in the spatial distribution of workshops as the East Kumars dominate the south-eastern corner of Kumartuli, with their businesses named after localities in former East Bengal.

Kumartuli, which is usually referred to as a caste based neighbourhood of image makers, is a partly segregated society, as the following narratives will show. In order to appreciate these narratives properly, we need to delve more deeply into the historical situation and contemporary experiences concerning mainly caste and the fight for independence that highlight the hostility between East and West Bengalis. A notion of caste does matter, but not in any way that would unify the two groups of Kumars. The concept of adibari or ancestral home is more important in creating solidarity. The Kumars are conscious of being a caste, but they are not caste-conscious in the sense that they have any deep knowledge of their caste or emphasize its importance in everyday chores or politics. What caste or jati, in a strict sense of the word, means to contemporary Kumars will also be discussed as part of the Partition narratives.

On the Ground

After Partition, the major lines of conflict that affected the Kumars were within the domain of caste itself. The narratives of especially the newcomers from the East provide an understanding of Kumartuli as a community were caste loyalty is not central. Rather they reveal a place where economic concerns and the notion of geographical origin (adibari) are highly important. The hostilities between the East and West Kumars cannot be explained simply in terms of xenophobia – a dislike of outsiders. While their dialects differed, the Kumars from both sides shared both gotra (subcaste, clan) and profession. Relations existed between the two groups before Partition; the East Bengalis were not complete strangers.

As mentioned earlier, the Kumbhakar jati was, at least in the second part of the nineteenth century, according to Risley, highly differentiated into various subcastes and gotras (1891a). Risley recorded the use of twelve different surnames or titles: Behara, Biswas, Das Deuri, Kunkal, Mahato, Majhi, Marar, Marik, Mehrana, Pal and Rana. He mentions more than thirty subcastes. The number of gotras is also more than thirty, but Risley recorded gotras for only a few subcastes. In Kumartuli, all the Kumars use the title Rudra Pal, regardless of ancestral home (adibari). This in itself does not tell us much, since all Kumars can use that title, as it is based on their shared story of origin. In the light of the complexity of subgroups that Risley recorded, the lack of knowledge when it comes to subcastes and gotras among even the most senior Kumars is interesting. A few are able to name one gotra, Aliman (or Alamyan) and no subcastes at all. Both East and West Kumars who are aware of their gotra say that they belong to Aliman. Two of my informants mentioned, after much thinking, two more gotras, before they mentioned some gotras belonging to Brahmans. Kumartuli formerly consisted of one single group of Kumars, who married within their gotra. None of the Kumars who told about Partition and the following hostility mentioned caste as the background of the conflict. The only indirect evidence of such notions comes from Nimai, who says that Kumars from the East and West did not marry each other. Knowing that the various subcastes of Kumbhakar practised endogamy (Risley 18: 518), this might indicate that the Kumars at the time of Partition recognized the two groups as two different subcastes. While gotras usually were exogamous clans in Bengal, according to the senior Kumars of Kumartuli they functioned as an endogamous group. To what extent there has been an intermingling between notions of subcaste and gotra is hard to say, but it is evident that notions of divisions and hierarchy at the level below jati are blurred to the point of being almost nonexistent. Historically, this state of affairs goes back as far as any living Kumar can remember today.

Thus, the Kumars are very much aware of their jati background, but not of any further divisions within the jati. As such, the Kumars are not very caste-conscious. In the decades leading up to Independence, the great majority of them came from the same district and with a similar background as potters of that area. The processes of caste unification and separation were different. An indication of the similarities is the knowledge among the senior Kumars concerning subdivisions like gotra and sreni within the jati. That they all mention alamyan gotra with relative ease, but not any other, suggests that they all came from that division. In one important respect is caste affiliation still important, and that is with reference to marriage. The geneaologies that I have collected show that even as intercaste marriages are getting more common, they are still rare.

When the newcomers arrived from the East after Partition, subcaste and gotra might well not have been classificatory categories which could easily be revalidated. As we shall see in the narratives presented, differences are described in a highly caricatural way: the Others were alcoholics with low morals, their artisan skills were poor and so on. I will argue that such notions were not the primary source of the hostility; rather the argument focuses on economic concerns, and a concept of proper image-makers based on their adibari played a prominent role. Only secondarily were such characteristics used as interpretations in explaining the conflict between East and West Kumars.

An important insight that the processes around Independence and Partition give is that this is a domain where politics trumps caste. This contradicts to a certain extent what Dumont argues in his *Homo Hierarchicus* (1980 [1970], Dirks 1992). Dumont approaches the structural foundation of the caste system, and argues that the hierarchical caste system encompasses politics. On the level of everyday practices, however, the realities look different. In short, referents of social identity other than caste, like territorial affiliation, family units, sectarian networks and economical concerns, were and are far more significant (also Dirks 1987 and 1992). The importance of the caste system should thus not be overestimated.

The narratives of Independence and Partition are centred on communalism, first between Hindus and Muslims, then, in a West Bengali context, between the East and West Kumars. Communalism in India is portrayed by Pandey as being opposed to secularism, and placed with reference to other binary categories: national/local (often read as antinational); progressive (economic)/reactionary (cultural) (1992: 29). Moreover, secular, national and progressive features are given as 'natural' qualities of the primary story of the (emerging) Indian nation-state; communalism (local and reactionary) and sectarian strife are secondary, aberrations from general Indian history (ibid.: 1992). Partition and the subsequent killings and mass escapes were a disruption, a hijacking of a noble Indian struggle, it was 'history gone wrong' – a puzzling and in effect inexplicable failure (ibid.: 32). Pandey argues that nationalist historiography, journalism and filmmaking have generated a 'collective amnesia' when it comes to Partition (ibid.: 33). While the sectarian conflicts of Partition are almost always explained and contextualized with reference to interreligious hostility, in Kumartuli, as in most of Kolkata and West Bengal, there were also intra-Hindu conflicts in the wake of Partition. East met West within the same jati of Kumbhakars. And the nationalist induced collective amnesia is striking. The antagonism, especially among the seniors, is still strongly felt, but is hard to communicate directly. At the same time, the Kumars still organize with reference to two separate samitis mainly based on a notion of adibari. Consequently, Partition in the caste based neighbourhood of Kumartuli highlights the subordinate importance of caste in a period of major change.

Before I turn to the Partition narratives, I will start with a short section on the fight for independence, as this highlights the politicization of, and increased sense of hostility in, Kumartuli and Bengali society in general. The sectarian conflict along religious lines that existed before Partition is more pronounced; yet it is a conflict that becomes replaced by that between East and West Kumars.

The fight for independence

In the early years of the twentieth century the fight for 'home rule' became more pronounced in Bengal: a struggle that later turned into a demand for complete independence. The fight gained significant momentum after the colonial administration's separation of Bengal into two parts in 1905. A few Kumars tell about how they remember the times of pre-independent India, with reference to mass gatherings around Mohandas Karamchand Gandhi (1869–1948), known as *Mahatma* (Great Soul) and Subhas Chandra Bose (1897–1945), known as *Netaji* (Respected Leader). As image makers, the Kumars participated in a special way through crafting images with a nationalist agenda, as when Durga was depicted as Mother India.

In fact, Durga Puja was a central site, occasion and symbol during the fight for independence, especially in Bengal. An important part of this was the connection created between India, the Motherland and the Goddess, especially as seen in Bankimchandra Chatterji's novel *Anandamath* (2005, in translation, first published in Bengali 1881–82). It is from this book about the Sannyasi Rebellion of the early 1770s that the famous nationalist slogan *Bande Mataram* (*Vande Mataram* in Hindi) is taken. As 'a cue-text for what eventually became the image of "the motherland", and then "Mother India", in the developing nationalist movement' (Lipner 2005: 145), the excerpt of the first occurrence of *Bande Mataram* is illustrative. The sannyasi (renouncer) Bhabenananda helps Mahendra into the jungle after he is separated from his wife during their quest to get help in a time of famine and riots:

> Then, with no other recourse, Bhabananda began to sing softly to himself:
> [*Bande Mataram*] I revere the Mother! The Mother
> Rich in waters, rich in fruit,
> Cooled by the southern airs,
>
> Verdant with the harvest fair.
>
> Mahendra was a little astonished when he heard this song, and was at a loss to understand. Who was this mother 'rich in waters, rich in fruit, cooled by the southern airs, verdant with the harvest fair'?
> 'Who is this mother?' he asked Bhabananda.
>
> Without answering Bhabananda began to sing
> The mother – with nights that thrill
>   in the light of the moon,
> Radiant with foliage and flowers in bloom,
>   Smiling sweetly, speaking gently,
>
>   Giving joy and gifts in plenty.
>
> Mahendra cried, 'But that's our land, not a mother!'
>
> Bhabananda replied, 'We recognize no other mother. "One's mother and birthland are greater than heaven itself." But we say that our birthland is our mother. We've no mothers, fathers, brothers, friends, no views, children, houses or homes. All we have is she who is rich in waters, rich in fruit, cooled by the southern airs, verdant with the harvest fair.'
> (Chatterji 2005: 144–45)

It was also within the realm of nationalist politics that the baroari, public puja, was turned into the sarbajanin puja. Stick fights (*lathi khela*), yoga and drill became a serious form of entertainment, as the festival provided a possibility of displaying in public people preparing to fight for freedom, under the guise of religious rites (Banerjee 2004: 50, Chaliha and Gupta 1990: 332). Together with the display of martial arts as practised by nationalist organizations, and movements disguised as fitness clubs like Anushilan Samiti and Yugantar (Sengupta 2001: 308), *swadeshi* (indigenous) goods were sold from stalls around the pandals (Chaliha and Gupta 1990: 332). Later on, central freedom fighters arranged their own Durga Pujas, as the Simla Byayam Samiti Puja started in 1926 (Banerjee 2004: 50). This puja was dedicated to the freedom movement by Atindranath Basu, the founder of the samiti. Other well known persons, as Saratchandra Basu, Bhupendranath Dutta (Swami Vivekananda's brother), Upenddranath Bandyopadhyay and Kiron Mukherjee were involved with this puja. It was used as a venue to showcase important events in the freedom struggle, like the Battle of Plassey and the 1857 uprising, together with slogans urging the public to rise and rebel, written on red cotton fabric (ibid.). Netaji Subhas Chandra Bose was involved in many pujas such as Kumartuli Sarbajanin and Bagbazar Sarbajanin. Niranjan, the well-read local historian, provides an account of Netaji's involvement in the Kumartuli Sarbajanin:

Niranjan: I have talked to Netaji. Once in Kumartuli we held pujas and Sir Harishankar Pal, who lived in that Dispensary [mentioned earlier], was the President for that [Kumartuli Sarbajanin] committee. He was very familiar to us and at that time there was a party called the Radical Democratic Party which was very active. Sir Harishankar Pal gave his vote to some European leader then. I do not remember every detail, I was young then. Some people did not like him, so they created some argument against Sir H. Pal against why he should be the president of our Puja committee. At that same time Netaji wrote a book called *Dream of Young Blood*.[1] I have read that book. Netaji was from South Kolkata, but he loved North Kolkata very much. Then, when he saw that this little issue with H. Pal was becoming big he arranged a meeting here. I was young then and I used to exercise a lot with the lathi: not to harm anybody, but to remain in good health. Netaji arranged a meeting here. And at that meeting I asked him how we can replace that person H. Pal once we have made him our president. Listening to my question, Netaji smiled, then he asked me what if I became a President? Then he became the President.

To people like Netaji, Durga Puja was an important venue for political agitation. Netaji could not let go of the opportunity to make an issue of the

---

1 Probably a pamphlet containing one of his speeches. I have found no book, pamphlet or speech labelled *Dream of Young Blood*.

Kumartuli Sarbajanin, and used the conflict with the sitting president to gain access.

Later on, in 1939, Netaji inaugurated the Simla Byayam Samiti Puja. It hosted a large pacchala (five frames, modern) image, with a giant Durga twenty-one feet high. While no other nationalist images, such as those of Durga as *Bharatamata*, Mother India, are connected to any certain Kumar, the maker of the giant Durga is known and it was Nitai Pal (Banerjee 2004: 50, Chaliha and Gupta 1990: 335). Nitai is not a name that recurs in the stories of any Kumar today.

While the pujas became politicized, the actual participation of the Kumars became less pronounced than in the nineteenth century tradition of sawngs, when comical caricature statues of the better-off classes were displayed together with the religious ones. Other, mainly high caste, people had entered the stage as leaders in the fight against the colonizers, a fight which included the general masses of lower caste people. However, Durga Puja as a political site became manifest and more or less institutionalized. The lower class and caste folk resistance of the sawng was replaced by a common (Hindu) Bengali resistance against the British with Durga as a manifestation of Mother India.

The freedom struggle hardened as the Second World War approached, with Hindu–Muslim riots, terrorist conspiracies and mass gatherings. The fitness clubs, which organized youths in physical training like lathi khela, were also visible in Kumartuli. According to Niranjan, he organized such a group of Kumar youths in Kumartuli. Lathi khela was practised and the motive was said to be self-defence. According to Joya Chatterjii's *Bengal Divided: Hindu Communalism and Partition* (1994), such groups were instrumental in the various communal riots in Kolkata and Bengal. She depicts them as more than mere self-defence groups; rather, they were sleeper cells that communally-minded activists activated, thus contributing to the creation of the riots, and to making them serious in terms of dead and wounded. Niranjan denies such actions on the behalf of the Kumar group he organized. Their group were organized in order to protect the rights of the inhabitants from the Kundos, the family who owned much of Kumartuli:

> **Niranjan:** The whole area [Kumartuli] used to belong to the Kundos: the Kundo family. Still there is one doctor here [from that family]. He is paralyzed now and he loves me.
>
> The Kundo family (*paribar*) used to be the landowners, they were jamidars. Among them there is left only one [the doctor]. They have no more land of their own. They used to be jamidars and they made the lower caste people suffer a lot in those days. Those Kundos oppressed poor people and grabbed their land. And now the family is destroyed.

> We had our exercise club and we used to lathi khela. I was my kind
> of leader, leader of the *para* [neighbourhood]. We did a lot to protect
> this area from this family.

Conflicts between the landowner and the Kumars who lived on his land are
rarely mentioned by the Kumars. Probably new lines of conflict overshadowed
this animosity in the narratives of the seniors. However, as Niranjan continues
to talk, we hear how the Hindu–Muslim conflict also affected his group of
young Kumars, but in a different way. Their group helped a few local Muslims
to escape from their Hindu–dominated area to safer places. He narrates:

Niranjan: Before the Famine (1942–43) we had a communal riot here
between Hindus and Muslims. But it will be a history if I tell you
everything. Many Hindus and Muslims were killed. The Government
arranged for the military to take control over the situation, and gradually the situation became normal.

At that time I did a lot of rescuing. I had a group with whom I did
rescuing from the locality where there were a few Hindus in a Muslim
locality or a few Muslims in a Hindu locality. We rescued them. In this
area there were some few Muslims and we made them move from this
area for their own security. We sent them to Muslim localities with the
help of [the] security [provided by us].

Still, in the times of riots, the Kumars felt the threat from nearby Muslim
localities.

Niranjan: At the opposite side of this (area), there is a slum called
Lalbagan. Many Muslims were living there. Many of them got killed
or beaten. We became aware that those Muslim people were trying to
arrange some attack in Kumartuli. At that time we worked as guards
throughout the night and we had our weapons too. But we did not kill
anybody.

To what extent the organized Kumar group participated in any of the atrocities around the time of Independence is impossible to say. While Niranjan's
narratives today seem credible, this might be part of the reshaping the history
which, according to contemporary judgments, has taken place where atrocities of Partition are concerned. He continues:

Niranjan: In our locality there were some Muslims whom we rescued. And the Government picked them up and sent them […]

I do not know where. Here few Muslims were killed. There was one Muslim labourer here from whom I learned Urdu. He was stout – he always respected me. When he was killed I did not get the news before [it had already happened]. I did not get the chance to protect him, keep him hidden in a secret place. I asked him not to get out, but he tried to get out and go to a Muslim community. But he could not manage it, and got killed. At that time, these groups of Muslims and Hindus killed each other. Many Hindus killed. Many Muslims killed. It happened based on the area, but we tried to provide protection so they did not dare to do something here. In each place you could see those communal riots in that time. In East Bengal this happened also. So Gandhi was in Beleghata for a few days to protect those Muslims, I do not remember the exact date, but he was there. And it was the main cause of killing Gandhi. Some Hindu of his group killed him.

With Gandhi in East Bengal in order to end the fighting in the aftermath of the Direct Action Day in 1946, Independence was in sight, together with an understanding that a partition of Bengal was inevitable.

Partition

The Partition of British India was and still is a defining moment of the subcontinent and its inhabitants' memories. Gandhi urged the people to 'leave India to God. If that is too much, then leave her to anarchy' (1942). And to anarchy India went. A short paragraph from the Bengali novelist Samagra captures the realties brought by Partition, when so many became refugees in the aftermath of the anarchy:

What is the meaning of refugee? *Udbastu.* That means he who has no home. But I do have a home. Still I am a refugee, because I am countryless [...]. So, this freedom that we have gained after driving out the English – this Hindustan and Pakistan – is it to produce refugees? [...] Is this the name of freedom? [...] Who are those who manoeuvred and manipulated to turn human beings into refugees after so many years? (Kayes Ahmed Samagra1993: 97 in Dasgupta 2001)

The Partition of British India into a Hindu dominated India and a Muslim dominated East and West Pakistan in the wake of Independence changed the social fabric of Kumartuli. Even now it is still an important incident evoked in the narratives of present day Kumars.

As part of 'dismantling their raj' (Bose and Jalal 1998: 165), the British finally found it necessary to partition India and create Pakistan along supposedly religious lines. The two nations were to be based on religious affiliation, but geographical constraints and not a small element of coincidence played important roles. The Hindu dominated Congress Party's attempt to create a secular and undivided state failed. The history of the initial 'two nation' theory of the Muslim League, and the process resulting in the violent partition has been and is the subject of fierce debate (Bose and Jalal 1998, Metcalf and Metcalf 2002). Pakistani mainstream historians say that there already existed two nations within British India, since the Indian Muslims 'were always a distinctive and separate community that had resisted assimilation into their Indian environment' (Bose and Jalal 1998: 165). Mainstream Indian nationalists blame imperialism for creating the divide between the two communities as part of their 'divide and rule' policy (ibid.). Even if these views are true to a certain degree, they do not tell the whole story. The creation of Pakistan was a result of the contradictions and structural peculiarities of Indian society and politics in the late colonial period (ibid.).

When the partition of India was eventually accepted by the Congress and the idea that was Pakistan had become a certainty, what to do with Bengal was uncertain. Some wanted Bengal to remain undivided and to become part of Pakistan as a Muslim dominated state, while a few others argued for an independent 'third' nation. However, soon afterward, in April 1947, the proposal for a partition of Bengal was first voiced. The majority of Hindus wanted partition, and they campaigned successfully (Chatterji 1994, Chakrabarty 2004). Consequently, when the decision to partition Bengal was broadcast by Lord Mountbatten on 3 June 1947, 'this was relayed through microphones on street crossings of Calcutta by jubilant crowds who saw in this proposal a liberation from the dark days of Muslim League rule' (Sengupta 2001: 514). They expected that the period of discontent, communal riots and postwar economic misery would finally end. The scale of the tragic outcome of Partition and the appearance of new communal lines that divided and created a hostile environment came as a surprise to most contemporaries.

The human consequences of Partition were enormous. Millions of people were forced to emigrate, to take whatever they could carry and escape from their old or new ancestral homes to a new life in a foreign place. While many managed to escape, it is estimated that between several hundred thousand and one million were killed, mainly in western India (Metcalf and Metcalf 2002: 218), in this massive population exchange of more than 14 million people (1951 *Census of Displaced Persons*). About 3.2 million or 22 per cent of the population transfer took place in eastern India, the bulk in Bengal. Large numbers of Bengali Hindus came to Kolkata. Those who had no family there or had not made any other arrangements settled on railway stations, parks, streets or wherever there was a place to create a shelter.

Many East Kumars went to Kumartuli, 'their' neighbourhood in Kolkata, in order to seek refuge and a new beginning. Within a few years the number of Kumars had doubled and a new social structure developed. A large group of East Bengal Kumbhakars settled in Kumartuli. They hoped to create a new living and a refuge among their own. Refuge was granted in the beginning, but as soon as the newcomers decided to take up work in Kumartuli, the divide became visible. It should be added that this was not something special for Kumartuli; the conflict and harassment of Bangals, East Bengalis, was common throughout Kolkata and beyond.

The stories about Partition are mainly told by the East Kumars, as it was they who were turned into refugees. A small group of the Kumars leaving East Bengal resettled in Kumartuli. They were initially greeted as persons in exile that needed help from their western jati brothers and sisters. But soon a majority of the West Kumars turned hostile; they treated the newcomers badly and tried to make them leave Kumartuli. In retrospect, East Kumars narrate their stories of hardship and suffering, while the West Kumars are not very proud of their unreceptive behaviour. Consequently, few West Kumars feel comfortable talking about the aftermath of Partition; it is not part of their narrative repertoire. When the narrators are the East Kumars, to whom I will turn now, the situation is the opposite.

Bangal, East Bengal

Partition was planned shortly ahead of Independence in August 1947. Many East Bengali Kumars felt the need to move and went to what should become their new home in the wake of Partition to see if it would be possible for them to make a new life there.

Among those who came after Partition were Gour and his family. I went to meet him at his house in Lake Town, just north of Kolkata, where he lives with his extended family. He is the senior member of the family, but is sick with cancer. Gour Chandra Pal is an elderly man; he sits cross-legged on a charpoy. His face bears visual evidence of his cancer – the upper lip on his right side is disfigured; it hangs down over his lower lip. In no other way is it possible to see that he is sick. I am offered a chair and his son Prodyut sits down by his father's side and helps me when I get stuck in the following Bengali conversation. Prodyut has told his father what kind of information I am after – that is, information about the time before Prodyut was born, about their travel to Kumartuli and the early days there. The story of Gour is representative when it comes to Partition narratives of the East Kumars, as it tells about the bad treatment they received from the West Kumars following their arrival in Kumartuli. Most of the Partition refugees do not feel comfortable when talking about these memories, as they think they have placed the antagonism behind them now. Gour, while commenting on the unease he feels telling me his story, also expresses satisfaction from narrating it.

> **Gour:** It is not that I have learned everything from history books or the Bible, Koran, etc.
>
> **Wife:** He did not have the opportunity to read. He began to work with his father when he was a little boy.
>
> **Gour:** I was in East Bengal. At the age of twelve I came here to Kolkata, after Independence. I know about Independence and the war. I know the time of 1940s when it was the great famine [1942–43]. Maybe you have also heard about it? I was then seven or eight years old. It was the time of fighting with the British. As you know, people speak about Netaji. In my childhood I heard that 'Netaji is coming. He is coming from Burma.' I have only heard about his escape. But then it was the time of war and then we got freedom [...] these things I can remember clearly. They killed Gandhi by shooting. And when Jawaharlal Nehru came to Kolkata the first time [after Independence] people gave him the garland of shoes.

Gour starts his story by relating to major incidents around the time of Independence, the Great Famine, the fight against the British, Netaji's warfare against the colonial powers and the killing of Gandhi. The garland of shoes 'given' to Nehru is a symbol of disgrace, a commentary upon the results of Partition. Memories of that time emerge as he remembers and recounts:

> **Gour:** They played many dirty games [...]. We are not educated people. My father was a partial participant of the *Swadeshi Andolon* [Fight for freedom]. My father helped many freedom-fighters to escape from the police. As I am not an educated person, I do not know very much about the proper history – but I heard all these stories from my ancestors.
>
> They killed Gandhi – and there was also a record [*with his hands he shows that he talks about a gramophone record*] of Gandhi. Then, they gave the garland of shoes to Jawaharlal Nehru at Shyambazar five-road crossing. At that time my father was here in Kumartuli [...].
>
> **Wife:** His father saw everything and told the story [...].
>
> **Gour:** Then it was after the Partition – no Hindus could live there in East Bengal – it was Pakistan. All the jamidars [landowners] started

to come to India. [*A phone is ringing in the room and Gour's wife answers it.*] Then this became Hindustan and that place was Pakistan.

And my grandfather had sent my father to observe Kumartuli in order to get a place – to see if they can start working here. Then my father came to Kumartuli, but it was not as it is today. My father went back and told my grandpa everything. They thought it would be better if they get a job here in Kolkata and then bring their entire family to settle down here.

There was a man named N.C. Pal who is no more – one of our relatives used to be there [in Kumartuli] with N.C. Pal. We did not have any relatives here in Kolkata then – N.C. Pal told us about the place where our workshop is now – it was a big building supposed to be a hospital – but as it was not made into a hospital, the owner of the building made it a rented house – you can see the building is separated into many portions...

Yes, then my father went back to Bangladesh. Then I started working with my father and uncle although I was only a boy of twelve or thirteen. My education had been stopped by then. It was something new – people were coming to India – it was the time of riots. Gandhi went to Noakhali[2] [in modern Bangladesh] – we have seen the whole riot in Bangladesh – we also escaped – running away – at the time of fighting.

The horrors of the Partition atrocities are quickly referred to. Noakhali is mentioned, a collective reference to the killings of Hindus in East Bengal. Gour is ill at ease when he talks, and his eyes move from me to an undefined point in the room. There is a short pause before he continues:

Gour: Then, after Partition – when Nehru [...] people began to come here [to Kumartuli] and to go there [to East Bengal]. Then we started to work here. Because in Pakistan there would be no more Hindus – but our business is to make idols – who will buy those idols if no Hindus live there? We have usually never done our ancestors' work – which is work with the wheel.

[...] We [my father, my brothers and I] have actually always done the work of making images. My Grandpa used to work with the wheel, but it was too hard work – so the main work was to make idols in

---

2 Gandhi visited Noakhali (Chittagong Division) in 1946 to ease communal riots of the Noakhali Massacre in the wake of the Direct Action Day (Bose and Jalal 1998: 182).

others' homes. In those days there was no such market of idols. Then we started living here and gradually we are in the state of – what you are observing now [among the better-off Kumars].

To what extent Gour and his family only made images is hard to say, since when asked later, he only recollects one landowner for whom they made images in East Bengal. It seems probable that when they settled in Kumartuli, they did not continue to work with the potter's wheel. Thus, his grandfather was the last member of his family who had pot-making on the wheel as his major source of subsistence. This becomes more evident as he continues:

Gour: I was 12 years old when I came with my family two years after independence in 1949, because of Muslim–Hindu problems. So we were refugees, you know refugees, here in Kolkata, in Kumartuli.

My father started working with making murtis. And we worked with him. There was no education then, we were too poor. We were seven brothers, I am the oldest.

Then we started to work, slowly we built up our own business.

Geir: But back to the time in Bangladesh, what kind of work did you do there, also thakur murtis?

Gour: No, very little. There was one jamidar where we lived and *Baba* [daddy] worked for him [making thakur murits].

Geir: So it was when you came to Kumartuli you really started to work with murtis?

Gour: Yes, *aste aste*, slowly, we built up and our work developed. We started to change all the idols, the traditional way they made them. From ekchala [one frame, traditional] we changed everything. We made murtis with normal faces that were very beautiful. We started with the Nataraj-type, Arjunta-type, we changed colour from the green skin on the [Mahisha] to proper human colour. We changed the singha, lion, giving it a proper lion's face; from black hair to grey. Then we changed the position of the thakurs, of Durga and the Mahisha. The old face of Durga was devoid of life, we brought life back to her face, life into the idols. Now our Devi murtis look alive.

While Gour's father had worked in a patron–client relationship with the local jamidar, making the images for his pujas, the move to Kumartuli meant that they also had to adapt to a new approach. Innovation became necessary to compete in the Kolkata image market. It was probably even more important for the newcomers to show off, through innovative images, in order to enter the market in West Bengal. And the Kolkatans liked what they were offered:

Geir: And what was the reaction of the costumers?

Gour: They liked it, and then the Bangla Durga was changed to pacchala Durga.

Geir [With surprise]: Did your father do that?

Gour: No, it was Gopesh[war] Pal. And then everyone started to make pacchala Durga. Then it all developed.

Gour continues narrating his recollections about his life: who he has met, what they have done, the economic problems – and the problems of being a 'refugee' in Kumartuli. The references to the names of powerful persons are a common feature in colloquial talk and discussions. In Kumartuli such evocations are used to position the narrator; the more powerful the persons he or she can mention being contact with, the more truthful the story or arguments he or she puts forth are supposed to be (a narrative feature quite similar to what one finds among academics).

Gour: [...] I know this much. I know many things, though I cannot tell you all, as I have forgotten many things.

Now for a few years I am forgetting everything. Look at this portion of my face [...]. [*Points towards his left side, where the lip on that side hangs down over his mouth*] [...] it was paralysed earlier. I went to Dr. Bidhan Roy [1882–1962, second Chief Minister of Bengal] also – I have this experience too. Then it was the high time for our work – my father took an order of C.I.T. Road – then Ashu Ghose [Ashutosh Ghosh, minister for various offices in West Bengal from 1957 to mid 1960s] was the minister – father told him that 'I have taken this big, big order, but my eldest son [Gour] is ill – what should I do?' Aashu Ghose wrote a letter to Bidhan Roy – and I was there the next morning for a check-up – but I was not able to visit him later – though he did give me medicine for my throat problem. But my next date to visit him was two days after his death. It was a sudden death. Then I could not mange to continue my treatment.

We were five brothers – and in order to maintain the family, we needed to do hard work. I have worked hard from my childhood – my grandfather was no more – my father was no longer able to do all the work by himself – it was also hard for my father to maintain the family and to give us education – then our family used to be in

Bangladesh – at the time of the war we had brought our family here to India. I have seen the Ayub Khan war – then Ayub Khan started military rule. From that time I had to work hard to maintain my family.

This is my life since childhood. I have learned everything from my father. All I have done – with my inner power. It was for me a challenge to establish myself in Kolkata. I have also discovered many new things with my father. Gradually my father's name became popular in Kolkata – it was the time of the 1960s or 1970s – everybody used to know his name – and everyone in Kumartuli agreed that my father is a real artist.

After again contextualizing himself and his narrative, he turns to the hardships they faced as refugees in Kumartuli:

Gour: Then, do you know what they [West Kumars] used to say to us? They said these people [East Kumars] came here floating with a flood. They used to mock us – they used to say to us Bangal [usually used derogatively for East Bengalis].

Yes, I could not tell these things – as I feared it might turn into an unhealthy quarrel [...].

Yes, they were jealous of us. We were ten to eleven families from Bangladesh there, within that range – and they could not tolerate us. In all respects we were growing faster than these people from West Bengal. They know that they cannot beat us within one hundred years. It was that high time when Kumartuli was changing – and they used to use slang words to us – when we showed them our good work, they were not able to say anything more. The Kumartuli became ours – Gorachand Pal [Gour's father] was the most popular artist in Kolkata.

There was also Ramesh Pal [East Kumar]. Have you heard his name? [*I nod in reply.*] He is also one of the best artists. They used to torture him too. He graduated from Art College. Then he used to do some big project (idol) in Fire Brigade, Park Circus [...]. He used to make two or three big projects. He was one of the good artists. You can get some information from him too.

There are many bad things I cannot tell you. We usually have to suppress all the pains. But in our minds we have tried always to show zeal to them. They are even now not growing as good artists. We are beating them in our work. They were not very educated people, they also had many addictions to tobacco or alcohol. They did not have any desire to make a name in the market. Now the situation has changed a bit, but the place is the same. Those people who have been living here for generations, they even cannot manage to build their own house.

As they were the addicted people, they usually spent their money in order to satisfy their addiction. Gopeshwar Pal and N.C. Pal [both West Kumars] they used to be the pride of Kumartuli. This is history. Bangladeshi people are beating them in all aspects – this is the truth – but I cannot tell these things as these are very personal matters. If you write these things then they will oppose it.

His daughter-in-law gives us some snacks and tea.

Others support the description of the reception as quite hard for most of the East Bengali Kumars.

Nepal: We were the artists from Bangladesh, here there were only people from Krishnanagar. There were a lot of quarrels, fighting, and beatings. The police had to come many times. [But] this is no more. Our relationship is close to marriage, there are also marriages between us.

Mohan Bhanshi, while not very talkative, says:

Mohan: Yes, these people around here made it difficult. They even did not give us drinking water.

Gour adds a comment on the hostile environment after Partition:

Gour: There was the high time when we used to do the work with our own hands. But the edeshis [artists from West Bengal] used to do their work only with the help of labourers. Then they spent their money and time in order to satisfy their addiction [to alcohol]. But now those old people are no more – and now the younger generation has become aware that this cannot be the proper work process. So edeshis with the help of their younger generation are moving forward, nowadays. Once they used to spread bad rumours against us, but now their children are following us in this profession. There are many things, we had struggled starving and spending sleepless nights. But the new generation, they cannot even think of it. This is hard work.

To sum up, most East Bengali Kumars belonging to the generation that remembers the time when they arrived Kumartuli, or in the following decade, have strong memories of the hostility they felt directed towards them. While the younger generations feel free to fraternize with each other, they also are aware of the divide between the two groups. Only during the last twenty to thirty years has marriage between the two groups taken place. Geneaologies that I have collected suggest that this is still rare. It seems that among a jati which used to be endogamous, marriage outside the jati used to be more acceptable (there are only a few incidents) than with a family belonging to the same jati, but from the wrong geographical area. As these topics are painful both to recall and talk about, the information concerning such relations is hard to gather. However, the testimonials given above tell their story of a new internal division that is still visible.

While the Kumars mentioned above talk about differences in the quality of work and morals, this is something that is contested by the West Bengalis. They say it was they who taught the East Bengalis to make proper images. There is also a common understanding that there used to be differences in artistic style, but no one is able to pinpoint what the differences actually were. Probably was it mainly individual styles that differed.

Nevertheless, it is time to present a view from the opposite side – from the West Bengalis' point of view.

Edeshi, West Bengal

The West Bengali Kumars seem to agree about the hostility. When I asked Nimai, one of the edeshi Kumars, if what I had been told about the reception they gave the East Bengalis was true, he told me: 'Yes, everything they have told you is true' and looked away, not saying anything more.

This is not a topic that Krishnanagar Kumars discuss freely, at least not with outsiders. Whether they are ashamed or not is difficult to say, but there is an understanding that within the society at large, the common and accepted perception is that they should feel ashamed. Communalism is history gone wrong and not what India should be and is all about. Consequently, most Krishnanagar Kumars do not openly admit the hostility they showed towards the newcomers, but some still privately carry a hostile feeling:

> **Niranjan:** Some people from East Bengal came here and made this place [...] [*pauses, shakes his head and looks sad, saying without words that they made it worse*]. Of course, they did not have any choice because they came here due to Hindu–Muslim riots.
>
> [...]
>
> At the time of partition many Hindu people escaped from their homes and many were killed. We took some responsibility for them; somehow we arranged for their food, looked after them to the extent that was possible for us. First we collected money from this community to give them food, and then the Government started taking care. Then those refugees started working in various places, doing their business,

any work they could do. Now we have many East Bengali people here in Kolkata. After Partition, here in Kolkata we have more East Bengali people than original Kolkata people. East Bengali people and their families [the tone and the gestures suggesting that they are no good].

The feeling of being pushed aside, of becoming a minority in their own place, is surfacing. The West Bengalis have 'belonged' to Kumartuli for at least 200 years. With Partition, the closely knit community became more complex. The commonalities that had existed among the West Kumars, the shared stories and experiences of emigrational labour from Nadia to Kolkata and back, the routines of how to compete in the readymade market and the fact that many of them had worked together as paid labourers in their youth (see Chapter 7) must have put old internal hierarchies and loyalties between families under fresh scrutiny. Competition to get a space for workshops increased, and already in the 1950s there was a lack of free space to establish a new business.

Geir: When they started working here after Partition, did they make competition very hard?

Niranjan: There was very little competition then. In the beginning there were a few people from East Bengal. The type of work they used to do then was usually not very good, not good enough to make a good business. We helped them a lot in order for them to learn. You know Rakhal Pal who is very popular now? He took a lot of help from us. Though Ramesh Pal has always been very original in his work, he took a lot of help from me. He made a very different style of work. He is familiar to me.

Artists from East Bengal were not aware of many important details about model making. They used our people and many times they took me to their workshop to help them. When I used to work in my workshop they came to observe my work. If announce this statement now, they will deny it.

Geir: When East Bengalis came, they were not qualified enough to suit the criteria of this kind of business?

Niranjan: They did not know how to make murtis.

Geir: They did not have this tradition in East Bengal?

Niranjan: Yes, they used to make some kind of murtis.

'Some kind of murtis', says Niranjan with a little contempt in his voice. The bangals were not as proper makers of images, not as the famed Krishnanagar

Kumars made them. According to Niranjan, they had to learn it from the West Kumars and then they stole their customers, a view not shared by the East Bengalis who emphasize that they already knew image making. The excellence achieved by the newcomers was a result of the teachings provided by the established edeshis. It was the Krishnanagar Kumars who were the proper image makers, other Kumars were pot makers, they belonged by the wheel. Again Niranjan refers to how his group of potters are of a different kind with abilities to create almost everything from clay.

Sundip, probably the oldest West Kumar in the neighbourhood, remembers the competition that arose between the settled and the newcomers. There is load shedding (interruption of power supply), the room becomes dark and the fan slowly stops. A young girl of the household provides us with a lit candle.

Geir: Just after Partition, the people from East Bengal came here, did that create any problem with so many new Kumars?

Sundip: No, we did not face too much of a problem with them, but on the other hand there were some problems, some people sold their land and […].

While not mentioned by many, this seems to be perceived as a significant cause for the hostility. Land in Kumartuli was and is a scarce resource. And I do not think I overanalyse my material when I emphasize this remark concerning selling of land. When the ten to eleven families of East Kumars settled permanently in Kumartuli, this must have resulted in the moving of others. Whether some poorer West Kumars in need of money sold their workshops, or a non-Kumar landowner decided to sell or rent to an East Kumar, the result was the same. Someone had to move, either to a different location (and occupation) outside Kumartuli, or to the streets. The West Bengalis at that time constituted a relative homogeneous group with a common geographical origin in Krishnanagar and its surroundings. When the East Kumars came to settle, for the West Kumars it meant that families of their group had to leave. It can easily be interpreted as a feeling among the West Kumars that a dismantling of the fabric of Kumartuli was taking place. Sundip continues:

Sundip: There was a lot of competition, work competition. For us there was a mixing of culture, we considered some things about them good, and we took their good aspects. And now the work has some excellence.

Geir: What were their good things and what were yours?

Sundip: The quality of the work […] The face of the Goddess was different. Our main quality, I can only say about the face, their idols had some different features as to face-cutting. And our idols had some different forms of face-cutting: I cannot say too much in detail about these things, but there was an exchange of how we do things. Now it is almost the same, the quality of our work and their work.

Interestingly enough, Sundip tells us that the East Bengalis had their own way of making images. Consequently, they did not have to learn everything from scratch. Still, to the edeshis, the immigrants from East Bengal were not proper image makers; they bought their land and made the competition even worse. Old family loyalties that had existed between the Krishnanagar Kumars, structuring and organizing relations within Kumartuli, did not matter anymore. At a point when the same Nadia families had more or less worked in Kumartuli for several generations by the time of Partition, suddenly a whole range of families came and settled to live there fulltime. The sensation of a rupture, a break with the past, must have been dramatic.

West Ghotis and East Bangals Today

While the hostility is not easily seen today, the feelings among the former East Kumars are still heated. They feel sad about how they were received and treated.

In the 1950s the East Kumars started a samiti, an association, to fight for the Maliks' causes, which mainly meant providing guarantees for bank loans. They wanted it to represent everyone, but some West Kumars – according to Niranjan he was the major advocate – opposed them and started a competing samiti. Ability to provide the respective members with medical and financial support also became a source of competition. While both samitis have members from both East and West, these are minorities of a few people. The fights for funds and 'development' for their members have been fields of high competition. Only during the last few years has there been some kind of collaboration, and then only concerning the possibility of developing a multistoried market-cum-workshop building in Kumartuli. More than anything else, the existence of these two samitis keeps the divide alive today

As discussed earlier, knowledge about gotras or subcastes is not reported even by elderly people today. Consequently, traditional divisions within the jati cannot be used as an explanation for the conflict of East versus West. Rather, the West Bengalis who already lived in Kumartuli experienced the newcomers as a threat, as aliens and not as caste-brothers and sisters. Caste loyalty, if such a thing has ever existed, was of no importance between the West Bengali ghoti and East Bengali Bangal. Richer East Bengalis bought places in Kumartuli and started their trade there. The poorer section of the West Bengalis sold their workshops, probably out of an urgent need for money or to pay off moneylenders who would not accept a further postponement (see next chapter). The intracaste hostility existed with no reference to caste as a power structure, a social hierarchy. Instead, I see it as instrumental in reducing the emotional attachment to belonging to a given caste. Caste mattered only insofar as it included, in an idealized way, a common source of income. And business and the attachment to the art of image-making were at stake as the root of the conflicts. The West Bengalis helped the East Bengalis until they understood that the Bangals wanted to work as image makers in Kumartuli.

Moreover, the West Kumars all had their adibari (ancestral home) in and around Krishnanagar. They were present in Kumartuli in Kolkata due to their traditional reputation within the clay artisan caste, based on the fact that the art of making Durga images as we know them today originated in Krishnanagar (Mukharji 1974 [1888]: 62). As a group of Kumars among many in Bengal, they were identified and historically given the job to also make the Durga images in Kolkata owing to their regional background. Their self-understanding as master artisans was based primarily not on caste, but on the notion of adibari. Thus, the Kumars of Kumartuli in the times before Partition were an occupational group with a common territorial background. This regional affiliation proved more important than the jati as such, when the once rather homogeneous group experienced the immigration of the East Kumars. Such a view supports Dirks' notion of jati as 'just one category among many others, one way of organizing and representing identity [...and that...] [r]egional, village, or residential communities [...] and so on could both supersede caste as a rubric for identity and reconstitute the ways caste was organized' (1992: 60). Thus, the jati as such became reconstituted after Partition and the immigration of East Kumars. It is evident that the jati was less important than territorial background and the connection that had to excellent craftsmanship where social structuring and communal self-understanding are concerned.

Chapter 5

TURMOIL AND ECONOMICS

The economic system within which the Kumars work has changed many times over the course of time, as it has in the rest of the society. As image makers, they began as clients of a patron, and then the slow introduction of community pujas turned Kumartuli into a permanent settlement and marketplace in the early years of the twentieth century. The Kumars started to use paid labourers in order to satisfy the growing market for readymade images for baroari and sarbajanin pujas. Innovative designs were necessary to please the customers. With Partition, competition hardened even though the demand for images increased. East and West Kumars started their respective organizations to get bank loans; and the labourers organized to get better conditions. The period of the Maoist Naxalite uprising from the late 1960s onwards created a sense of emergency in Naxalite-demarcated Kumartuli, making customers afraid to go there to purchase their murtis. Economically strained as they were, Indira Gandhi's policy of nationalizing the major private banks in 1969 (Chandra et al. 1999: 353) came as a relief to the better-off Kumars, while the problems remained for those who ran smaller workshops. The nationalized and politically controlled banks started to grant loans with low interest rates. The new policy had limited success within Kumartuli, at least in the initial decade, and the private moneylenders remained important. During the 1960s and 1970s, a few Kumars were able to accumulate the necessary capital to turn their image making business into a small-scale industry. The divide between the successful and ordinary Kumar widened as Kumartuli left much of its patron–client economy during the 1970s and entered an economy dominated by a capitalistic mode of production, characterized by ready-made images, organized wage labourers and surplus accumulation that was reinvested in the business. From then on, Kumartuli became a place with a strong divide not only between Maliks, but also between the class of Maliks at large and wage labourers, even though they both generally belong to the same jati.

In this chapter I aim at providing an overview of the economic developments, with political turmoil, nationalization of banks and the establishment of a labourers' union in the 1970s as the main cases. The changes taking place in this period have altered life and work in Kumartuli radically. Contemporary Kumartuli is a product of these changes, as it exists in a fairly similar way to the renewed Kumartuli of the late 1970s. Before we enter this decade when the major changes are manifested, I begin with a short economic history of earlier times.

Patron–Client Economy

As the autumnal festival of Durga Puja gained popularity among the petty rajas and landowners of Bengal in the eighteenth century, the demand for images grew accordingly. During the time of Raja Krishnachandra of Nadia there were probably several quarters of potters in the vicinity of the his palace – potters that are still famous especially for their skill in making realistic clay dolls. The Kumars travelled both within and outside the district of Nadia to make clay images on commission (Robinson 1983: 179), much as the Krishnanagar Kumars are doing even today. When the landed gentry moved into Kolkata from various localities in Bengal in the early decades of the eighteenth century, the Krishnanagar Kumars that they had patronized were hired again to make clay images for them in the new city.

A household hosted a group of artisans in order to make the clay images for their pujas. The Kumars made the clay image; the paṭua (painter: a profession, not a caste) painted it, while the mali (*malakar* or garland maker caste) decorated it. The artisans lived and worked in the household until the image was completed. They were given board and lodging as well as grants of land as their payment (Robinson 1983: 185). A story relates to the time when Raja Nabakrishna Deb brought the Krishnanagar Kumars to Kolkata to create a clay image for his Durga Puja in 1758. The puja became so popular that the Kumar working there became overwhelmed by work, and travel to and from Krishnanagar became rather troublesome. Thus he asked for permanent residence for himself and his apprentices, which was granted by Raja Nabakrishna Deb at the place where Kumartuli is today (Robinson 1983: 182). While probably not entirely true, the story at least shows the reputation of the Kumars of Krishnanagar and the custom of paying for their service through grants of land. It should be noted that all Kumars rent the land, most of them from the Government. So the land was never actually given to the Kumars; they were only given the right to live, work and make a small garden for vegetables there, without paying the same taxes others had to. This follows traditional liaisons of the rich, who would express their generosity and gain merit through gifts to temples, Brahmans and so on. Moreover, such generosity underlined the client–patron relationships of the time.

During the following 150 years, Kumars mainly from Krishnanagar came to Kolkata every year to supply clay images to the rajas and bourgeoisie. For from three to six months they made clay images, while the rest of the time they spent in their native homes making pots and models/dolls. Initially they lived in the households of their respective patrons. Later, they rented a space in Kumartuli where they lived while working for the wealthy residents of the town, many of who lived in the close vicinity of the potters' neighbourhood. Still, they worked only in the households of those who ordered production of the images.

Kumartuli Bazaar

Towards the end of the nineteenth century, the Maliks running the approximately fifty workshops in Kumartuli began to find that they no longer needed to supplement their work as image makers with making pots and/or clay dolls (Goldblatt 1979: 50). Gradually they gave up pottery, while some continued to make small models. By the first decades of the twentieth century, all the Maliks had given up pottery as an income supplement.

The growing importance of community pujas described in Chapter 4 increased the demand for murtis, and in the end this changed the way the Kumars worked. The Maliks could no longer depend only on labour from their families, thus the engagement of wage labourers became important (Goldblatt 1979: 320). This early employment of wage labour marks the beginning of a capitalist mode of production of murtis. At this time there was almost no class divide between the owners and the labourers, who both were mainly Kumars from Nadia. Until the mid-1950s it was common for workers to establish their own workshop; sons of Maliks worked as labourers before they become Maliks in their own right, and there was a high degree of intermarriage between the two groups (Goldblatt 1979).

During the same time, there was a significant change in producer–consumer relations. While for a long period the Kumars had produced murtis to meet fixed orders from their patron-customers, they now started production for the open market directed towards communal pujas arranged by various associations. The change came gradually, and only in the late 1920s and early 1930s did the output from Kumartuli intended for such pujas show a clear rise (Goldblatt 1979: 111). Still, from around the beginning of the twentieth century, some Maliks found that the only way to meet the increasing demand for murtis was to start production before the usual orders were placed. At the same time, the puja associations dependent on subscriptions from the locality had problems placing orders so far in advance of the pujas. They neither had the money at hand so early, nor the organizational capabilities necessary for planning so far in advance for the festival. A situation thus developed where an increasing number of Maliks produced murtis for sale on the open market, so-called 'readymade' murtis. In practice, this did not result in a marked increase of risk, since the Kumars of Kumartuli enjoyed a monopoly and the market was expanding fast (Goldblatt 1979: 112).

Due to the seasonality of the murti making after the Kumars left regular potting, and the increasing production of ready-mades, the Maliks soon became dependent on borrowed money. Until the nationalization of banks in 1969, the market was dominated by private moneylenders with a non-Kumar background. The rates of interest charged in the early years are unknown, but just as today it must have depended on the degree of security provided and the size of the workshop. As is the case today, Maliks who defaulted on their loans would have found it exceedingly difficult to get further loans. It is always possible to negotiate with private moneylenders, as it is in everyone's interest that the money is repaid. But even though the Maliks are dependent on annual loans in order to make images for sale, the moneylenders for the Kumars will seldom provide them with infinite loans if they repeatedly default. This would effectively force such Maliks to close down business, as no moneylender will provide an indebted Malik with the new annual loan that is necessary to continue in the occupation. According to the Maliks, private moneylenders at present might turn to the use of force to 'persuade' the debtor to pay back. The high rates of the private moneylenders were seen as, according to Sundip, 'making them all losers', although the ease of getting money at any time with a minimum of formality was seen as positive (Goldblatt 1979: 189).

However, the gradual growth of arranged pujas made the risks of making readymades and borrowing money from a private moneylender minimal. Kumartuli and the number of workshops grew steadily until the mid-1950s, when there was no more available land to establish a new workshop. While there probably were around fifty workshops making murtis in Kumartuli in the late nineteenth century (Goldblatt 1979: 42), the number in the late 1950s was around 140. In the last half of the 1970s, the number was 148 (ibid.), while today there are around 180 families running their own business of making clay murtis. Some of these present day families do not have a proper workshop, and run their business more or less from the streets.

The growing unavailability of land resulted in a marked increased in workshop rent. While most Kumars had kept their family homes outside Kolkata until after Partition in 1947, they soon had to let them go. They could now only afford to keep one home, and had to sell their rural homes and start living in Kumartuli for the entire year. As mentioned earlier, many had done this even before Partition.

Another consequence of the increased rent was that it became difficult for Kumar labourers to start their own, independent workshops. Until the 1950s it had been rather common for skilled labourers to start as Maliks. While sons of Maliks did usually start their own workshops after spending time as regular wage labourers, after Partition it became more common that the sons interested in the profession inherited their father's business. As a result the divide between Maliks and wage labourers grew. Marriage between the two groups became rarer and towards the 1970s, tension grew and the dividing interests became more visible.

In 1974, an open conflict between wage labourers and Maliks occurred, something which is discussed in a later section of this chapter. But by that time, turmoil had been the order of the day for some time.

Political Turmoil

Even though most Kumars lived on borrowed money and with increasing loans taken from both individual moneylenders and banks, some were able to create profitable art businesses. After Independence the Indian National Congress was in charge and performed rather well until the mid 1960s (Chandra et al. 1999: 312, Metcalf and Metcalf 2002: 243). At the national level, the first twenty years of Independence gave India the image of a model developing country. Then things changed. An agricultural sector beginning to show signs of stagnation was further burdened with monsoon failures in 1965 and 1966. With droughts and the wars of 1962 (with China) and 1965 (with Pakistan), inflation rose steeply. The balance of payments got worse, with foreign exchange reserves enough to cover only little more than one month of imports. Food shortages made foreign aid more important at the same time, as the then most important donor, the USA, suspended its aid as a response to the Indo–Pak war of 1965. The World Bank, the IMF and the USA wanted India to liberalize its trade and industrial controls, devalue the currency and adopt a new agricultural strategy. The central Government attempted liberalization and devaluation, but condemned the policies before any possible effects could take place (Chandra et al. 1999: 251–53, Metcalf and Metcalf 2002). In the end the problems were met with a reversal of earlier policies of state intervention and control.

In West Bengal, the Congress Party ruled for twenty years after Independence in 1947. During this period the Government was able to provide economic stability and secure West Bengal's position as an important state for industry at the same time as it made progress with its public health program, electricity production and road infrastructure. Progress occurred despite the problems created by Partition and the continuing refugee influx of more than four million arriving from East Bengal until 1965. There were two main fields where the Congress Government did not succeed: unemployment among the educated and the growth of the landless. At the same time the jurisdictionally abolished jamidari system still functioned and secured the jotedars and landlords power over the sharecroppers and tenants (ibid.). Still, for the Kumars of Kumartuli, the general economic improvements meant a good market for their art products.

The West Bengal Congress lost power in the 1967 election after a split of the party in 1966. The splinter group formed a government coalition with the Communist Party of India (CPI) and the Communist Party of India (Marxist) CPM, which was named the United Front (UF), but was however ousted due to internal conflicts later that year. The CPM was itself formed as a splinter group of the CPI in 1964, and soon became the stronger of the two left parties. The growth of the CPM as a, or the, major party in West Bengal is said to be mainly a result of the urban elitist radicals' abilities to attract the impoverished peasantry (Ruud 2003: 28). When the CPM joined the first UF Government it caused disappointment among many of its supporters, who accused the party of betraying the revolution through succumbing to reformism and parliamentarianism (ibid.: 28–29, Chandra et al. 1999: 230). Rebel CPM leaders wanted the party to initiate peasant insurrections and form liberated areas in order to fight for a gradual expansion of the armed revolution to the entire nation. As a consequence, a small peasant uprising in the Naxalbari area of North Bengal started: an insurgency that became a popular alternative for many disappointed activists. The rebel CPM leaders were immediately expelled from the party and became known as the Naxalites. The Naxalites consisted of a large number of factions, of which the Communist Party of India (Marxist–Leninist) formed in 1969 under the leadership of Charu Majumdar was best known.

The Naxalite movement attracted many young people, especially college and university students. While the years from the first uprising until 1970 left Kolkata calm, apart from noisy street demostrations in support of the more violent struggles, together with counter-insurgency in the countryside (Dutta 2003: 188), the situation changed after the second UF Government. This Government lasted from 25th February 1969 until 19th March 1970, when the administration of West Bengal was taken over by the Central Government in New Delhi. Then the peasant insurgency hit the urban areas and Kolkata became a central site for its armed struggle until 1973.

The popularity of the CPM, however, grew and in West Bengal the political establishment's fight to suppress the Naxalites was largely successful. Around 1973, the Naxalite Movement had split into numerous splinter groups and factions, marginalizing and limiting its influence. Nevertheless, the few years of Naxalite insurgency in Kolkata made an impact on the entire city. Also the Kumars became captives of the fight, as Partha Chatterjee describes in the following words:

> What has left its imprint on the life of the city is the memory of deserted streets, bomb blasts and running footsteps in the night; of combing operations and 'encounters', of torture in police stations and jails, and of the extinguishing of a few hundred young lives symbolizing the predictable death of a never-to-be-fulfilled dream.
>
> The intensity of state repression unleashed in the city between 1970 and 1973 was of such a magnitude that, unlike many other parts of India, Calcutta saw little in the year and a half of Emergency to add to what it already knew about the ways of an authoritarian regime. (1990: 32)

Charu Majumdar ordered his comrades to target policemen and government officials, businessmen and college teachers. Criminal elements took advantage of the turmoil and started to loot and vandalize, and assassinated people from opposite gangs in the name of political activism (Datta 2003: 189). Cinema halls and theatres were burned down, embassy officials harassed, robbery and mugging became widespread. The Government did not make a distinction between Naxalites fighting for a political revolution and criminal *goondas* (thugs) operating in disguise as politically engaged revolutionaries. It should be added that the distinction was rather fuzzy. As Chatterjee writes, the repression was hard. The Governor of West Bengal suspended the Constituent Assembly and got the Government to send in the army. Thus, the military took over the streets of Kolkata with orders to shoot to kill. The journalist and researcher Sumanta Banerjee writes in his book *In the Wake of Naxalbari*:

> Clumps of heavy, brutish-faced men, whose hips bulged with hidden revolvers or daggers, and whose little eyes looked mingled with ferocity and servility like bulldogs, prowled the street corners. Police informers, scabs, professional assassins, and various other sorts of bodyguard of private property stalked around bullying the citizens. Streets were littered with bodies of young men riddled with bullets. (1980 in Datta 2003: 190)

The atmosphere in Kolkata during the Naxalite uproar was one of fear and terror. People spent as little time as possible on the streets. Kumartuli was (seen as) part of one of the more Naxalite infested areas of Kolkata and, thus, the army and the police hit hard on the residents of the neighbourhood. While this was a great problem for individual Kumars who got beaten, arrested and jailed, the main problem was that customers did not risk travel to Kumartuli in order to purchase images. The police regularly combed the area for Naxalites, abusing everyone at hand, damaging images, and demanding money from Maliks. Not only did the customers fear the bombs the various parties threw at each other, they as visitors to the area were also subject to the harassment of the police. The consequence, as the situation became known throughout Kolkata, was a dramatic fall in the income from image sales. Customers turned to other localities to buy their murtis and the Kumartuli Kumars were economically strained.

Returning again to Niranjan, in one of our conversations, I ask him about the situation during the time of the Naxalite insurgency in Kolkata. He says:

Niranjan: This area [Kumartuli] used to be a Naxalite area, while across the Chitpur road there was a Communist area. One of my friends used to live near Sobha Bajar Rajbari in a rented house [in the Communist area]. We used to play cards there [...] then we used to come back late at night to our homes. There was a narrow lane going through Madhan Mahan palace. And my friends knew my home was in a Naxalite area, but I did not like to be involved in those dirty politics [...] all of them knew that. They used to say: 'Today you should not go home [...] today they [Naxalites] have made load-shedding [power-cut], they will kill you [...] your neighbour will kill you. You better make a telephone call to your family and stay at your friend's place.' This was the Naxalite Movement's area. Opposite the Chitpur road was a communist area.

Geir: Were many people working here Naxalites?

Niranjan: No, our people were not that involved in the Naxalites. The clay modellers and the others did not belong to any party at all. Today the situation has changed and people are almost bound to belong to a political party: selfish, greedy – politics for their own needs. But in our time, we had only our ideals to live by. We could give our lives for the sake of ideals, but the present day situation is rather changing. Today, if a person gets money [...] that person can do anything, he can forget everything.

Geir: When this was a Naxalite area – I would like to go back to that. At that time I was just born and in a country far away – but I have been reading a lot and heard stories about that time. There was a lot of shooting, much violence. It must have been a scary time?

Niranjan: Yes, there was a lot of killing, shooting and violence, but clay modellers and others were not engaged in those actions.

Niranjan is probably right that the image makers were initially not inter-ested in politics generally, or in joining the Naxalites. In Kolkata it was mainly younger middle class students who entered the streets to fight for the Naxalite revolution. However, as the army and police entered the area in their 'comb-ing operations', the attitude among many Kumars changed, turning the neighbourhood into a truly Naxalite area. Pasupati was just a kid at that time, but he recalls the troubled 1970s as told by his elder brothers:

Pasupati: My elder brother and other brothers, the second and third eldest brothers, became involved with the Naxalites.

Geir: Was there any ideological motivation behind this?

Pasupati: No. First they were not in the movement, but the police came and caught so many people. They beat them and tortured them to get the leaders; because of this they joined the movement. They were thinking, if the police torture us anyway, we will be members and fight the police.

Geir: So these were hard times for your family? What happened to your brothers?

Pasupati: They were taken to jail. Now everything is okay, they joined the family again. In those days nobody escaped, you had to join.

Sundip, a senior Krishnanagar Kumar, can recall that the Naxalites had a firm foothold in the area and that business suffered as a result of it:

Geir: But later during the sixties and seventies there were a lot of politi-cal campaigns in West Bengal; to what extent was there any political uprising in Kumartuli?

Sundip: People believed then […] then people believed that the revolu-tion would come, they had a club or strong community here […].

Geir: The Naxalites?

Sundip: Yes, it was the reason that our business was hampered, because people were afraid to come here and buy idols.

Stories from the Naxalite insurgency told by other Kumars echo the same topics and form: there were many Naxalites here, the police arrested and tor-tured many people, some joined from the Kumar community, and business suffered badly. It is evident that it is a topic that is easily mentioned, but they do not like to dwell on the theme. The memories seem still to be causing pain, recollections are excruciating.

At the same time another incident occurred, this time at the national level, when Indira Gandhi decided to nationalize the major private banks. This resulted in economic relief for the some of the Kumars, but many others got further indebted due to the low sales at that time.

Indira Gandhi – the Nationalization Redeemer

The strained economy of India was a severe political challenge and many radical economic policies were launched in order to regain control over economic development. One of these policies, which was to have long term effects on India's development, took place in July 1969 (Chandra et al. 1999: 252–53). Late in that month, the Prime Minister, Indira Gandhi, nationalized the major Indian-owned private banks as an attempt to make more money available to assist the development of small-scale industries and aid the self-employed (Goldblatt 1979: 190). According to Goldblatt, the image makers of Kumartuli were an obvious target for the positive attention the Government sought to achieve. They were famous for their products, and a successful financing of their business would provide good publicity for the scheme (ibid.).

Initially the bank loan scheme was given a positive welcome, but it soon became evident that the scheme would not free the Kumars from the money-lenders' high rates of interest. Goldblatt writes about the implementation of the scheme among the Maliks, a story that no one I met in Kumartuli could remember in such detail:

Late in 1969 an official of the United Bank of India (U.B.I.) came to Kumartuli. He sought out Lakshmi Kanta Pal, whom he had met whilst the latter was working on a series of models for a Government sponsored patriotic exhibition at the time of the 1965 war with Pakistan. [...] The official explains the bank's plan to provide cheap finance for the image makers, so that they could rid themselves of their dependence on the money lenders. He asked Lakshmi Pal to arrange a meeting of all the image makers, so that everyone could learn of the new opportunities that waited them. After the first meeting, the East Bengalis, who run only eighteen shops in Kumartuli, decided to have nothing to do with the scheme; they simply distrusted the intentions of the bank. Many of the West Bengalis were enthusiastic though. Further meetings were held, at which the bank insisted that the image makers form a committee, the officials of which would both represent the image makers to the bank and be responsible for the collection of dues at the end of each season. (1979: 190–91)

Thus, the interested Maliks rejuvenated the old organization of the West Bengalis, Kumartuli Mritshilpa Sangskriti Samiti, which at that time was inactive. They elected a new President, Sudhir Chandra Pal, and a Secretary, Sudhir Pal's friend Sankar Pal. The two men then made a list of interested Maliks and what their needs were for the approaching Saraswati Puja. Loans ranging between 1,000 and 2,000 rupees were given at an interest rate of 9.5 per cent per annum on behalf of the nationalized bank. All the debtors repaid, except one, who was given an interest free loan from a few other Maliks in order to settle the loan.

The East Bengalis changed their minds after they had seen the scheme in operation, and decided to take part. However, they rejuvenated their own organization, Kumartuli Mritshilpa Samiti. This time both East and West Bengalis applied for bank loans for the Durga Puja of 1970. As the Durga Puja is a much bigger event, the loans applied for and granted were respectively higher, ranging from 2,000 to 5,000 rupees (Goldblatt 1979: 192). With the Puja season completed, it was time to repay. All the East Bengalis managed it, but only around a quarter of the West Bengalis repaid their dues in full.

In the following years the East Bengalis took bank loans and repaid them regularly. Thus, the upper limits of available capital were raised. The West Bengalis did not get a raised limit; simultaneously those who could not repay were denied further loans. An explanation for this divide is that the East Bengalis, who at that time represented a minority in Kumartuli, were running larger businesses (ibid.).

While the bank loans were initially not very popular, at present the situation has changed and both groups have positive views on the nationalization of the banks and the service they still provide. There is no difference among East and West Bengalis when it comes to praising Indira Gandhi and her bank scheme. Sundip, a senior West Bengali Malik, says:

> **Sundip:** At that time [before Indira Gandhi] it was very difficult, because we had to borrow money at a high rate of interest and we were always the loser. However, Indira Gandhi [...] our Prime Minister [...] did us a favour. She said that the banks should give us the money at low interest, and then the situation changed.

As a consequence the Congress Party is popular among the Maliks of Kumartuli.

> **Sundip:** We have a strong support for Congress, we always vote for them. And most of the time the Congress have won from this area, not the CPM.
>
> The Congress like us the best, they helped us with bank loans and this was good for us artists.

Recollections of past events are always flavoured by the current situation. Sundip runs a reputed and larger business and was among those West Bengalis who could repay his loans. What thus were major problems during the initial years have changed, and the Maliks are now comfortable with the bank scheme. They have become familiar with the process and know how to utilize it. For well established workshops with a rather predictable economy, it is easy and economical to turn to a national bank for loans. Nimai, a central member of the West Bengalis' organization, estimates that of the total loans made by the image-makers, around 60 per cent of loans are from banks while the remainder are from private moneylenders. Again, bank loans are most popular among the larger workshops.

Consequently, during the difficult years after the general stagnation of the Indian economy and political turmoil with frequent periods of President's rule in West Bengal, Maliks running a larger, more industrial, art business had better chances of success. This was reinforced by the introduction of bank schemes by the nationalized banks. The businesses that survived became more successful; a few grew even larger, also establishing workshops outside Kumartuli. The better off were able to accumulate money, making their business even more financially secure. Many invested the excess capital in better education for their children.

During the 1970s the businesses became larger, the divide between wage labourers and Maliks was evident and a few could expect to accumulate surplus money. In many aspects, the business of image making bore marks of a capitalist mode of production. This was further cemented with the establishment of the first union of wage labourers in 1974 and their following conflict with the Maliks, to which I now turn.

Maliks and Labourers

Until the end of the nineteenth century, when the main work of clay modelling for the religious festivals was done in the homes of the rich, the Kumar made the murtis by himself with the help of his son(s) or other family member(s). The need or practice of engaging labourers came with the growth of community pujas and the sale of readymade murtis from workshops in Kumartuli. Labourers were then, as now, almost exclusively from the same jati as the Malik. While a labourer until the mid-1950s often established his own workshop when he had acquired a high level of competence in the art of making clay murtis, this is not the case anymore. The wage labourers in contemporary Kumartuli constitute a class of their own, with a professional and organized relationship to the Maliks.

At present the working hours for the labourers are, at least in theory, regulated based on the agreement between the two Malik organizations and the labourers. According to the contract, workers should be categorized as either local or non-local workers. A local worker is one who has his home close enough for him to be able to commute every day to and from Kumartuli. Non-local workers have their homes too far away to commute, and as a consequence the Malik provides the worker with shelter and food. Local workers, among whom almost everyone lives outside Kumartuli, have an eight-hour working day. They start at 9:00 a.m. and work until lunch break at 1:00 p.m.; they resume work at 2:00 p.m. and continue until 6:00 p.m. Non-local workers commonly live within the workshop from Monday to Saturday; on Sunday they are free to visit their family homes. They work ten hours each day, starting at 8:00 a.m. and working until their lunch break at 1:00 p.m. Since they are not able to bring their own lunch from their homes, they are given a two-hour break in order to prepare lunch and get some sleep before they resume and work until 8:00 p.m. In contrast, it should be mentioned that the Malik's lunch break is from 1:00 to 4:00 p.m. However, the working hours change throughout the year. During the periods with little or no work, the labourers are not hired. Similarly, during periods with a lot of work, especially as big pujas are close at hand, they have to work overtime (Figure 5.1).

The salary is based on the type of work provided by the given labourer and his level of expertise. An experienced labourer with a reputation for providing

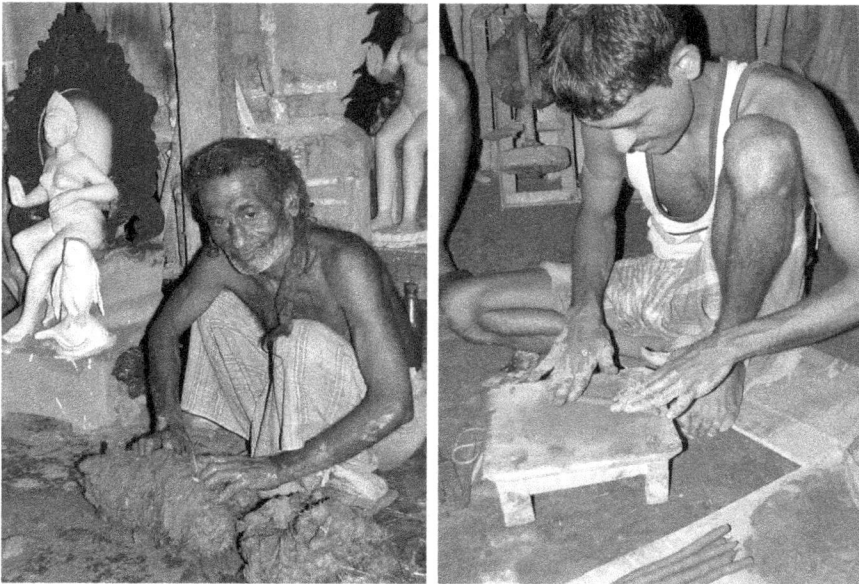

Figure 5.1 Labourers at work. Photo by author.

high-quality work is much in demand; he can earn a rather good income. There is a lot of animosity among the Maliks concerning the labourers. Since many of the labourers are taught the craft at a workshop, the Maliks feel a certain time-honoured right to the labourers' expertise and qualifications. Thus, if a labourer changes employer on the promise of a higher salary or better working conditions, the Malik who he leaves feels that he has been cheated both by the labourer and the other Malik. Many discussions among the people of Kumartuli concern this topic. It should be noted that (almost) every Malik has snatched away a labourer through providing him a higher salary; otherwise it would be difficult to understand why every Malik states that they have experienced that their labourers are seized regularly, and that everyone (except himself) does it.

The formal agreements made between the Maliks and the labourers, which regulate the latter's working conditions, were made in 1974. They came as a response to a demand from the labourers to improve their situation. Most Maliks are still dissatisfied with the new arrangements, something the outspoken Asit readily mentions. Asit is among the senior Maliks in Kumartuli. By caste he is a Brahman and as such he is an anomaly. As a young boy he ran off from his family, and after drifting around for some months he ended up in Kumartuli. There a Kumbhakar Malik took pity on him and he started as an apprentice in his workshop. When he reached young adulthood he was experienced enough to rent his own, very small workshop and become a Malik in his own right.

> **Geir:** What about the working conditions for the workers? I believe they have been fighting for shorter working hours?
>
> **Asit:** Yes, it was in the 1970s they wanted an eight-hour work [day]. When the labour committee was on strike, we the artists did all the work ourselves. We helped each other. But we did not accept the demand.
>
> Previously the Maliks and the labourers were like a family. There was a family bond between us. The labourers took their food in the Malik's home, they slept there. We could beat the labourers, in order to teach them. But when the labourers won, this family unity was gone.

A common feature of patron–client relations is the use of a family terminology to name the various relations (Waldrop 2001).

> **Asit:** The strike ended in a meeting between the labourers' committee and ours; there we decided to try eight hours for three years. There was also another proposal, to divide the labourers into three classes

based on their working quality and what payment they should get. But until now the labourers are not divided, so the payment is almost the same for every labourer.

Then he points towards a boy around fifteen years who is working with a clump of clay in front of his kharkhana.

You see this boy, he is new. This is his learning period; I have to teach him, but still I have to pay him.

The new regulations concerning the wage labourers have made it necessary for Asit to give his young apprentice a salary. The patron–client mindset of this senior Malik protests against this, but there is nothing he can do. Even during the long period of learning, he has to pay. The relationship between him and the boy is not like one of belonging to the same family. Instead it is a regulated relationship between an employee and an employer. I continue the interview:

Geir: How much do you have to pay?

Asit: The payment is not fixed. There are now two types of labourers: one who works eight hours and one who works ten hours. Those who have their family home nearby work for eight hours, then they go home. But labourers from distant villages, who have no place to sleep, they work for two more hours and get food and a place to sleep in our house.

While Asit is nostalgic about the way it used to be, most Maliks accept the regulating of their relations with the labourers. It is one of the most evident indications of the processes of professionalization that have taken place within Kumartuli. To be a labourer, one needs a long period as a novice learning the skills of image making. A proper labourer is highly experienced and much in demand. Thus, while unemployment is high in Kolkata and Bengal, the excess of labourers does not provide the Maliks with the possibility of denying the labourers the right to organize. They cannot hire random people from the streets; they need experienced and qualified labourers.

The emphasis of this book is on the Maliks and their world and work. In a certain sense, they represent continuity, as their work is hereditary. The labourers are also mainly Kumbhakars by caste, and they start as apprentices while in their early teens. They usually have family connections to the profession. Still, they experience it as only one out of many possible professions. Important to them is the possibility of starting when they are young, and that all the necessary education is done within Kumartuli by senior labourers and the Malik. There is no need to be literate or have any other official educational background. Thus, it is a low threshold, manual profession for youngsters who need a job.

It would have been a desirable part of the fieldwork to talk with and interview the labourers, but this proved to be difficult. They were unwilling to talk, and when they did agree to talk, they seemed uncomfortable and answered as briefly as possible. While they do not have the same possibility of administering their own time as do the Maliks, the reluctance most probably is due to fear of what the result of talking to me might be. They do not want to create any conflicts, and being uncertain of my role (I spent time mainly with the Maliks), they preferred to keep a certain distance from me. Except for more informal small talk, I made only a few proper interviews. What follows is an excerpt from one of these interviews. I borrowed the office of my Kumar friend Pasupati's Photo Shop in order to keep the Maliks at a distance; still the anonymous labourer spent most of the time staring out the door and at his wristwatch. My offers of tea and a cigarette did not ease the atmosphere as it usually does. My main intention was to learn about the labourers' samiti.

Geir: So now I would like to know about your organization and your work here. Can you tell me about it?

Labourer: The samitis deal with working hours. Earlier the workers worked the whole day, but then the committee decided that they should work ten hours in a day. This is the first task.

Geir: Then?

Labourer: Then they thought the work should be eight hours. When they tried to make it eight hours, there was a quarrel between the owners of the shops and the workers, but now it is eight hours, now all workers work here for eight hours per day. It starts from early morning at 9:00 (*sokal*) a.m. and at 1:00 p.m. we have our lunch. And then there is work from 2:00 p.m. to 6:00.

Geir: What kinds of labourers are organized in your samiti?

Labourer: There are people from all quarters, but they used to come from Nadia, Rannaghat, Krishnanagar, and also from Kumartuli. [...] Also from different [...] from different places in Kolkata, we come here, work here and then go home.

Geir: But this task with working hours was before, what is the samiti doing now?

Labourer: Now the committee has no work.

The labour samiti or union was started to provide the labourers with regulated and better working hours in order to prevent exploitation. It is interesting to witness the professionalism of the labourer when he ticks off the schedule: 'we come here, work here and then go home'.

Geir: But do you have a place where you come and meet once a week or so?

Labourer: Yes, whenever there is a meeting we come and join the meeting.

Geir: At these meetings what do you come and discuss?

Labourer: There are many problem between the labourers (*karighor*) and Maliks.

Geir: What kind of problems?

Labourer: Sometimes the labourers do not get paid, and sometimes those who invest in the idols do not pay the entire cost of the thakur.

Geir: When was the samiti started?

Pause, the labourer thinks and looks out the door.

Labourer: In the seventies.

Geir: When you fought for eight hours, did you have to go on strike?

Labourer: Yes, there were two strikes to solve this problem.

Geir: Were the strikes peaceful?

Labourer: Yes it was peaceful. Everything was settled within one month.

Geir: Was there any support from political parties?

Labourer: No, the political parties wanted to help us, but we did not take their help.

Geir: Why not?

Labourer: Because if we wanted some help, the political parties [...] the strike would not happen peacefully, there would be some [...].

Stops talking, looks at his watch

Geir: Which political parties wanted to help?

Labourer: All, Congress, CPM [...] But we said no, we do not want your help.

Non-involvement from political parties is an interesting way of handling such a labour conflict. The labourer is probably entirely right when he states that in order to keep it peaceful, they refused the help of any parties, since otherwise the conflict would have soon reached a level of interpolitical fighting between various parties.

Geir: Has the treatment of the labourers changed during the existence of the samiti?

Labourer: Yes, earlier the Maliks gave us money and food, but the money [wages] was too little. Then we had the strike for eight hours' work, then our salary increased, but we no longer get food from the Malik.

Geir: How is the present situation for labourers here in Kumartuli?

Labourer: So so [...] not very good. Not too much development, just good enough to earn a living.

Geir: What kind of development do you want?

Power cut while the labourer talks; this makes him stop. He really wants to get out of this situation. Some candles are provided.

Labourer: We want four holidays in a month, the Sundays, but we do not get it. We have only two days off [each month]. Some time ago there were some talks with the Maliks that we need four holidays, but the Maliks do not respond. We also have other needs, but we have not talked about these needs.

Geir: Yes, which needs?

The labourer does not answer, there is a long pause and I change the topic.

Geir: Do you, the labourers, live here with your families?

Labourer: No, we have no home or quarters here. We live in the house of the Malik and our families live in the village.

Geir: When do you visit your families?

Labourer: Those of us who are daily passengers generally go at six p.m. and some of us who live in villages far away go when they have their day off.

Geir: Do the labourers get the same payment from every workshop?

Labourer: No, there are different rates from different shops.

Geir: Is the competition big between the different shops?

Labourer: Yes, there is big competition. Those who want to make something big, they need good labourers.

Geir: Do good labourers get good payment because of the high competition?

Labourer: Yes.

Geir: How much for a good labourer?

Labourer: 7,000 per month.

Geir: And for an ordinary labourer, not that good?

Labourer: 3,000–5,000 each month, there are different categories.

Geir: What are the different categories?

Labourer: It depends on the work [...] the quality [...].

An income of Rupees 7,000 in a month is relatively speaking a high income in Kolkata. A teacher without an M.A. earns 8,000 rupees, but has in addition better working hours and other benefits. A taxi driver earns between 3,000 and 5,000 rupees per month, working longer hours. It should be added that there are periods during the year when few of the labourers have work in Kumartuli.

Geir: How is the Maliks' general treatment of the labourers?

Labourer: It is always a leader–labour relationship, nothing much. We work and get paid.

Geir: How much does a Malik get in average every month?

Labourer: It is tough to say; only the Malik can answer that question [...].

Since the labourer is so uncomfortable, looking out the door, answering in single words, I end the interview asking:

Geir: How many are members of the labour samiti?

Labourer: Around 800.

I express my thanks for the interview and the labourer leaves at once.

My few conversations with labourers were all similar, and displayed an interesting consensus concerning their relative satisfaction with the existing state of affairs. The labourers speak with an almost single voice. The reasons for this are difficult to explain with certainty, but it suggests that their samiti is rather successful in organizing the labourer in their joint efforts for better working conditions.

A Renewed Kumartuli Emerges

As the 1970s passed, an additional change occurred concerning the main economic unit of Kumartuli: the families. Until the problematic years of the 1960s and early 1970s, joint families were common. Throughout the last thirty to forty years, an increasing number of Kumars have established their own families outside their parents' homes, often entering a different profession. This change in the Kumars' family structure is identical to changes taking place in India at large at the same time.

To the elders of Kumartuli the decline of joint families is a sad fact:

> **Nimai:** Now there are no longer joint families, everyone lives separately, with separate shops within one family. I want joint families, I like that. When united our strength is better.
>
> **Geir:** Has it damaged the art and the profession when children go off on their own?
>
> **Nimai:** The work of art is stronger if we work together, live together. Of course it hurts when we are not together and the family breaks up.

The establishment of nuclear families by those Kumars deciding not to follow the family profession; the existence of relatively large art businesses run in an industrial manner; regulated work hours and payment for the wage labourers, and the possibility of accumulating surplus money from murti making are salient features of the Kumartuli of the beginning of the twenty-first century.

There is only one major difference: the children of the parents who were able to give them a good, and higher, education are now grown up. And today it is the educated Malik Kumars who are responsible for the changes taking place. As the families of the better-off Maliks are able to provide their children with an education that is highly esteemed, not only in society at large, but also within Kumartuli, the reproduction of inequality in the neighbourhood takes place at the level of the family. This follows what Béteille writes concerning the Indian middle class, as being the 'retreat of caste as an active agent for the reproduction of inequality' (2005 [1991]: 313), when he emphasizes the 'significance to the active role of the family in reproducing inequalities in the new occupational system in India' (ibid.). With the emergence of Maliks who run their business as a small scale industry, and who in terms of the actual image-making mainly pay attention to the creative aspects of style, the occupation of the Maliks has changed rather dramatically compared to what it was before the time of Gopeshwar. As the surplus gained by these successful Maliks is invested in education for their children, they reinforce the inequalities. Moreover, being a Malik is reinvented as a modern profession 'based on formal qualifications that can in practice be secured by only some and not all members of the society [...] through] high levels of education [...] and [...] the expenditure at least of time and usually also of money' (Béteille 2005 [1991]: 305). And it is the impact and importance of education which is the main topic of the following chapter.

Chapter 6

ACCUMULATED VALUE: EDUCATION AND CASTE AS ASSETS

This chapter is about recent processes concerning mainly education and recent modernization, which are changing, and will further change contemporary Kumartuli. With a dramatic increase in the level of education among Kumars, the need for middlemen to reach a global market for their products is diminishing. Moreover, with its further integration into global markets, education and contemporary and pan-national ideals of development can be seen as an integral part of the life of most Kumars. The concept of Kumartuli as a neighbourhood outside the passing of time (Fabian 1983, Heierstad 2009), a living museum of 'the age-old art of murti making', must be rejected – again. No need to be deceived by the simple conditions under which most Kumars work, and the seemingly pre-historic process of making status-giving objects with unbaked clay. Kumartuli is a hub of modern capitalism and globalization.

The opening up of the Indian economy in the early 1990s made no immediate impact on Kumartuli. Indirectly however, it created better connections with clients abroad through the globalization of the local economy and the growing impact of information technology in India. When a few Kumars started to use the Internet at the beginning of the twenty-first century, they also started to take control and empower themselves in opposition to local intermediaries. With education from colleges and universities in Business and Art, the new Kumars take their trade into a new area in a way comparable to what the likes of Gopeshwar Pal did seventy years earlier.

However, not every aspiring Kumar comes from a family who can afford the expenses of a higher education. This suggests that the economic divide is gradually being cemented in Kumartuli, as those provided with a higher education are able to develop the business and earn more money.

At the same time, all Kumartuli is facing a radical makeover. In late 2007, plans were finalized to convert the neighbourhood of rundown and inexpensive, but convenient, workshops into a multistoried building. The result is set to be a combined shopping centre and working area for those Kumars who can afford the transition. Views on need and possible impacts vary greatly.

One thing is, however, certain: if the multistoried centre gets built, it will be the end of Kumartuli as we know it. A caste based neighbourhood turning into a caste based shopping centre would definitely be something new, truly epitomizing the ongoing commodification of the image trade and of the caste inhabiting the neighbourhood. Again we see that the landscape of Kumartuli is highly contested. The remaking of Kumartuli into a 'murti mall' is supported by a large majority of both East and West Kumars, but opposing voices are often raised.

Before I enter into this discussion, the everyday world of the younger Malik generation of contemporary Kumartuli is presented and analysed with an emphasis on the successful ones.

Successful Kumars of the Twenty-First Century

From the nineteenth century artisan working in his patron's rajbari or palace, to the artist in Kumartuli making innovative images for sale mainly to the community pujas in the twentieth century, the Kumars metamorphosed from high-status shudras to successful artists. Among them a few families were able to generate a relative high income; they hire labourers and run a small-scale art industry.

The success of some of the Kumar families of Kumartuli, especially after Partition, gave the Kumars new choices. Among the more important ones was that of what kind of education they should give their children. For the first time, they had the possibility of taking their children out of the workshop and giving them an education, even at a college or university level. While many of the younger generation left for different jobs with their newly obtained degrees, some returned to Kumartuli. And with this new generation of Kumars, Kumartuli again changes and moves in new directions. The artist Malik, with a total practical knowledge of every step of image making, steps aside; and the Malik as an administrator, businessman and/or designer steps in. A higher education is the most prominent hallmark of the successful Kumar of the twenty-first century.

Education, modern technology and a new approach to marketing the images are signs of a new Kumartuli. Even so, most workshops are run like they have been for the last century, but a growing number of Kumars can be described as modern in a way that would easily be recognized as such by outsiders. Furthermore, globalization has become an asset. The main competitors to this generation are puja designers from outside Kumartuli. After a period when the theme pujas were in the hand of non-Kumar outsiders, many with an art degree, some Kumartuli Kumars are now working actively in order to gain access to this lucrative market.

The old divide in 'new' Kumartuli between East and West Bengalis is next to nonexistent among the younger generation; instead, there is a divide between those who have an education and those without. These young people are children of the more successful Maliks of the 1970s and 1980s, who reinvested their surplus not only into new workshops, but also into their children's education.

In the following pages, we will meet three young artists who all make or try to make a living within the new paradigm of Kumartuli where education is seen as the road to artistic success and a healthy business.

Prodyut – broadband connected

Prodyut is the son of Gour Pal and grandson of Gora Chand Pal. He is the third in a line of very successful Kumars of Kumartuli. His father and grandfather came from East Bengal after Partition. They soon established themselves as innovative artists, serving many important pujas. Like his older brothers, Prodyut was given higher education at a city college affiliated to Calcutta University, and he got a master's degree in commerce from a Kolkata university. While his older brothers soon found jobs outside Kumartuli, Prodyut did not know what kind of job he wanted when finished with his education.

His father found him lazy and unwilling to work, enjoying the comfort and security of their extended family with high earning relatives. So a few years ago his father asked him to join him in Kumartuli to see if there were aspects of their business there that he might get involved with. Prodyut had spent much time in Kumartuli, both as a child and teenager. He knows parts of the work, especially that of making ornaments; and feels he has it in his blood. But being a regular Kumar, a Malik of a workshop was not his idea of a good source of income. However, with his education in mind, he started to think that there could be better ways to run the old business of image making, and that the market abroad could be better utilized, bringing in a better income.

My first meeting with Prodyut is in their Kumartuli workshop. It is one of the larger ones, with a proper office with a cement floor. We start talking about his family and their background, but he says he does not know enough about it and asks me to talk about such things with his father. The we go on to talk in a mix of English and Bengali about his work and what he perceives as the major problems in contemporary Kumartuli:

> **Prodyut:** After my education at City College I came here [to Kumartuli]. I especially made ornaments, the ornaments of the idols.
>
> **Geir:** Did your father or your uncle give you training in making the [...].

Prodyut: No, training, *mane* [starts to speak Bengali] means I had no training. I just watched them work, I was just watching.

Geir: Did they give you any training in making thakur murtis, in working with clay?

Prodyut: I am engaged in practical work [...] colour, *shadanjo*, ornaments, but I do not work with clay.

Geir: But you also [...] you run the website, it is your responsibility?

Prodyut: Yes, I am now mainly involved in marketing [...] marketing for sale abroad. For the last seven to eight years, Durga Puja has been dominated mainly by theme pujas. Students from an art college will make theme thakurs. People like that will make the thakur, and not us in Kumartuli. Different artists [from us Kumars] will make the Durga idol. They will not make it for earning, but in order to get famous. We, on the other hand, work to secure an earning for living.

It has become commonplace that students from an art college try to get the job to create the design for the pandal and the image. They do not engage in the design work as a necessary source of income, but in order to gain experience and a name. Thus, they take on the job without demanding a high price; all they need is to cover their expenses. This quickly became popular among the puja committees, at least for some years, since it has meant a drastic reduction in expenses. At present, it is not that much in vogue, as, once again, to display the name of an already popular designer or Kumar as the maker is valued more highly.

Prodyut: Then, when Kumartuli was having big financial problems I started to think: the foreign market is very high, foreigners [diaspora Bengalis] come from abroad to purchase Durga idols.

I think, I think [...] I want Durga modernization. Modernization must be [...] like if you want to buy anything [...] just click, payments you make by credit card and then you have purchased what you desired. [...] Then I started. I bought a computer, a digital camera and started my website. Next year I will make it possible to pay online with credit cards. If you want to purchase, the payment is done with a credit card.

Geir: On the Internet [...].

Prodyut: Yes. On the web. Now payments are wire transfer or bank transfer. I want to [...] do more modernization.

When Prodyut is talking about modernization, he uses that English word and not any Bengali equivalent. To him, modernization conceptualizes a whole range of things, of which marketing is the major one. He wants to reach new customers, people who are living far away from Kolkata and who are not mainly concerned with the price. Modernization means the utilization of new technology to reach customers and interact with them.

Geir: Do other workshops modernize in this way?

Prodyut: Other workshops are not involved in or interested in websites […] eh […] the others do not think about this, they cannot. It is I who conceptualized this idea; it is done entirely by me. Last three years from […] [*Stops talking*]

This is not entirely true. There exist some other similar websites, though not with the same professional interface. Prodyut started with a self-made site, but in 2006 he had professional web designers from a small company named CIGMA make him a new site with a proper content management system (CMS) to ease the publishing of new information.

Geir: Do you get good response on the website?

Prodyut: Yes, yes – in 2004 I sent a fibreglass Durga to USA, Dallas, Texas. In 2004, that was the first time. The second time, in 2005, I sent three Durgas abroad, one to San Fransisco, one to New Zealand and one to Australia. This year it is six!

Geir: It is very good progress […].

Prodyut: Yes, good progress. My work is to secure the orders, three to four Durgas, and the price is not very expensive.

Geir: But the price difference between your online Durgas and ordinary one purchased here […].

Prodyut: But my work is fine quality, I maintain my quality, then my price compared to others is high.

Geir: Quality means much work, means higher price […].

Prodyut: Yes, my order book now contains one Kali, one Kali for Dallas this year, it will go by air. And two Swaraswati idols for Swaraswati Puja.

Geir: And the income for your new enterprise, selling abroad, is paying off, is good for the workshop?

Prodyut: Yes, yes.

Geir: The others must be happy for you?

Prodyut: Yes, In Kolkata there is one season for Durga, when we make and sell Durga idols. The USA Durga Puja is at the same time, but the sending time is two months […] by ship. Then we can make the USA

Durgas when it used to be our off time. The USA Durgas give us work when it is out of season here. I send all the Durgas complete in the end of June, by then they are already totally finished at the time when we start working on Kolkata Durgas.

Geir: But in this workshop you also make other murtis for Ganesh, Devi Ganga […] [*no response*], for Saraswati?

Prodyut: Swaraswati, Laxmi, Kali, Jagadhatri, Ganesh, Radha-Krishna – we make all kinds of murtis.

Geir: And the customers abroad are mainly Bengali people,

Prodyut: Yes, yes, all are Bengalis. Purchase is only done by Bengalis. I have exported […] do you know Laxmi Mittal? He is the third richest in the world. Laxmi Mittal lives in London [a non-Bengali from Rajasthan]; I sent them images of Durga, two times. Two times I sent them images.

[Prodyut's uncle enters and asks what Prodyut is going to do after the interview, he answers that he is going home.]

Geir: […] But you told me about the artists from art colleges starting to make idols, being in competition with proper Kumars, doing it for free, for fame. Do you think that their work is very different from your Kumartuli work?

Prodyut: Yes, Kumartuli work is […] others, their work is different. Their works are total, total work […] they work with the pandal, lighting, we only make the Durga image. They make the pandal and the decoration with Durga. For the Durga puja they make the total environment, for competition. We only make Durga idols.

Geir: I have also been talking to other Kumars and they tell me about a lot of difficulty […].

Prodyut: There are many problems here. The number one problem is electricity. The electricity problem in my workshop is the 'DC-line'. In the rest of Kolkata, the DC-line is gone, but in Kumartuli there is still the DC-line. There are two types of lines, AC-line and DC-line, you know. The DC-line here is old; there has been no modernization. I cannot use my computer when there is a DC-line here. The DC-line is a very old system. This system is very old, from the time of the Raj. This is a big problem.

Prodyut is not alone in experiencing electricity as a problem, but their reasons differ. Others complain about the electricity as expensive and of 'poor quality'. Only Prodyut states that the problem is that it makes it impossible to have a computer within Kumartuli.

The second problem is moisture, the damp weather. The environment is not healthy. [...] Sunlight is not reaching the shops.

And the third problem is the clay, from the Ganga [...] eh [...] how to say it? The hospital people say the clay is not good, dangerous clay for [...] [*Pauses*] There are some problems with Ganga water, and we use clay from the Ganga for our work. With the clay from Ganga, we get some disease.

Geir: What kind of disease? Skin disease?

Prodyut: There are some skin diseases; then we get problems with our eyes. There is an 'eye problem' here, we all use spectacles, as I do just now.

The expenses of electricity render the use of electric light rather limited. Together with the meticulous work of image making, eye problems are probably more frequent in Kumartuli than in rest of Kolkata. The problem is so acute that the two samitis of Kumars also work in order to provide inexpensive access to eye specialists. This is done with money from NGO donors and through inviting a 'friendly minded' eye specialist to carry out checkups within Kumartuli for a day or two annually.

An elderly labourer dressed in lungi enters the doorway with two cups of tea.
Prodyut: Tea?

Geir: Yes

The man serves us tea in clay cups.

Geir: So water from the Ganga poses a problem [...].

Prodyut: Yes. And the younger generation is not entering into this business.

Geir: Why?

Prodyut: Many reasons [...] Making murtis is very expensive; the price of a murti is not high enough, except in our workshop. To make one murti it takes 20,000 [rupees] [...] by selling that *murti* people earn 15,000, 14,000 [...] competition [...] meaning [...] if the demand is 100 Durgas, a person will make 150 Durgas. We only make 12 to 15 Durgas.

This creates a big problem. People borrow money from the bank in March or April, but the following year they will not be able to repay it. For many years they take loans, but without the ability to repay. This is a problem and the younger generation is not entering into this business [due to this financial insecurity].

Geir: But what is the younger generation doing, then?

Prodyut: A lot of different things; art college, they go to art college and become different kind of artists. Some enter into altogether different professions.

We continue to talk about future prospects with reference to the current proposals for a multistoried building for the Kumars, a project which he believes will be of great help in renewing the neighbourhood both in terms of facilities and the approach to work. Then we move to the office desk and Prodyut shows me their albums with pictures from many years back; among them the clay Durga they sent to Laxmi Mittal in London in 1996. Most of the murtis are for local Kolkata Durga Pujas. Prodyut keeps repeating 'Our art work is very fine; please compare to other artists'. There are many ekchala or pacchala Durgas, in various styles and colours, with modern faces, theme Durgas, Nataraj style Durgas, Durgas made of clay, fibreglass, jute and papier mâché, where the chala, decoration, ornaments and dresses are made of clay, and so on. A majority of the Durgas for abroad are again of the traditional ekchala style.

The most common way for the Bengali diaspora to purchase an image for Durga Puja is to use intermediaries, mainly people they know who live in Kolkata. The problem is that many of these intermediaries demand a percentage of the payment; thus the price gets relatively high. With direct contact with the Kumars, the purchasers can get a better price, but even better, they get more opportunity to take part in the modelling of the image. Prodyut sells their images for a higher price than most others in Kumartuli do. He gives their high quality as the main reason. It can be added that their workshop is well reputed and due to this, a murti from them is in fact rather prestigious.

It was in 2003 that Prodyut established the Internet site www.kumartuli. com, and he sold his first murti through the website in 2004. The website provides potential customers abroad the option to select from a wide range of murti-styles from their catalogue and order online. When the first contact is established, usually via email, communication is channelled over to an Instant Messaging (IM) client like Yahoo or MSN Messenger. Thus, through the Internet, size, style, colour, material and price are discussed. Production time is estimated at two to three months while the sending time is two months. The total time from purchase to the delivery of the murti is thus five months. When the order is made, the communication does not end. Prodyut brings forth updates throughout the entire process of making the given image. He sends photos regularly, and chats with the clients even more frequently.

He spends little time in Kumartuli. His office is in his and his wife's bedroom where the computer with a broadband connection is situated. On one occasion I visited him at home, and he showed me all the various newspaper clippings he has collected and scanned into his computer. He has also recorded television and radio interviews that he shows me on the computer. His new enterprise has created a lot of attention and he has become a sort of Kumar celebrity, one whom both insiders and outsiders identify as belonging to the new breed of image-makers. While his family's workshop became famous due to his grandfather's and father's innovation of Durga images, Prodyut has preserved its position as an innovative workshop through utilization of new channels of marketing, even if his father does not recognize this. The knowledge he gained at college about Internet marketing has paid off.

Through particularly the work of Prodyut, Kumartuli is accessible from anywhere in the world with an the Internet connection. It is fully possible for everyone who would like anything that can be made by the Kumars, from full-scale images of Durga to smaller pieces in clay, to order it on their PC. There is no need for middlemen or the telephone. Just a web-browser, e-mail or an IM client. To entrepreneurs like Prodyut, the understanding of what the work of a Malik constitutes represents a change from customary conceptions. Prodyut is in the workshops in Kumartuli almost daily in order to supervise every step, from decisions on style to applying colour and ornaments of the actual image-making. However, he spends most of his working hours as a Malik in front of a computer. This is hard for most of the Kumars, including his father, to imagine as part of the work. But as his investments concerning both time and money in this new form of marketing and public relations are paying off, the others understand that this is not a waste of time.

Parimal – presenting one's portfolio

Parimal is in his early thirties. He lives with his parents in Kumartuli and is the youngest of three brothers. The family's adibari is in Krishnanagar and it was his grandfather who settled permanently in Kumartuli. His family runs two workshops, and they have had enough success to give him a higher education, something that his elder brothers do not have. When he obtained his master's degree from the Government College of Art and Craft in Kolkata in 2001, his approach to his work in the family's workshop turned out to be quite different than that of his father and uncles. Providing designs for the whole puja is his main job. He suggests 'concepts' or themes, how the pandal should be constructed, and the look of the image.

When I visit him, he takes me to a room on the second floor. He brings with him his portfolio with a collection of drawings and pictures of realized and unrealized projects. It is March 2006, and we find time to have a lengthy conversation, seated on the bed that occupies most of the space.

Parimal: I have my Government Art College background; there I did my master's degree. I do everything in connection with the puja from the concept to the murti. We have two workshops and usually we get orders to make twenty-five Durga murtis annually. I also draw the eyes of the murtis. This is the work.

Geir: Which college did you attend?

Parimal: Mine? 'Government College of Art and Craft'. I graduated in 1998 and got my master's degree in 2001.

Geir: Was it your decision to go to art college or was it your family's decision, because education is very expensive and [...].

Parimal: No, it was my own decision.

Geir: Why did you want to go to art college?

Parimal: We make traditional murtis, to make it different in some way and to make sculptures – to think in a different way – I choose to go to an art college.

Geir: So you also make different types of sculptures, not only images of gods and goddesses?

Parimal: Yes.

Geir: But in terms of income, what is most important, images of gods or secular images?

Parimal: I have done a few exhibitions of my art work, but I am still not well known [as a secular artist]. Thus the main source of income for me and my family derives from the thakur murtis.

Geir: Do you think that your education is important in order to secure a good income for your family and their work in the future?

Parimal: Yes, I think so, because Kumartuli has not that much business these days, since there are now many other places where people can purchase murtis. We do not have a good market now in terms of income, at present it is decreasing. Then, the making of thakur murtis is a seasonal work; it is six months with work and six months without. So with this background we can make other kinds of sculptures out of the regular season.

Geir: This way of having a higher education is getting more common in Kumartuli. Some have completed art college, while others have an M.A. in business – and they are working here in Kumartuli. Do you think they are transforming Kumartuli in this way?

Parimal: In fact, if we have an art college background this can help us in this business. We can get good orders. Yes, we have many young boys who have, or study to get, an art college background. And other boys from Kumartuli […] they are now mainly graduates. Many boys are getting an education. This business is not financially secure, so if a father has two or three sons, one is set to take care of the business while the remaining two are given an education in any other profession.

Geir: I will return to your making theme or concept pujas. For some time there have been people from outside making the themes, and the Kumars were just told to make the murti. Do you think that education is a good way to be able to take control over the entire process of making a puja?

Parimal: Yes, I think we should take control over the entire process of making the theme, including the murti. Then it becomes a total artwork. Earlier, people just ordered Durga murtis [from us] and they got for instance people in Midnapur, Nadia, to make the decoration and the pandal – that was very popular. And they got people from Chandranagar to arrange the lighting. But now, if we take control of the entire process […] like if we want to make Orissa [a neighbouring state] the theme, then we can take one man from Orissa […] one or two artists from Orissa, then they can work here with us […] making the murti and the pandal. So, then we can arrange for some local Orissa music to be played. That is a total artwork […] the kind of work we should do.

Geir: But for you, is this important in terms of income or for your own satisfaction as an artist?

Parimal: The satisfaction is most important, satisfaction of taking control of the entire concept. When I was in art college, we did not manage to make much investment [necessary in order to make larger murtis], we [the family] used to make small art works. Now we have a big budget, making theme pujas – so now we can do whatever we want to in order to make our concepts clear and beautiful.

Geir: Since your graduation in 2001, how many theme pujas have you designed?

Parimal: Every year I generally make five or six murtis. Among these five or six there is one theme puja annually.

Geir: Is the competition to make theme pujas hard?

Parimal: Yes, it is highly competitive now. Actually, these theme pujas are very much connected to prizes like Puja Perfect. And some reputed artists who get these kinds of prizes usually get three or four orders per year. There are five or six reputed artists who get to do three to four theme pujas each year. And then the others compete for orders for the few remaining pujas.

The various prizes Parimal mentions are awards given by a number of different corporations, newspapers and various organizations. Awards are given to categories like the best murti, best pandal, best ambience, most environmental puja and, most importantly, best overall puja, which usually includes only the theme pujas. The ordinary Kumar wants to receive the prizes for best murti or to be providers of the murti for a puja that wins one of the best puja prizes. That will give them reputation and consequently more and better orders the following year. For concept artists like Parimal, the best puja prize is of great importance.

Geir: Are these 'reputed artists' from outside Kumartuli?

Parimal: Yes, from outside Kumartuli.

Geir: How many within Kumartuli are doing all the work of theme pujas, from concept to the actual organizing of the work?

Parimal: There are two of us from Kumartuli, Pradip Rudra Pal [M.A. from an art college, son of Mohan Banshi Pal, one of the most famous contemporary Kumars] and I. The most reputed artists who get the orders for theme pujas, they only make the concept and have the Kumars here make the murtis.

Geir: When you are making a theme puja, you have to work with the committee to decide the theme. Can you describe the process of working with the committee to conceptualize the entire theme?

Parimal: For us [...] we prepare two or three different themes, we show them to various committee members, then the choice is theirs. They decide and discuss with us which theme they want to have. It is like that when we are doing a work with a new committee. But if we have been working with a committee for some years, then they trust you and it is entirely up to you what you will do. And such as [...] I have not done this [...] someone did a theme puja with Khiral paintings. Then they brought in some artist who was a specialist in Khiral paintings to do this special way of painting. This is how.

Geir: How much can you earn for one theme puja?

Parimal: We have two ways of being paid. One is when we get a budget of four or five *lakh*[1] [rupees]. That is without lighting, only the murti, the decoration and the pandal […] That also includes the labour costs. And sometimes it is ten or twelve lakh […] But another way to work is to get the payment for only my design, my own ideas – my own supervision. For that I charge one lakh or eighty thousand. Then the labour and the material will be the committee's responsibility.

Geir: But when you do this total four or five-lakh project, there is a lot of material, labourers involved for a long period – what is the profit for you when you are finished with all this?

Parimal: It all depends […] but approximately fifty thousand […] for two months of work.

Geir: When you are in this business of creating theme pujas, the most important thing must be to win one of the big prizes. Would that change the business much for you?

Parimal: Yes, I have got many prizes. In Asian Paint I got to the countdown of the last ten. From one to six and from six to ten they have special countdowns – and I have been many times in this six to ten, but I have never been in the group of one to six. But in Puja Perfect I have become third and sixth. And there are many little prizes that I have won. This increases the importance of the artist.

Prizes depend much on luck. I have compared my work with others and I think it is good. To get prizes you also need experience and time to study.

The committees who arrange these prizes are quite familiar with my name. I have a little reputation. Before every puja, you can see small or big news items in the newspapers about my work. So I am already a little reputed. Those who are very much reputed will do these ten or twelve lakh pujas, but we and other artists like my usually do five to six lakh pujas.

Geir: But these competitions, do you think they are completely fair?

Parimal: Yes, it is more or less fair, but reputed names have of course a better chance. Like Amitabh Bachchan [India's most famous and beloved actor] stands higher compared to anyone, so more people will give him votes. This is quite common in other fields too. It depends much on reputed names. First they give prizes based on names and reputed artists get much more publicity.

---

1 One *lakh* is equal to a hundred thousand / 100,000.

Parimal has little more to say about the actual fairness of the competitions. We continue talking about the plans for the multistoried building, then he opens up his portfolio and we delve into his artwork.

As one out of two Kumars who try to capitalize on the theme puja market, Parimal is quite extraordinary in Kumartuli. The other person he mentions, Pradip Rudra Pal, is among the East Bengal Kumars. Pradip works with his father and brother, and runs perhaps the most successful business in Kumartuli with large workshops outside the neighbourhood. In contrast to Parimal and the other Kumars, he was not very comfortable talking to me and told me that I had to do the interview with his father (whom I had already met). What Pradip said was that he did not want to work as a Kumar making thakur murtis, he would like to focus only on art sculptures made of bronze. Torn thus between loyalty to his father and his individual artistic desires, it is not strange that Pradip did not want to answer questions on behalf of his family as a Kumbhakar making thakur murtis. Parimal, on the other hand, feels he can satisfy his personal artistic ambitions within Kumartuli through working with theme pujas, while making different styles of sculptures on order in the off-season.

Parimal belongs to the new breed, which really tries to reinvent the work of the Kumbhakars. It is a long distance between the life of his grandfather, who worked mainly with his potter's wheel, while occasionally making a Durga murti, to Parimal who with his M.A. from a reputed art college sells 'my design, my own ideas – my own supervision'. Still it is the same jati-based trade.

Joyanta – aspiring artist

Joyanta is 17 years old and attends a private art school. In his spare time he works in his father's small workshop. His dream is to get access to a government-run art college. His father does not make many regular murtis for pujas. Instead, they make smaller models, used as decoration in pandals and wherever they are needed.

Joyanta sits next to a table in the back of the workshop the first time I meet him. It is a small room in a pucca building, with a cement floor elevated from the road. In front of the workshop are several boards lined with small newly painted figures placed to dry. His father and a worker sit on the floor and paint more five-centimetre tall mini-murtis made with moulds. I ask the father for Joyanta, who is rather surprised that it is him I want to talk with. He agrees to talk, but leaves the workshop and asks me to follow him. We find a wooden bench in front of a Kali pandal close to his father's workshop. It is February 2007, and the Kali pratima who looks down upon us is being made for a local puja.

Several passers-by stop next to us, trying to find out why Joyanta is sitting next to the researcher. He talks very quietly, making sure that no one can eavesdrop, and politely. I start asking what kind of work he is doing. I initially speak in Bengali; he answers in a mix of English and Bengali, so I copy his mixed way of speaking:

> **Joyanta:** Basically, my subject is painting. I go to a private art college; in P.C. House in Park Street, third floor, Oriental Art. There we do painting, drawing and sculptures, sculptures with cement. I am also trying to get into a government art college.

In India as in many other countries there is a pronounced ranking of schools (Béteille 2005 [1991]), and when it comes to getting an art education in West Bengal, the government-run colleges are placed at the top. Thus, the highest educational aspiration for Joyanta is to get admission into a government art college.

> **Geir:** With an education from this art college, do you want to continue working here [in Kumartuli] or do you hope to get some other kind of work? Or what are your plans?
>
> **Joyanta:** Speaking of plans [...] mainly sculptures, this is the work of my caste. But we have difficulty, problems with studies and nowhere to exhibit our caste's work. We can make regular statues and statues of gods. Making miniature sculptures as you saw me doing is one way of getting publicity as early as possible. If I make sculptures with clay (proper murtis) it will take a long time [to finish, and get publicity]. And I do not have that many opportunities, as I am still learning; I have many things to learn. I want publicity. The younger generation has few possibilities to display their work; there is no exhibition place to show our paintings and our work. There are no chances for us anymore.
>
> I do not know if my work is good or bad, that is secondary. What I need first is to get my work into the public. People should see my work; I need a platform to show it to other people. That is the primary thing. I have many friends who are facing the same situation. If you want to get into Government Art College, you also need a lot of money – that is also a problem.
>
> **Geir:** Is the market for the kind of sculptures you are making better than the one for ordinary images of gods?
>
> **Joyanta:** Yes, the market is obviously better.

Geir: Where do you sell those sculptures? Who buys them and for what purpose?

Joyanta: The purpose [...] people buy them for decoration in the house. And we have some occasions, like memorials for Netaji or the Mother, when we can sell portraits.

A machine starts in a workshop next to the pandal. The noise forces us to take a short break while we wait to be able to talk again. It runs for almost one minute, then falls silent.

Joyanta: I will help you with information, if you help me.

Joyanta's drive to get publicity, to reach out of his father's workshop, is noticeable from the first minutes of conversation, and did not diminish during the rest of this meeting and the subsequent coonversations, chats and meetings we had. To sit next to his father and learn the profession of working with clay, be it making thakurs or large and small mundane sculptures, is not enough for him. He has a clear conviction that in order to succeed in Kumartuli, he needs to obtain both a proper education and to get his work displayed to an audience as soon as possible. Publicity, publicity, publicity – there is no end to his felt need of getting publicity. This firm focus on what he has to achieve in order to make a satisfying, profitable profession as a Kumartuli artist is not common among other artist apprentices of his age. We continue talking about what his drive for an education actually means and the desires of the younger Kumars.

Geir: Your art school background is quite different from your father's. Many young people here in Kumartuli are attempting to get an education and get a job outside – a different kind of job than making murtis. What is, for instance, your father's thinking about this development?

Joyanta: My father thinks that I need a platform to show my work, like I need to arrange an exhibition. We [young people with an art school or college background] want to work, we want to work very well, but as we do not get any chance, gradually we will turn to murti making as our only source of income, nothing else.

While there is a desire to earn money in various ways, it is seen as quite difficult to succeed as an artist outside the realm of sacred image making.

Geir: What will be the best place for an exhibition? What kind of place are you dreaming of?

Joyanta: We have many places in Kumartuli that we can use. We have the exhibition hall of the samiti [a small room facing Chitpur road], which is closed now. But there are also other places here or outside [Kumartuli]. These places are too expensive, one or two persons cannot afford them. It is a huge amount of money.

Geir: Do you think that the samiti should also be working to help people like you?

Joyanta: Yes, I think the samiti should help us, because we are only apprentices, and there are many who are much more experienced than we are, who do much better work than we do – they could work with us. As we are inexperienced, we will make many mistakes – it is quite natural.

There are many places outside Kumartuli where people are making thakurs. Therefore, it is now a very competitive market and the younger generation do not want to throw themselves into this work of image making. So they are choosing other models and aspects of sculpting.

Geir: But your father is also doing sculptures now, this kind of small model. Did he make thakurs earlier?

Joyanta: Yes.

Geir: When did he stop making thakurs?

Joyanta: When our business was running at a loss, he could not make thakurs anymore.

Geir: If you could choose, would you prefer to make thakurs?

Joyanta: No, no. There is too little work in making thakurs, just a few months. But I do get my lessons from Mantu Pal on making images.

There are many problems with making murtis. We have problems during the rainy season, great problems. We have very little room, if anyone wants to make a business here, a larger business; he has no space to do it. We also face many other problems. […] And the bank loans we get are not very easy to pay back. And every day the raw materials we get are more expensive compared to the little money we get selling images. So that is also a big problem.

Joyanta does not see good prospects in the conventional business of making only or mainly thakur murtis. The competition is too tough, and with just a small workshop, they will never be able to make images for the larger pujas, which would have generated a higher income.

During our conversations it becomes clear that Joyanta has decided that he wants to become an artist, and he wants to work in Kumartuli. What kind of work he will actually do is secondary. He wants to make clay sculptures, to paint, make portraits and busts: in short, whatever people want. He is confident that provided a possibility to exhibit his work, he will be able to thrive as an artist. To search for other possible products to manufacture is common within Kumartuli. Many other established Kumars make secular statues utilizing various materials from clay to cement, from plaster of Paris and fibreglass to bronze. They manufacture household décor, pillars, sculptures for commercial enterprises, furniture – everything that can be modelled in some way or another. While the Kumars have done various works with clay, like house décor, from their early days in Kolkata, the use of other materials is rather new. Joyanta has sold a few of his paintings, but that is all. He is still young and works persistently in order to create an alternative living within Kumartuli.

Kumartuli reinvented, reimagined, reconfigured

What these three young Kumars represent is something quite astonishing. Connected, as they perceive it, through blood to an age old tradition of making images with unbaked clay, they attempt to and succeed in reinventing the work of the (Kumbhakar) Kumar. While maintaining that they are successors to an old family tradition that links them and Bengalis as a whole to their heritage, they represent a development of a Kolkata modernity far away from the city's hi-tech and IT hubs. Modernistic architecture and city planning are not prerequisites for the presence of modernity. Behind the bamboo mat walls of Kumartuli, modernity is as present as anywhere else in the world.

Even though they, as most people of Kumartuli, are not very aware of their own history, they have a firm understanding that they represent a change. It is a change that they actively promote; they are the new breed. Kumartuli with its conventional emphasis on the making of sacred images for a local puja market does not present them with all the answers to the question of what they are going to do as individuals who want to make a living in the neighbourhood. They are pursuing different ways of marketing, various approaches to image making and new art objects that they can, and feel a desire, to make. As Kumars, they are appropriating both the work and attitude of professionals outside the business and art of Kumartuli. They respect their forefathers, but do not necessarily follow their desires when it comes to choosing how to live and work as image makers. They see new possibilities in the market and try to capitalize on these, based on an education acquired with difficulty. Image making is not a sacred profession, it is a possibility of living and developing as an artist, as a way of earning an income that compares to middle class aspirations for a comfortable living with exciting holidays and money to purchase consumer technology for their nuclear family. While senior image makers to a greater extent emphasize their work as a sacred business, in terms of, for example, the ritual of painting the eyes, and with some references to rituals when starting to work at a house (see Chapter 4), the new generation is far removed from this reality. In the actual approach to the work, the young Maliks try to create images and themes that can evoke religious feelings – or a sensation of the shared creativity. 'Tradition' as the actual murti is their trade, but they do not think that it provides all the answers.

Returning to the dilapidated surroundings of these Kumars, one gets the sensation that most Kumars do not think that they are suited to their life and work. Many of the young Kumars look forward to the emerging of a new Kumartuli. They are people like Prodyut, who are concerned with aspects of marketing. To them, the slum of Kumartuli does not represent the new approach to public relations that they represent. The narrow streets lined with dilapidated kaca workshops do not resonate with their self-image. But some oppose the project. Among the more outspoken opponents to the transformation of Kumartuli to a multistoried murti-mall, we find Parimal and others from the younger generation. This is the topic of the following section.

A Kumartuli without Mud Floors

Unnayan or development is a much-used word in Kumartuli. There is an urgent feeling that they live in a slum, that they are underdeveloped and that the government does not do anything to help them in any way. When asked to be specific about what kind of development they want, the most react rather uncertainly. They point to the workshops made of bamboo, plastic sheets and sheet metal; they mention the lack of water and medical facilities, the need for an exhibition space and so on.

The Kolkata Municipal Corporation provided an underground drainage system in the late 1970s; there are a few common water pumps, and an NGO run by a non-resident Bengali offers free medical examinations. Still, there is a feeling among the majority of the Kumars who do not earn a good income that they lag behind the city's general development. They feel stuck in a dead end, and doubt that the profession of the Kumbhakar can provide the future generation any prospects of a better life. They cannot afford to give their children the education the better-off Kumars have managed to provide.

However, there is an ongoing project to rehabilitate the entire neighbourhood of Kumartuli. The Kolkata Metropolitan Development Authority (KMDA) has worked to finalize an economically supported plan initiated in 2007 during the Left Front rule to build a multistoried building with exhibition rooms and spaces for workshops. The idea is to provide the Kumars with both better working conditions and a more convenient place to interact with the customers. The project is highly debated for a multitude of reasons. Nevertheless, in the autumn of 2007 the samitis and the Government agreed to go for the long planned project that by 2013 still remains on the paper:

> Now, with the five-day festival of the Bengalis set to start this week, the West Bengal government is drawing up a blueprint for its makeover. 'We have transactions of around Rs. 90 million every year at Kumartuli. Despite doing good business, we are still living in unhygienic conditions,' Mintu Pal, general secretary of the Kumartuli Mrith Shilpi Association, told IANS. 'There is a serious space crunch, filthy environment and no civic amenities in terms of road infrastructure and drainage.' (Bhabani 2007)

It was an MP of the state's ruling Communist Party of India-Marxist (CPI-M), Sudhanshu Seal, who initially led the committee that is set to administer Kumartuli's makeover. According to an interview with him quoted in the same article cited above, the rehabilitation plan is ready and will be part of the Jawaharlal Nehru Urban Renewal Mission (JNURM) project worth Rs. 260 million. KMDA has decided to construct a three-storied building for the artisans, with over five acres of land, at Kumartuli. It will also build an art gallery for artisansto showcase their work. The KMDA renovation project will start in early 2008, and the entire work will take one and a half years to complete. Cost-wise, 35 per cent of the total amount needed will be provided by the central government, 15 per cent by the state government, while the remaining 50 per cent will be arranged through loans. Mintu Pal adds: 'We want the Kumartuli development project to be implemented. It will not only be for the betterment of existing artisans working in the area but for rejuvenating the art of ancient Bengal. [...] We think there will be a huge employment opportunity if the Kumartuli rejuvenation project is done in a proper manner' (Bhabani 2007). Another interviewed image maker, Somnath Pal, adds: 'We are now in talks with the state government and KMDA officials regarding plot-related matters. A location near Kashipur in north Kolkata is likely to be chosen for shifting artisans temporarily in November this year' (ibid.).

According to the ICICI – West Bengal Infrastructure Development Corporation Limited's project I-WIN, a joint venture between the ICICI Bank Group and West Bengal Industrial Development Corporation Limited, the assignment for the renewal project is completed and Kolkata Metropolitan

Development Authority (KMDA) is responsible for the project. Among the goals cited are:

- Improvement of Livelihood & Living Condition at Kumartuli – A World Class Heritage Site and a *sine qua non* for Durga Puja – the most grandiose festival in Kolkata / Eastern India.
- Decongestion of Trans-municipal drainage system across five municipalities, prevention of Water-logging, improvement of economic activity & ensuring a high economic rate of return. (ICICI Winfra 2007)

The KMDA says that the project will cover 3.22 acres and 298 shops, of which 166 are clay workshops, 51 workshops for decorative material, 81 other establishments and 524 residential flats. The project will include, in addition to workshops, community facilities like an exhibition hall, community hall, health centre, post office, banks, art gallery and so on. The total project cost is set to be Rupees 30.69 *crore*[2] (KMDA 2007).

Due to the sheer size of the project, every Kumar is affected. He or she has to decide if they want to continue as image makers in Kumartuli or outside, if they at all desire or can afford to continue. In order to get a workspace within the new multistoried building they have to pay a rather large sum of money. Many Kumars fear they do not have the economic strength to do that. Still, a majority of the Kumars agree with the project, expecting that it might give them a better chance to succeed in their profession. Secondly, the construction of the new heritage centre means that the Kumars will have to move for a period. Many fear they will lose clients. Some mention that only those who have additional workshops outside Kumartuli will have a possibility of keeping their clients – that is, the already successful among them.

Besides the pressing economic constraints that are discussed, several point towards actual practical problems of doing business. And interestingly enough, this is quite common among the juniors, perhaps because they do not feel the same loyalty towards the group as a whole, or because they have a more professional outlook and understanding of how a modern multistoried building will affect their profession. The young apprentice Joyanta, for instance, remarks that: 'Some people say they will rebuild Kumartuli. There is also a problem that after the development of Kumartuli, we cannot dry the thakurs in the sunlight.' The images they manufacture are mainly made with unbaked clay, which needs to dry in the sun. The image lined alleyways of Kumartuli are thus not only evidence of cramped conditions, they are also a necessity.

---

2 One *crore* = ten million (a hundred lakh).

Other ways of drying the murtis artificially is of course possible, but at what cost? Drying in the sun is free to anyone.

Parimal, the puja designer from Government Art College, is very critical of the project. He said in spring 2007:

> **Parimal:** The multistoried building is still a plan and not very much a reality. At first it was a 200 million rupee budget, then it was cancelled, then it was started again with a 100 million rupee budget, then it was again cancelled, then it was an 80 million rupee budget, then it was also cancelled, then it was a 47 million rupee budget, and then again it was cancelled, and now it is a project with a budget of 27 million rupees. And still they have only arranged for 17 millions, and 10 they have not been able to collect. We get to know about this project through the samiti [both of them supported the project when I discussed it with them] and newspapers, so we have no clear concept of what we will get, if we will get the same place that we own now, where we will get it, on the ground or middle floor or on the roof. So if they make us aware of all these things, then we can see [...].

> **Geir:** So the people [local samitis and individual Parliament members] behind this project have not been able to involve all of you?

> **Parimal:** Actually, it is very difficult to communicate with all the people of Kumartuli, because there are different types of people living here. For instance, we have our own home here and our workshops. Here in Kumartuli there are also some people who only have their homes here and who are involved in other professions. And there are also some who live in rented houses in this area. These are also problems that have to be solved –where shall these people live, and who will get a place in the new building? The Government never discusses such problems with us common people. We get information from the samiti and newspapers, and this makes a lot of confusion. Once they arranged a meeting here, which was cancelled because of all the confusion.
>
> What they are publishing is that they want to develop Kumartuli, so if an artist here does not get enough space for his business [...] he can never be included in this project.

> **Geir:** But if this project gets realized, do you think it will be of any good for most of the Kumars?

> **Parimal:** In fact, the concept is not clear within us and also for me it is very hazy. They have published many things, like it will be a multistoried building with a swimming pool and so on [...] which is only a story. And in real life [...] how many square feet we will get for our

business, that is not clear. Therefore, it is difficult for me to say if it will be good or bad.

In addition, the Government does not have a clear idea about our business and the kind of place that we need for our business. We do not need a big concrete building; actually it is not good at all for our use. A government engineer can never build the kind of place that we need. Because it is best for our profession to have a mud floor, it can absorb the dust and such things. If we want to cut some bamboo or [...] a mud floor is good. We do not need big concrete walls, we need such a room through which enough air and light can pass. I think the Government should involve the experts from Kumartuli; they can give concepts to the Government. It is not possible for an engineer from the Government to have an idea of what kind of place we need for our business.

The government officials are not very conscious about these things; they are only thinking that we need a very clean place. That that will be good for our business, but that is their idea, not ours. You need different types of space, workshops, for different kinds of businesses. Such as when I went to visit one place that worked with the acid industry, they have mud floors – so it is important.

The practicalities of constructing the 'murti mall' are not discussed or, at least not communicated to, the people of Kumartuli. Like other craft traditions in India, 'the unchanging technology is not a sign of tradition or stagnation' (Venkatesan 2009: 19). Why artesans and artists resist development agents differs: among many of the Kumars it is mainly due to lack of resources to take part in and/or the unsuitability of the proposed development. When talking to leading members of both samitis, they are not very responsive about this aspect. Their major concern is the cost for getting a new work space in the new building and not if or how it should be built.

Geir: When one talks to the samiti members, they seem to be very much in favour of the new building. Their only concern seems to be the price the individual Kumar will have to pay in order to get a working space. I have heard no details about floors or walls, or anything else [...].

Parimal: The samiti wants to start the work of making this building first, then they will see later. In addition, they are not very much clear about how many years it will take to make this multistoried building. They cannot tell us properly when we have to move, to where we have to move [while construction is going on] or if it will be possible to run our business in that place; or when we return to this place again, if we will get the market that we once had. This is a very scary thing.

The business that we run here in Kumartuli is very much based on its name [...] of the place. Like [...] I prefer to buy some new clothes from the New Market, not from Sobha Bazaar [...] it is like that. The Kumars working in other places in Kolkata are doing very well in murti making. If you get a murti from Kumartuli then it is very reputed, it is very famous. And among us it is only from 20 per cent of the workshops that you can get really good works of art. The remaining 80 per cent does very simple kind of work. If people start making murtis in a different locality, there will be competition. And that will not be very helpful for us Kumars.

The uncertainty of what the future will bring is evident. Wild rumours and lack of knowledge make it difficult to comment upon how the new project might affect the Kumars' life. It is easy to imagine the new Kumartuli with its multipurpose, multistoried building buzzing with life from Kumars communicating and marketing through the Internet in front of widescreen LCD monitors, while others are running to and from their studios with a portfolio or two containing various concepts for pujas and other artworks under their arms, disturbed only by local visitors and tourists spending time in the various art galleries and enjoying a cappuccino in one of the coffee shops while discussing whether they should buy this or that painting.

To many Kumars, such a place might provide a new possibility to develop the art and business of image making. To many others, it might equally well imply the end of a lifestyle and profession. Many Kumars in Kumartuli want to see some material improvement, even if not properly defined, but whether the new project has the potential to meet their vague concepts of that is impossible to say. The samiti members, who after all know the plans best, support the plan. The rest do not know what to think. What is for certain, when the new, in reality, jati-based murti-mall is built, Kumartuli as people have known it will have changed dramatically. The most critical claims concerning the new Kumartuli are raised by some educated and inventive members of the younger generation of Kumars together with the poorest section of Maliks. While the former see the practical problems, the latter are afraid they cannot afford to pay the necessary charge to get a new workshop in the new locality. Although these two groups constitute a small majority in Kumartuli, their critical arguments have not been considered properly. It is interesting to see that someone like Parimal, who in many ways represents the new modern type of Malik with his education and attempts to capitalize on the theme puja market, is by the majority of the Kumars seen as anti-development and anti-modern.

Another aspect of the growing urge for development and modernization can be seen with reference to globalization. With the increasing impact of the transnational economy, cable and satellite television and other kinds of information technology, the outlook among the Kumars has changed. While their artist forefather Gopeshwar went abroad and brought with him inspiration that changed their professional approach, at present many among the younger generation of Kumars look beyond the borders of Bengal. They search for inspiration in popular movies like some of their senior predecessors, but perhaps more importantly, they come to imagine their life as different from that of their seniors. With increasing globalization, modernity becomes even more visible among contemporary Kumars, a modernity with a life as members of a middle class connected through mobile phones, with references to the same transnational television shows like *Who Wants to Be a Millionaire?* (*Kaun Banega Crorepati*), *Big Brother* (*Big Boss*), *Pop Idol* (*Indian Idol*), soaps and so on; with styles of dressing where jeans are for everybody, and education is provided by English medium schools. Self-understanding is marked by references to objects and practices that are transnational, rather than local. A growing number of Kumars have gone global.

Modernity at Large: Caste for Sale

Since at least 1851, Kumartuli's products have reached a global market (Mukharji 1974 [1888]), even if in a limited way. With the ever-growing Bengali diaspora, the market has become quite large. Whilst it used to be common for middlemen to arrange for 'bringing out' the images, lately Kumars themselves have started to approach potential and existing clients outside the boarders of West Bengal and India. In this way the Maliks have connected directly into the global market of images. The main parallel between those global entrepreneurs is that they have an education above the primary level.

Appadurai writes in his formative book *Modernity at Large* (1996) that globalization has shrunk the distance between elites, shifted key relations between producers and consumers, broken many links between labour and family life, obscured the lines between temporary locals (immigrants) and imaginary national attachments. With reference to the Kumars of Kumartuli, who are never depicted as a hub of globalization, it is evident that globalization has also created local elites or affected others than the elites – due to education for one. They relate more directly to consumers, avoiding intermediaries – owing to education. Still, it seldom affects the links between labour and family life, although a few are given the possibility to travel in order to make murtis in other states orrarer still, abroad. The Bengali diaspora has entered Kumartuli more directly, thus Kumartuli has entered the Bengali diaspora.

Appadurai continues, 'Locality itself is a historical product and […] the histories through which localities emerge are eventually subject to the dynamics of the global' (1996: 8). The locality of Kumartuli is a historical product and the histories through which Kumartuli emerges are subject to the dynamics of the global. The question that has to be asked is which 'histories' and what 'dynamics of the global'? The histories that make Kumartuli are those of the old days of patron–client relations, of working in the palaces, of Gopeshwar Pal and innovations, of Partition and various phases of economic difficulties. In addition, there is the continuing history of how one makes a good image with both cult and exhibition value. When it comes to the dynamics of the global, important processes are the emphasis placed on getting a reputation, especially through television and newspapers, and the drive for a useful higher education and the use of modern media like the Internet in reaching new markets more directly. Kumartuli is a trajectory of its histories, reinvented and remarketed by the younger generation of Kumars as they capitalize on modern technology and global concepts of what constitutes a good and modern living.

Through the Internet, other media and education, the locality of Kumartuli emerges in a globalizing world (Appadurai 1996: 18). Contemporary Kumartuli becomes visible to the attentive observer through these ongoing processes. Media (increasingly) links producers and customers across national boundaries (ibid.: 22), and in the context of providing murtis for pujas we witness the globalizing twist of what Fredric Jameson called 'nostalgia for the present' (ibid.: 28–29), epitomized in the successful attempts in selling Kumartuli – for example, Kumar-made – images.

With the growing importance of trade outside Kolkata and West Bengal, the Maliks are capitalizing on new markets by promoting themselves indirectly in regular news coverage or directly through the Internet. A new way of understanding what the work of the Malik should be has emerged: as the art college-educated Maliks think in terms of theme pujas and seek inspiration for total concepts, or as the business-educated Maliks seek to reach new markets directly through the utilization of information technology, at the same time as they stress the authenticity they represent as being image-makers by caste.

Even when, or if, the new multistoried building is completed and the Kumars return, Kumartuli will continue to exist as more than part of the name of a heritage centre and 'murti-mall' that makes the Kumars' art products easily recognizable as commodities. The histories will remain; the Kumars with their experience of a blood relationship, and the art of making unbaked clay images that with ease lend themselves to the immersion into Ganga at the end of the puja will survive.

Chapter 7

COMMODIFICATION OF CASTE

The contemporary Maliks of Kumartuli live their life in this jati-based neighbourhood, making images of unbaked clay. While they might not work with the actual clay as much as their forefathers, they engage with it on a daily basis, supervising the process from making the wooden frame and the straw binding to the application of clay and painting. They represent themselves as both carriers of an ancient tradition as well as innovators and creative artists of a new type. And in contemporary India with its liberalized economy, the markets have not disconnected themselves from caste (Harris-White 2003: 196). In the case of Kumartuli the opposite seems to happen (Figure 7.1).

If the rundown, slummy workshops of Kumartuli are replaced by the new multistory building, the competitive, modern and capitalist realities of the Maliks might become even more visible both to themselves and to outsiders. The possible loss of a practical workspace in the new 'murti-mall' is rarely addressed, as ideas of development and modernity seem to have the upper hand among the majority. At present the Kumars and Kumartuli are understood and presented as archaic, as lost in time, both by themselves and outsiders. On behalf of the commenting outsiders, this allochronism, or displacement of others in the Third World to the past (Fabian 1983), is often based on an essentialist understanding of caste and modernity as oppositions.

An important question that this book has sought to address is: what is caste as practised by the Kumartuli Maliks, and how does this relate to the contemporary sacred art market that has developed in Kolkata during the last 150 years? In order to answer this question, the caste system is approached as historically and geographically situated, and not as defined by any unchanging structural basis of pure–impure oppositions. Moreover, the kinds of lived realities of the Kumars of Kumartuli is described with reference to a capitalist modernity that does not emphasise its specific origins in each case, as this often remains mere speculation.

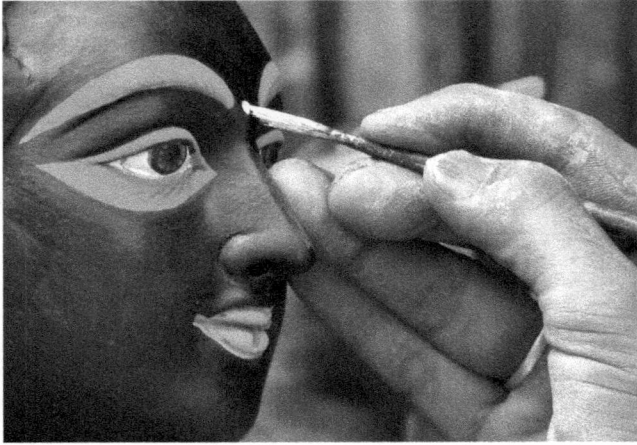

Figure 7.1 Painting of Kali Ma. Photo by author.

Caste versus Modernity

Caste and modernity are not two randomly chosen concepts with relations established only by the anthropologist, mutually used in order to guarantee that this book does not appear 'chance erected, chance directed', to paraphrase Kipling's infamous description of Kolkata.

In the sociology of India, from colonial times to the present, caste and modernity are almost isomorphic in a certain, negative way. While many studies during the last decades have challenged this view (Gupta (ed.) 2004), it is still very much alive among laypersons outside and within India. Being the hallmark of everything Indian, seen as the all-encompassing organizing principle, caste is also depicted as essentially nonmodern. A telling historical example is provided by Rev. Matthew Atmore Sherring's (1826–1880) *Hindu Tribes and Castes*, published in 1872 (1974), which is among the first empirical studies of castes that occurred after a century of textually based studies of the early orientalists (Dirks 1992: 66–67). In his concluding essay he writes on the prospects of Hindu castes, and sums up: 'Caste is sworn enemy to human happiness'; 'Caste is opposed to intellectual freedom'; 'Caste sets its face sternly against progress'; 'Caste makes no compromises'; 'The ties of caste are stronger than those of religion'; and 'Caste is intensely selfish' (274–96, Dirks 1992: 67).

Even as caste is portrayed as denying the Hindus everything from happiness and freedom to intragroup empathy and progress, Sherring does not recommend that they should convert to Christianity or do away with their tradition as 'some caste-emancipated Bengalees' have done. The Hindus are not fit or ready for human happiness, intellectual freedom or progress, traits that constitute central features of modernity. Thus, as Hindus they are organized, (self-) governed, represented and enact their roles based almost totally on their caste affiliations and the structures of the caste system. As such, they can never be modern; modernity is the opposite of everything Indian, and Indianness as defined by the omnipresent existence and realties of caste is definitely the reverse of the West and its modernity. The orientalists' depiction of the Other as the negative reflection or image of oneself, as discussed by Said (1978), is evident in this kind of study.

Much later, Dumont provides a rather similar representation of caste regarding its structural/structuring importance. Caste is still the single most important expression of a principle of hierarchy and social organization among the Indians. Slightly caricatured, Dumont's concept of caste is non-political and leaves little space for any individual freedom. Dumont conceptualizes modernity as an academic discourse, one concerning an emphasis on the individual. Thus, holistic or individualistic – hierarchical or egalitarian – societies can at least in principle all be modern. The Indian reality is however not such a case. Introduction of modernity involving mainly individualistic values does not pose a challenge to caste. In the words of Dumont, 'Caste values envelop and encompass modern ferments' (1998: 224) and Indians will somehow remain premodern or traditional (Dumont 1980 [1970]: 9, Searl-Chatterjee and Sharma 1994: 4). The new is subordinated to the old and even when individuals participate in modern education, the end is still the traditional rank. He goes on to talk about the incompatibility of the two sets of values: traditional and caste-based, and modern and individualistic, and how 'traditional Indian values' are not destroyed by the introduction of 'everything accompanying modern values in Western society' (224–25). Caste prevails and encapsulates modernity in order to heighten/increase/achieve certain values defined by the society, a society that is still defined by traditional values rooted in the caste hierarchy. Again, caste and modernity are counterposed. It is telling that Dumont writes in the very first line of his introduction that 'the modern reader is doubtless rarely inclined to study' the 'caste system' fully as it 'is so different from our own social system' (1980 [1970]: 1). Does this imply that a 'modern reader' is by definition distanced from the Indian caste system? If non-European modernity (Narayan Rao et al. 2003, Woodside 2006) exists, as argued above, then this conception of modernity is somewhat Eurocentric. It seems that not even Dumont managed to put aside his own prejudices when it came to what constitutes modernity or the modern man and woman.

Caste and modernity are both 'social facts' in the sense that they are empirical realities. Caste does exist, according to the Kumars, even if it does not look very much like the kind of caste that Dumont describes. Modernity as an attitude among the Kumars also exists, and has done for a long time. While the caste system as described by Dumont might be opposed to a certain sense of modernity, a more empirically grounded description of the caste system is not opposed to modernity as a comparative and empirical category. Thus, if one extrapolates from the stories and practices of the Kumars, one can state that both exist simultaneously as a 'state of mind' (Dumont 1980 [1970]: 34). (I use the term 'extrapolate' since I know of no device or method that gives direct access to peoples' minds.) Consequently, a society with a caste system can be both modern and non-modern (or traditional). The picture is further complicated by the awareness that knowledge (in every sense of the word) is unevenly distributed within most societies. And since modernity is a certain kind of knowledge and practice, we have to admit that within any given society some might be modern while others are not.

This venture into modernity and caste points to some of the major questions that this book addresses. Being responsive to the continually growing impact of modernity raises the question of what makes modernity appeal so strongly to so many people. A study of the role of caste on the ground in contemporary India will also contribute to the understanding of what caste actually means and how it is practised today. The historical perspective on caste discussed above will help us to see the caste system as a historical product with a multitude of local manifestations, quite unlike the universal and never-changing system Dumont depicted. Thus, we can ask empirical questions concerning what caste means to the contemporary Maliks and how it manifests in their practices. Changes that are described as the emergence of modernity are traced without the need to link them to Western modernity.

Caste in twenty-first century Kumartuli

In the first decade of the twenty-first century, Kumartuli is still a caste based neighbourhood. Kumbhakars making unbaked clay images as their main or sole source of income dominate it. Most fathers are followed by at least one son in the profession, with both stating that the hereditary transition is natural and in the blood. This belief in a substance that contains at least an important part of their identity is common in India (Östör, Fruzetti and Barnett (eds.) 1982, Hanssen 2001). While they maintain such a view, the young Kumars often emphasise that it is not enough. They need education as well in order to succeed as Maliks. Marriages also take place primarily within the jati. Thus, two commonly cited aspects of caste, those of hereditary profession and endogamous marriage, still exist within Kumartuli. In an urban context like Kolkata, such consistency over time is rather rare. Only a small minority of the population works within their caste's profession; a growing number of youngsters are even not aware of their jati-background and/or its traditional professional affiliation. Jati endogamy is also commonly depicted as a traditional aspect of caste that soon decreases in importance and frequency when members of a jati move to an urban context (Uberoi 1993, Béteille 2005 [1996]).

In the context of Kumartuli this atypical consistency can be explained mainly with reference to the stable demand for murtis. This has created a sustainable living for the Kumars – thus the existence of Kumartuli as a hub for image-making. The continuation of not only a viable hereditary profession, but also one which is growing and which opens opportunities for at least a small minority to earn a middle-class income, also secures the continuation of endogamy. The potter community is relatively large, but still geographically concentrated in a few centres, and it has a relative success, both factors which sustain the actual possibility of continuing the practice of endogamy after resettling in an urban area. The Kumars' ability to transform their profession from rural artisanship into a small-scale urban art industry while keeping their good reputation, has, ironically enough, contributed to protecting them against change when it comes to some aspects of the caste system. Innovative abilities and an understanding of the changing conjunctures of the market are probably the reasons why Kumartuli is even today a neighbourhood dominated by Kumbhakars working with clay. As innovation and artistic abilities are central to the modernistic turn in Kumartuli, modernity can be said to have sustained this particular community.

The caste system as it was practised 50 years or 100 years or 150 years or 200 years ago has changed (continuously) among the clay artists. Caste does not have the same connotation, does not entail the same practices and rituals and is not perceived in the same way as it was earlier. As caste changed from pre-colonial to colonial times, it has also changed during colonial times and afterwards. A major point of divergence concerns the aspect of purity with reference to the caste hierarchy today, which is next to nonexistent from the point of view of most Kumars. The young, contemporary Kumars are proud of their jati-based neighbourhood and profession, but awareness of former practices and stories connected to caste has almost totally vanished. To them caste is an asset, a source of self-respect, which they utilize in the competition to succeed in the market. Their concept of purity fits in better with the Government's desire to give them clean and hygienic surroundings.

Hierarchy and purity

The concept of purity and the structural opposition between the impure and the pure are perceived by many scholars as an important pillar of the caste system. In contemporary Kumartuli, purity is not an important aspect of how the Kumars perceive or act with reference to caste. This was not always the case. Purity did, unsurprisingly, matter some six to seven decades ago among the Kumartuli Kumars. A central question that the diminishing role of a caste-based concept of purity raises is whether it is possible to describe Kumartuli as caste-based in the twenty-first century? Put differently, can the caste system exist among people who act without a notion of purity? It must be emphasised that the discussion here is not concerned with the 'fruitless debates about whether caste has changed its "essential" character in the modern period' (Searle-Chatterjee and Sharma 1994: 9). Instead of seeing caste as simply something the Kumbhakars 'are', I stress how they act with reference to caste, as caste is seen as something people 'do' (ibid.).

Conceptions of purity have always been central in the depiction of caste and the caste system. The hierarchy that caste is said to constitute is described by many mainly as a hierarchy of decreasing levels of purity. As mentioned earlier, for Dumont the caste-system is composed by hereditary groups placed in a hierarchy founded by the opposition of the pure and the impure (1998 [1970]: 43). Still, Dumont does not suggest that this opposition can account for all distinctions or segmentations of caste (ibid.: 44). The opposition is mainly seen on a macroscopic level between the pure Brahmans and the impure Untouchables, and thus more visible on the varna-level of the caste system.

At present, few Kumars make images in the homes of other people. Nevertheless, no one cares for such notions of purity as to whom to accept food from anymore, as mentioned by Niranjan in Chapter 4. Does this imply that the caste system does not function as a proper hierarchy anymore? The opposition between the pure and the impure is said to define the hierarchical *form* of the system that is its underlying structure (Dumont 1980 [1970]: 44). Remembering that the Kumbhakars are clean Shudras from whom a Brahman would accept water, and that within the Bengali caste system (as it is depicted in what is seen as the traditional form) they have a relatively elevated position, it seems probable that at least among the 'purer' jatis, concepts of purity have decreased in importance.

Dumont argues that the opposition between the pure and the impure underlies the whole hierarchical structure of castes. As such, it is a hierarchy of value which places individuals in relation to an encompassing whole, the structure that informs Indian society at large. In this depiction, status is detached from and subordinated to ritual purity: the king is inferior to the priest. Even if we accept this explanation as partially valid, caste within Kumartuli does not support such a notion of what constitutes the Kumbhakars as a caste. It seems that the notion of hierarchy as such, be it derived from purity or status, has lost its importance among the greater number of jatis on the level of relations between various castes (Parry 1994).

Intra-jati notions of status are, as seen in Chapter 6, quite important. The opposite seems, however, to be the case in the urban context of inter-jati notions of the present-day Kumbhakars. Neither with reference to purity and pollution, nor as materialistic and ritual-religious ideology (Searle-Chatterjee and Sharma 1994: 15) does status matter.

Caste, as a language, is often used in the context of Kumartuli with reference to the authentic or traditional. 'Real' murtis must be made by a proper Kumar. In such a context there is no need of ritual purity, only a notion of hereditary traits. This brings us back to blood, and the contradiction between common statements such as the work 'is in our blood', indicating that there is no need to actually learn the trade on the one hand, and the emphasis put on education as necessary to succeed in the competitive environment of Kumartuli on the other. Hence, caste, in the same manner as education, is used as an asset in order to sell products. And as such, caste gets commodified. It provides the murtis purchased by the customers with a heritage, a genealogy. Thus every murti purchased in Kumartuli is, in a sense, seen as traditional.

Returning to the three young Kumars we met in the beginning of the last chapter, we get a sense of how caste and the concept of purity are unfamiliar terrain for them. When asked questions concerning their caste affiliation, they have problems answering beyond stating that they are Kumbhakars. If pressed for more details, they tell me to ask someone senior, like their fathers. They cannot talk about clans or gotras, about ritual purity or their jati's position within the system. Jati matters only as a signifier of inherited profession and as a guide when it comes to marriage – and as a source of pride and commercial success.

The introduction of a market model for selling murtis, with its increase in the level of competition, might provide a partial explanation of the decreased importance of ritual purity in the context of Kumartuli. No one can afford to make caste and concepts of ritual purity significant in the murti market of Kumartuli. As elsewhere in the urban society, earning money is more important than sustaining ideals of ritual purity. There is a constant flow of people entering Kumartuli in the months before the great pujas. Kumartuli becomes caught up in the 'urban swirl' (Hannerz 1992), making interaction based on caste notions problematic. As customers enter the workshops and show their interest in the images, the ongoing discussion is all about price, size and style. Education also provides a part of the explanation. In Bengal there has long been a conscious awareness concerning the role of the caste system as a discriminatory practice. Thus, varna or jati play a small role in Bengal, compared to many other states, in the educational system. Through the practices of the schooling system, the pupils and students must forget, if they even remember, the laws of the system.

This does not imply that notions of purity no longer have any impact in the lives of the Kumars or of urban Bengalis in general. Collecting garbage is still an impure profession, and one does not place one's feet on top of a pile of books. But their concept of purity does not play any significant role as a ritualistic foundation of the caste system.

The lost relevance of purity and the diminishing complexity of the caste system as a practice might very well be a part of the impact of a modern and competitive attitude in the neighbourhood. However, as modernity is not in opposition to the caste system as such, this might not be the case. Modernity entered the world of Kumars through selling images to the neighbourhood pujas and via an internal change in their practical approach to the process of making images, not as part of pressure to change as a caste-based neighbourhood. What modernity conceptualizes is important in this respect.

A Kumartuli Lesson

The hybrid nature of Kumartuli's modernity is an important part of its definition (Gaonkar 2001) as well as its genealogy. If modernity as attitude and practice has existed in India before the colonial encounter, this rules out emphasising solely Western influences. Moreover, modernity as a concept must also be redefined so that it doesn't necessarily have one historically situated beginning with a single line of development that follows, as modernity does not belong exclusively to one place and one period.

Thus, the first step in reconceptualizing modernity is to accept the existence of independent or lost modernities that do not stand in a genealogical relationship with European modernity as this originated during the Enlightenment. Secondly, we have to agree upon certain common processes that the concept seems to denote. The last step is to scrutinize the possible benefits and/or disadvantages of such a concept.

Modern practices and attitudes do not necessarily have a common origin, as various modernities have existed independently of each other (Eisenstadt 2005, Wittrock 2005). Accounts of independent, that is non-European, forms of modernity are not uncommon nowadays (Kaviraj 2005, Narayana Rao et al. 2003, Woodside 2006). It is not controversial any longer to state that there exists a multitude of ways of being modern due to 'the fact of difference' (Gupta 1998). If one is able to accept the existence of modernity outside the metastory of the Western Enlightenment, one also needs to discard the standard evolutionistic features often attributed to that specific development. These features are commonly mentioned as capitalism, industrialization, colonialism, bureaucratization and a formal scientific rationality (Gaonkar 2001, Woodside 2006); as well as views that came to stand in opposition to these features (Gaonkar 2001). In fact, one should probably not engage in endless tasks of mapping the genealogies without being able to being able to incorporate the complexity and hybrid nature of most practices (Latour 1993). Thus, what needs to be asked at this point is what we are left with in our understanding if we discard the common 'creation myth' of modernity?

As Akhil Gupta writes, modernity manifests differently from location to location because 'the *fact of difference* itself is a constitutive moment that structures the experiences of modernity' (1998: 36). For the Maliks of this book, one major difference that has been discussed is a change of style in the making of Durga images. This change forced the Maliks to reinvent themselves as image makers and created a new sense of historicity through which a sense of tradition was also born. The way of being modern, as it became visible in the work of the Maliks after community pujas and Gopeshwar, is unique to Kumartuli at the same time as it is based on the same 'fact of difference' connected to modernity in other locations (Appadurai 1996, Gupta 1998, Gaonkar 2001). Through not only the break with the common style of the Durga image, but also through the appreciation it received, a sense of tradition emerged – a tradition that contemporary Kumars use as part of their self-representation: They belong to a tradition with a special emphasis on caste-affiliation, while at the same time, their imaginations have been freed, and they make art images.

It is exactly the break or caesura that results in an experience of a new departure, through which the past becomes seen in contrast to the present, which contains the most important process that might eventually emerge as modernity. Thus, we see that tradition is no longer experienced as something taken for granted, and its quasi-natural quality is questioned. Self-reflexivity becomes possible in new ways, as the caesura makes comparison and evaluation possible. 'The Other' might equally well be the perceived past of one's own society as an altogether different society. As one loses the previously unquestioned connections to the past, the present becomes a more important point of reference. One starts to look around, at one's neighbours and the society at large. The past failed to provide all the answers to questions about how to proceed in everyday chores, or to explain more existential questions like (for a Kumbhakar Malik) how did pottery emerge as a profession? An understanding of oneself as part of historical developments and not as a natural given seems to be a common result of such breaches (Narayan Rao *et al.* 2003), as does the related conception of having a tradition (Rudolph and Rudolph 1984 [1967]).

When we turn back to the narratives of the Maliks of Kumartuli, we get stories that simultaneously provide us with their self-understanding and self-representation. The overall history or itihas of their development was entrusted to me, the university-educated Saheb, to write. But their stories or golpas are as historical as my rendition of their history. Recurring stories that they told to explain who they are refer to their historical migration to Kolkata, the change of occupation after Gopeshwar, the new realities created by Partition, how the economic situation developed and how formal education became an important asset. At the same time, the Kumars expressed their jati affiliation as important, an affiliation that connects them to a practice of working with clay which demanded no other education than that orally transmitted by relatives, without the use of any scriptures like the *Silpa Sastra* (Robinson 1983: 10). Jati affiliation does not however imply the impossibility of individual achievements and aspirations. It does not succumb under the influence of formal education or other aspects of modernity. The conceptualization of belonging to a jati changes when capitalism and modernity hits Kumartuli. In the world of competing Maliks they use this affiliation in marketing their products and their artistic capabilities. They still argue that working with clay is in their blood and part of their heritage (*bangsher dhara*), at the same time as they emphasize formal education as being important to compete for the best-paid jobs in the Durga market.

The stories of the Maliks do not necessarily fit within common conceptions of modern development, at least not as far back as Gopeshwar and beyond. And even though he went abroad, it is not that fact that contributed to the modernistic turn in Kumartuli. Rather it was the consequences of the stylistic changes he introduced, as they resulted in a demand for 'art-er' images and thus made imagination more relevant for the Maliks than the use of old moulds. The special flavour of this life-experience, as represented in the stories of the Maliks themselves, is most powerfully described and communicated if one breaks free of an understanding of modernity that enforces notions of beginnings in Western capitalism, bureaucratization, rationalism, and so on. This is so because no simple explanation for indigenous sources of inspiration can be identified. Modernity in Kumartuli is not a simple mimicry (Gupta 1998) of Western modernity. Thus, the evolution of modernity in the West – through phases of capitalism, rationalism, et cetera – does not have to be replicated in other modernities if one understands modernity as primarily a set of attitudes and practices.

When modernity is stripped of its Western origin and understood in terms of a caesura that enforces self-reflexivity and individualization, historicity and a sensation of having a tradition, an important step is taken that also gives caste-based societies and neighbourhoods their place in a shared history. Being part of a caste-based profession does not imply that one is non-modern. One is as much part of history as others, even when one's occupation is atypical and seemingly old-fashioned. Realizing the existence of tradition, and constantly comparing present reality to a concept of tradition, are important parts of being modern. Kumartuli is no time capsule with a group of pre-modern Kumars. In fact, modernity came to Kumartuli at least several decades before India's independence in 1947.

An image of the Kumars of Kumartuli

Kumartuli as a jati-based neighbourhood fits with the fact that almost all the image-makers belong to the same jati, and visually, as well as in ordinary Bengalis' consciousness, the Kumars dominate the area. But that does not imply that jati is of any great importance in reproducing inequality in terms of a ritually sanctioned hierarchy. However, belonging to a jati is important as a source to self-representation, as it is seen as part of an important tradition that one should be proud of. Still, there are other aspects and characteristics that are just as important when it comes to self-representation among the Kumars as jati – aspects concerning creative abilities, a sense of belonging to a 'home place' as captured in the concept of adibari, and economic situation. As these aspects become important in self-understanding and self-representation among the Kumars, the understanding of what belonging to a jati means changes as well. To work as a Malik in the last century is to a large extent best described as living a modern life. To be a contemporary Malik means, for the great majority, to run a modern small-scale business that values formal education and entrepreneurship as well as artistic abilities.

The free individuals usually attributed to the new form of civil society as it was constructed in the new and modern nation-states of eighteenth century Europe also existed in the colonies. In Kolkata, at least, this is true of the former uneducated groups as well as of the *bhadralok*, the educated Bengali elite. The caste system never became the totalizing factor for organizing and representing identity that the British thought it was, and thus made it into. Among the Kumartuli Kumars, Gopeshwar was perhaps the first free individual, at least in the recollections of the contemporary Kumars. As such, he is also the first artist in the narratives of both the Kumars themselves and the society at large. Gopeshwar's evidently strong connections to the Kumbhakar jati as an artist of Kumartuli and an image maker never reduced his individual capabilities and recognition to a 'position of relative unimportance' (Dirks 1992: 58). Gopeshwar was an individual-within-the-world, not a *sannyasi* or renouncer, which is the only individual that Dumont seems to recognize within India (1980 [1970]: 184–85). Within artisan communities, this is perhaps more prevalent than elsewhere in the society and it is possible to find references to individual Kumars working before Gopeshwar (Mukharji 1974 [1888]). However, they are remembered not for their artistic innovative skills but for their abilities to refine their work within a given artisan tradition. Hence, even in the later days of colonial India jati was not all-encompassing in the sense of denying the individual any importance. Important characteristics or processes like self-reflectivity and presentness, usually explained with reference to a modernity said to have originated in Europe, are evident. At the same time, explaining these processes with reference to a European modernity is not satisfactory, since doing so evidently does not explain very much at all. Consequently, in Kumartuli we witness the beginning of a modern era that stands on its own. It is not indigenous or alternative – that is a sort of imitation of the 'official' Western modernity born out of the European Enlightenment. The modernity of Kumartuli Kumars is simply a modernity as much as other kinds of modernity.

As seen in the special situation created by Partition, jati was less important than perceptions of artistic skills with reference to a vague notion of adibari. Nicholas B. Dirks' conceptualization of caste (1987) seems to explain more than, for instance, that of Dumont (1980 [1970]), with the exception that it appears obvious that the British never were able to reify and transform the caste system to the extent that Dirks argues in *Hollow Crown* (1987). Later on, when the modern Indian nation-state is well established and working, we witness the conjunction of the abovementioned Kumartuli modernity with a modernity that can be easily explained with reference to processes concerning Western development and nationalist discourses. Strangely enough, this conjunction takes place in times of emergency, when many parts of the modern civil society are heavily suppressed, as was the case in India in the late 1960s and throughout most of the 1970s.

Recently, education has replaced the emphasis on adibari at a time when the Kumartuli Kumars have lost their 'monopoly' on image-making. Moreover, the Kumars' quest for 'development' and utilization of new forms of marketing cannot be understood simply as 'modernity at large' (Appadurai 1996). The Kumars, young and old, are carriers of a tradition of change and ruptures, of a modernity that both provides new spaces of agency and restricts old ones. In both their historical narratives and their present lives, the Kumars act as free individuals who navigate within a framework that encompasses, among many other processes, both an indigenous and an alternative modernity. Common views (within anthropology) concerning the impact of modernity on non-western societies seem thus to be too simplistic in their indirect denial of the existence of non-European modernities. Approaching modernity in terms of tradition-creating breaks without referring to the Western Enlightenment is more in tune with historical evidence (Narayan Rao et al. 2003, Woodside 2006). Returning to this book's conceptual frame of caste, it becomes even more evident that any contemporary notion of caste has to be very complex. What caste was, is, signifies, represents, et cetera appears to be so contextual with reference to – in the context of this book – time and, probably, to space, that it is hard even to call it part of a Wittgensteinian language-game. Caste consists both of historically situated societies' notion of what it implies, as well as of actual practices. In Kumartuli caste is an asset and a source of pride. It is also a framework defining potential marriage-partners, but not a set of rules that defines how to interact in other ways with other groups in the society. Moreover, caste and modernity in the context of Kumartuli do not represent two opposites. They exist and develop together in the lives of the Kumars.

Talking in terms of alternative modernities invokes a notion of an original modernity. In the context of Kumartuli there is no such thing as an alternative or indigenous modernity. Here only modernity as such can be said to exist. It is impossible in most cases to craft a genealogy of a given society's modernity without riding roughshod over the hybrid and complex nature of most attitudes and practices. One might find important sources of influence and/or inspiration, such as Gopeshwar's travel to Europe provided him with, but that does not tell the whole story. Modernity did exist in India, before the colonial encounter, in a multitude of manifestations. That the Kumars of Kumartuli did not belong to any of these traditions is impossible to declare with certainty. In all probability they did.

Conceptualizing modernity in terms of a caesura that creates a new sense of self-reflexivity, historicity and of having a tradition is enough. There is no need to establish a genealogy that dates back to the European Enlightenment in order to describe attitudes and practices of a society as modern.

Commodification and the Illusions of Tradition

The narratives presented and the argument made in this book are not about either praising the commodification of caste identity or critiquing the conditions under which the processes took place. Rather, it is an attempt to narrate an emic history of a seemingly historyless group. Moreover, inspired by John L. and Jean Comaroff, it seeks to 'identify, scrutinize and anatomize, and merging historical phenomenon: on that, being scattered and dispersed, has escaped scholarly treatment' (2009: 140) concerning how, here, caste consciousness and identity have changed and reconstructed themselves in accordance with the unfolding political and ethical economy in relation to 'the affective dimension of commodification' (ibid.).

While the Kumars of Kumartuli have operated in a capitalist-like market since the advent of community pujas, it was especially with the introduction of theme pujas that they got substantial competition from people outside their caste. This made them feel sidelined, unable to capture the big customers with the big money. Through formal education some of the Kumars sought to encroach on the path followed by successful non-Kumar theme puja artists. At the same time they started to advocate more fully their caste's deep, almost existential connection with image making. In a struggle over *legitimacy* (Bourdieu 1982) the Kumars seek to project their *knowledge from the blood* as providing 'the right to define what counts as competence, as authenticity, as excellence, and over who has the right to produce and distribute' (Heller 2003). It is in their blood, they know every part of the work from binding the straw to painting the eyes. They can provide contemporary Bengali worshipers with the authentic protimas, like they provided for their ancestors. An image from a respected Kumartuli Kumar is value added for the worshipers and puja committees. It is caste as a brand; it is the commodification of caste.

The importance of originality, of artistic quality and authenticity has been important to the Kumars of Kumartuli for decades. They operate in an economically strained and global market with merciless competition. They use their descent, caste background and historical knowledge in an attempt to gain an upper hand in the market. As Kumartuli has not yet been turned into a shopping mall of Kumar artists, it is still concealing their modern approach to the art, the trade and what caste affiliation could be all about. They sell not only objects of cult and exhibition, but also the authenticity of tradition

Kumartuli's images are given value by the Kumar's by emphasizing the caste affiliation of the producers and the historical background of the place. Caste is a 'raw material' brought into the production and marketing that is not depleted by mass circulation (Comaroff and Comaroff 2009: 20). The commodification of caste by the Kumars changes the meaning, implication and practice of caste identity. The result is not that the commodified caste gets diluted and unrecognizable. Quite the contrary, it strengthens the caste identity of the Kumars both within the group and in society at large.

REFERENCES

Abu-Lughod, Lila, ed. 1998. *Remaking Women: Feminism and Modernity in the Middle East.* Princeton: Princeton University Press.

Agnihotri, Anita. 2001. *Kolkatar Protimashilpira.* Kolkata: Ananda.

Agnihotri, R. K. and A. L. Khanna. 1997. *Problematizing English in India* (Research in Applied Linguistics, Vol. 3). New Delhi: Sage Publications.

Amin, Shahid. 1995. *Event, Metaphor, Memory: Chauri Chaura 1922–1992.* Delhi: Oxford University Press.

Appadurai, Arjun. 1991. 'Global Ethnoscapes: Notes and Queries for a Transnational Anthropology'. In *Recapturing Anthropology: Working for the Present,* edited by Richard G. Fox, 191–210. Santa Fe, NM: School of American Research Press.

Appadurai, Arjun. 1992. 'Putting Hierarchy in Its Place'. In *Rereading Cultural Anthropology,* edited by George E. Marcus, 34–47. Durham: Duke University Press.

Appadurai, Arjun. 1996. *Modernity at Large: Cultural Dimensions of Globalization.* Minnesota: University of Minnesota Press.

Ashcroft, Bill, Gareth Griffins and Helen Tiffin. 1995. 'General Introduction'. In *The Post-Colonial Studies Reader,* edited by Bill Ashcroft, Gareth Griffins and Helen Tiffin, 1–4. London: Routledge.

Banerjee, Sudeshna. 2004. *Durga Puja: Yesterday, Today and Tomorrow.* New Delhi: Rupa.

Banerjee, Sumanta. 1980. *In the Wake of Naxalbari: A History of the Naxalite Movement in India.* Calcutta: Subarnarekha.

Banerjee, Sumanta. 1989. *The Parlour and the Streets: Elite and Popular Culture in Nineteenth Century Calcutta.* Calcutta: Seagull Books.

Barth, Fredrik. 1967. 'Economic Spheres in Darfur'. In *Themes in Economic Anthropology,* edited by Raymond Firth, 149–74. A.S.A. Monographs, 6. London: A.S.A.

Bayly, Susan. 1999. *Caste, Society and Politics: From the 18th Century to the Modern Age.* Cambridge: Cambridge University Press.

Benjamin, Walter. (1936) 1984. 'The Work of Art in the Age of Mechanical Reproduction'. In *Illuminations: Essays and Reflections,* 217–51. New York: Schoken Books. First published 1936.

Bernstein, Richard J., ed. 1985. *Habermas and Modernity.* Cambridge, MA: MIT Press.

Berreman, Gerald D. 1972. *Hindus of the Himalayas: Ethnography and Change,* 2nd ed. Berkeley: University of California Press.

Béteille, André. 1991. *Society and Politics in India: Essays in a Comparative Perspective.* London: Athlone Press.

Béteille, André. (1991) 2005. 'The Reproduction of Inequality'. In *Anti-Utopia. Essential Writings of André Béteille,* edited with an introduction by Dipankar Gupta. Oxford: Oxford University Press.

Béteille, André. (1996) 2005. 'Caste in Contemporary India'. In *Anti-Utopia. Essential Writings of André Béteille*, edited with an introduction by Dipankar Gupta. Oxford: Oxford University Press.

Bhabani, Soudhriti. 2007. 'Potters' Town Kumartuli May Finally Get Makeover'. IANS/ IndiaeNews.com. Accessed 26 April 2008. http://www.indiaenews.com/pdf/75147.pdf.

Bhanu, B. V. and B. R. Bhatnagar, D. K. Bose, V. S. Kulkarni, J. Sreenath, with general editor Kumar Suresh Singh. 2004. *People of India: Maharashtra, Part Two, Vol. 30*. Mumbai: Popular Prakashan.

Blackburn, Stuart. 2007. 'Oral Stories and Culture Areas: From Northeast India to Southwest China'. *South Asia: Journal of South Asia Studies* 30(3): 419–37.

Blaut, J. M. 1993. *The Colonizer's Model of the World: Geographical Diffusionism and Eurocentric History*. New York: Guilford Press.

Bloch, Marc. (1952) 1954. *The Historian's Craft*. Translated from French by Peter Putnam, with a foreword by J. R. Strayer. Manchester: Manchester University Press.

Blurton, T. Richard. 2006. *Bengali Myths*. London: British Museum Press.

Boas, Franz. 1909. "The Kwakiutl of Vancouver Island." In *The Jesup North Pacific Expedition* 5, Pt. 2, 301–522. Leiden E. J. Brill Ltd Printers & Publishers.

Bose, Sugata and Ayesha Jala. 1998. *Modern South Asia: History, Culture, Political Economy*. New York: Routledge.

Brown, Percy. 1942–1943. *Indian Architecture*. Bombay: D. B. Taraporevala.

Chaliha, Jaya and Bunny Gupta. 1990. 'Durga Puja in Calcutta'. In *Calcutta: The Living City Volume II, The Present and Future*, edited by Sukanta Chauduri, 331–36. New Delhi: Oxford University Press.

Chakrabarty, Bidyut. 2004. *The Partition of Bengal and Assam, 1932–1947: Contour of Freedom*. London: RoutledgeCurzon.

Chakrabarty, Dipesh. 1997. 'The Time of History and the Times of Gods'. In *The Politics of Culture in the Shadow of Capital*, edited by Lisa Lowe and David Lloyd, 35–61. Durham: Duke University Press.

Chakrabarty, Dipesh. 2003. '*Adda*, Calcutta: Dwelling in Modernity'. In *Alternative Modernities*, edited by D. P. Gaonkar, 123–64. Durham: Duke University Press.

Chakrabarty, Dipesh. 2009. *Provincializing Europe: Postcolonial Thought and Historical Difference*. Princeton: Princeton University Press.

Chakraborty, Sudhir. 1985. *Krisnanagarer Mritsilpa o Mritsilpi Samaj*. Calcutta: K.P. Bagchi Publishers, on behalf of Centre for Studies in Social Sciences.

Chandra, Bipan, Mridula Mukherjee and Aditya Mukherjee. 1999. *India after Independence 1947–2000*. New Delhi: Penguin Books.

Chandra, Uday, Geir Heierstad and Kenneth Bo Nielsen, eds. 2015. *The Politics of Caste in West Bengal*. New Delhi: Routledge.

Chatterjee, Jaybrato. 2004. *Kolkata: The Dream City*. New Delhi: UBS.

Chatterjee, Partha. 1990. 'The Political Culture of Calcutta'. In *Calcutta: The Living City Volume 2, The Present and Future*, edited by Sukanta Chauduri, 27–33. New Delhi: Oxford University Press.

Chatterjee, Partha. 1993. *The Nation and Its Fragments: Colonial and Postcolonial Histories*. Princeton: Princeton University Press.

Chatterji, Joya. 1994. *Bengal Divided: Hindu Communalism and Partition, 1932–1947*. Cambridge: Cambridge University Press.

Chatterji, Bankimchandra. 2005. *Anandamath, or 'The Sacred Brotherhood'*. Translated with an introduction and critical apparatus by Julius J. Lipner. Oxford: Oxford University Press.

Chatterji, Shoma A. 2006. *The Goddess Kali of Kolkata*. New Delhi: UBS.

Chekuri, Christopher. 2007. 'Writing Politics Back into History'. *History and Theory* 46 (October): 384–95.

Childers, Joseph. 2004. 'Outside Looking In: Colonials, Immigrants, and the Pleasure of the Archive'. *Victorian Studies* 46 (2): 297–307.

Cohn, Bernhard S. 2004. 'The Census, Social Structure and Objectification in South Asia.' In *An Anthropologist among the Historians and Other Essays*, collection of works edited by B. Cohen, 224–54. Delhi: Oxford University Press.

Cole, Stroma. 2007. 'Beyond Authenticity and Commodification'. *Annals of Tourism Research* 34 (4): 943–60.

Comaroff, John L. and Jean Comaroff. 2009. *Ethnicity, Inc.* Chicago: University of Chicago Press.

Das, Soumitra. 2007. 'Once a European Enclave'. *The Telegraph*, 2 November. http://www.telegraphindia.com/1071102/asp/frontpage/story_8502672.asp.

Dasgupta, Shubhoranjan. 2001. 'Creativity's Mirror'. *Refugee Watch*, 14 June. http://www.mcrg.ac.in/rw%20files/RW14.DOC.

Davis, Marvin. 1983. *Rank and Rivalry: The Politics of Inequality in Rural West Bengal*. Cambridge: Cambridge University Press.

Davis, Richard H. 1999. *Lives of Indian Images*. New Delhi: Motilal Banarsidass.

Deb, Chitra. 1990. 'The "Great Houses" of Old Calcutta'. In *Calcutta: The Living City Volume I, The Past*, edited by Sukanta Chauduri, 56–63. New Delhi: Oxford University Press.

Dirks, Nicholas B. 1987. *The Hollow Crown: Ethnohistory of an Indian Kingdom*. Cambridge: Cambridge University Press.

Dirks, Nicholas B. 1992. 'Castes of Mind'. In 'Imperial Fantasies and Postcolonial Histories'. Special issue, *Representations* 37 (Winter): 56–78.

Dirks, Nicholas B. 2001. *Castes of Mind. Colonialism and the Making of Modern India*. Princeton: Princeton University Press.

Dubois, J. A. (1816, 1879) 1992. *A Description of the Character, Manners, and Customs of the People of India and of Their Institutions Religious and Civil*. 3rd ed. New Delhi: Asian Education Services.

Dumont, Louis. (1970) 1980. *Homo Hierarchicus: The Caste System and Its Implications*. Complete revised English edition translated by Mark Sainsbury, Louis Dumont and Basia Gulati. Oxford: Oxford University Press.

Dumont, Louis. 1986. *Essays on Individualism: Modern Ideology in Anthropological Perspectives*. Chicago: University of Chicago Press.

Dumont, Louis. 1994. *The German Ideology: From France to Germany and Back*. Chicago: University of Chicago Press.

Dutta, Krishna. 2003. *Calcutta: A Cultural and Literary History*. New Delhi: Lotus Collection, Roli Books.

Eisenstadt, Shmuel N. 2003. *Comparative Civilizations and Multiple Modernities, vols. 1 and 2*. Leiden: Brill.

Eisenstadt, Shmuel N. 2005. *Multiple Modernities*. New Brunswick, NJ: Transaction Publishers.

Errington, Fredrick and Deborah Gewertz. 1996. 'The Individuation of Tradition in a Papua New Guinean Modernity'. *American Anthropologist*, n.s., 98 (1): 114–26.

Fabian, Johannes. 1983. *Time and the Other: How Anthropology Makes Its Object*. New York: Columbia University Press.

Ferguson, James. 2005. 'Decomposing Modernity: History and Hierarchy after Development'. In *Postcolonial Studies and Beyond*, edited by Ania Loomba, Suvir Kaul, Matti Bunzl, Antoinette Burton and Jed Esty, 166–81. Durham: Duke University Press.

Foucault, Michel. 1980. *Power/Knowledge: Selected Interviews and Other Writings 1972–1977*, edited and translated by Colin Gordon. Brighton: Harvester Press.

Gaonkar, Dilip Parameshwar. 2001. 'On Alternative Modernities'. In *Alternative Modernities*, edited by Dilip P. Gaonkar, 1–23. Durham: Duke University Press.

Geertz, Clifford. 1973. *The Interpretation of Cultures: Selected Essays*. New York: Basic Books.

Ghose, Benoy. 1981. *Traditional Arts and Crafts of West Bengal: A Sociological Survey*. Calcutta: Papyrus.

Goffman, Erving. (1959) 1971. *The Presentation of Self in Everyday Life*. Harmondsworth: Penguin Books.

Gold, Ann Grodzins and Bhoju Ram Gujar. 2002. *In the Times of Trees and Sorrows: Nature, Power, and Memory in Rajasthan*. Durham and London: Duke University Press.

Goldblatt, Beth. 1997. 'The Image Makers of Kumartuli: The Transformation of a Caste-Based Industry in a Slum Quarter of Calcutta'. PhD diss., Faculty of Economic and Social Studies, University of Manchester. Unpublished.

Guha, Ranajit. 2002. *History at the Limit of World-History*. New York: Columbia University Press.

Gupta, Akhil. 1998. *Postcolonial Developments: Agriculture in the Making of Modern India*. Durham: Duke University Press.

Gupta, Akhil and James Ferguson. 1997. 'Discipline and Practice: "The Field" as Site, Method, and Location in Anthropology'. In *Anthropological Locations. Boundaries and Grounds of a Field Science*, edited by Akhil Gupta and James Ferguson, 1–46. Berkeley: University of California Press.

Gupta, Dipankar. 2004. 'Introduction: The Certitude of Caste; When Identity Trumps Hierarchy'. In *Caste in Question: Identity or Hierarchy?*, edited by D. Gupta, ix–xxi. New Delhi: Sage Publications.

Gupta, Dipankar, ed. 2004. *Caste in Question: Identity or Hierarchy?* New Delhi: Sage Publications.

Habermas, Jürgen. 1987. *The Philosophical Discourse on Modernity: Twelve Lectures*. Translated by Frederick Lawrence. Cambridge, MA: MIT Press.

Hall, Stuart. 1992. 'The West and the Rest: Discourse and Power'. In *Formations of Modernity*, edited by Stuart Hall and Bram Gieben, 275–331. Cambridge: Polity Press in association with the Open University.

Hannerz, Ulf. 1992. *Cultural Complexity: Studies in the Social Organization of Meaning*. New York: Columbia University Press.

Hanssen, Kristin. 2001. *Seeds in Motion: Thoughts, Feelings and the Significance of Social Ties as Invoked by a Family of Vaishnava Mendicant Renouncers in Bengal*. Doctoral dissertation in economics, University of Oslo. Unpublished.

Hardgrave, Robert L. 2004. *A Portrait of the Hindus: Balthazar Solvyns & the European Image of India, 1760–1824*. New York: Oxford University Press in association with Mapin Publishing.

Harriss-White, Barbara. 2003. *India Working: Essays on Society and Economy*. Cambridge: Cambridge University Press.

Harvey, David. 1999. *The Limits to Capital*. London: Verso.

Harvey, David. 2002. 'The Art of Rent: Globalization, Monopoly and the Commodification of Culture'. *Socialist Register*, https://mediatropes.com/index.php/srv/article/view/5778/2674.

Heierstad, Geir. 2001. *Nandikar: Staging Globalisation in Kolkata and Abroad*. Doctoral dissertation in social anthropology, University of Oslo.

Heierstad, Geir. 2009. 'Etnografiske representasjoner, et spørsmål om tid'. *Norsk antropologisk tidsskrift* 20 (3): 151–66.

Heller, Monica. 2003. 'Globalization, the New Economy, and the Commodification of Language and Identity'. *Journal of Sociolinguistics* 7 (4): 473–92.

ICICI Winfra. 2007. 'Ongoing Projects, Real Estate'. *ICICI Winfra*, http://www.iciciwinfra.com/restate.html#8, Accessed 5 March 2008.

Jayaram, N. 1996. 'Caste and Hinduism: Changing Protean Relationship'. In *Caste: Its Twentieth Century Avatar*, edited by M. N. Srinivas, 69–86. New Delhi: Viking.

Kaviraj, Sudipta. 2005. 'Modernity and Politics in India'. In *Multiple Modernities*, edited by Shmuel N. Eisenstadt, 137–61. New Brunswick, NJ: Transaction Publishers.

Khare, R. S., ed. 2006. *Caste, Hierarchy, and Individualism: Indian Critiques of Louis Dumont's Contributions*. New Delhi: Oxford University Press.

Khare, R. S. 2006. 'Introduction'. In *Caste, Hierarchy, and Individualism: Indian Critiques of Louis Dumont's Contributions*, edited by R. S. Khare, 1–35. New Delhi: Oxford University Press.

KMDA. 2007. 'The Fact and Figures of the Kumartuli Urban Renewal Projects'. KMDA Online, http://www.kmdaonline.org/plans_stat-projects-kumartuli.html. Accessed 5 March 2008.

Knight, Donald R. and Alan D. Sabey. 1984. *The Lion Roars at Wembley: British Empire Exhibition, 1924–25*. London: Barnard & Westwood.

Kolenda, P. 1986. 'Caste in India since Independence'. In *Social and Economic Development in India: A Reassessment*, edited by Dilip K. Basu, and Richard Sisson, 126–28. New Delhi: Sage.

Kundu, Nitai. 2003. 'Urban Slums Report: The Case of Kolkata, India'. In *Understanding Slums: Case Studies for the Global Report on Human Settlements 2003*. London: University College London.

Lal, Vinay. 2003. *The History of History: Politics and Scholarship in Modern India*. Oxford: Oxford University Press.

Lipner, Julius J. 2005. 'Introduction and Critical Apparatus'. In *Anandamath, or 'The Sacred Brotherhood'*, by Bankimchandra Chatterji, translated with an introduction and critical apparatus by Julius J. Lipner, 1–130. Oxford: Oxford University Press.

Losty, Jeremiah P. 1990. *Calcutta: City of Palaces*. London: Arnold.

Latour, Bruno. 1993. *We Have Never Been Modern*. New York: Harvester Wheatsheaf.

Madan, T. N. 2006a. 'Foreword'. In *Caste, Hierarchy, and Individualism: Indian Critiques of Louis Dumont's Contributions*, edited by R. S. Khare. New Delhi: Oxford University Press.

Madan, T. N. 2006b. 'Louis Dumont and the Study of Society in India'. In *Caste, Hierarchy, and Individualism: Indian Critiques of Louis Dumont's Contributions*, edited by R. S. Khare, 52–84. New Delhi: Oxford University Press.

Marriott, McKim, ed. 1955. *Village India: Studies in the Little Community*. Chicago: University of Chicago Press.

Metcalf, Barbara D. and Thomas R. Metcalf. 2002. *A Concise History of India*. Cambridge: Cambridge University Press.

Miller, Daniel. 1994. *Modernity, an Ethnographic Approach: Dualism and Mass Consumption in Trinidad*. Oxford: Berg Publishers.

Mines, Mattison. 1994. *Public Faces, Private Voices: Community and Individuality in South Asia*. Berkeley: University of California Press.

Mintz, Sidney. (1979) 1990. 'The Anthropological Interview and the Life History'. In *Oral History: An Interdisciplinary Anthology*, edited by David K. Dunaway and Will K. Baum. 2nd ed., 298–305. Walnut Creek: Altamira Press (Sage Press).

Michelutti, Lucia. 2004. '"We (Yadavs) Are a Caste of Politicians": Caste and Modern Politics in a North Indian Town'. In *Caste, Hierarchy, and Individualism: Indian Critiques of Louis Dumont's Contributions*, edited by R. S. Khare, 43–71. New Delhi: Oxford University Press.

Mukharji, T. N. (1888) 1974. *Art-Manufactures of India* [Specially compiled for the Glasgow International Exhibition, 1888]. New Delhi: Navrang.

Nair, P. Thankappan. 1986. *Calcutta in the 17th Century*. Calcutta: Firma KLM.

Nair, P. Thankappan. 1990. 'The Growth and Development of Old Calcutta'. In *Calcutta: The Living City Volume I, The Past*, edited by Sukanta Chauduri, 10–23. New Delhi: Oxford University Press.

Napier, A. David. 1992. *Foreign Bodies: Performance, Art, and Symbolic Anthropology*. Berkeley: University of California Press.

Narayana Rao, Velcheru, David Shulman and Sanjay Subrahmanyam. 1992. *Symbols of Substance: Court and State in Nayaka Period Tamil Nadu*. New Delhi: Oxford University Press.

Narayana Rao, Velcheru, David Shulman and Sanjay Subrahmanyam. 1994. *When God Is a Customer: Telugu Courtesan Songs of Kshetreyya and Others*. Berkeley: University of California Press.

Narayana Rao, Velcheru, David Shulman and Sanjay Subrahmanyam. 2003. *Textures of Time: Writing History in South India 1600–1800*. New York: Other Press.

Narayana Rao, Velcheru, David Shulman and Sanjay Subrahmanyam. 2007. 'A Pragmatic Response'. *History and Theory* 46 (October): 409–27.

Nicholas, Ralph W. 2003. *Fruits of Worship: Practical Religion in Bengal*. New Delhi: Chronicle Books (an imprint of DC Publishers).

Ortner, Sherry B. 1984. 'Theory in Anthropology since the Sixties'. *Comparative Studies in Society and History* 26 (1): 126–66.

Östör, Ákos. 1984. *Culture and Power: Legend, Ritual, Bazaar, and Rebellion in a Bengali Society*. New Delhi: Sage Publications.

Östör, Ákos. (1980) 2004. *The Play of Gods: Locality, Ideology, Structure and Time in the Festivals of a Bengali Town*. New Delhi: Chronicle Books (an imprint of DC Publishers).

Östör, Ákos, Lina Fruzzetti and Steve Barnett, eds. 1982. *Concepts of Person: Kinship, Caste and Marriage in India*. Harvard: Harvard University Press.

Pandey, Geeta. 2008. 'Caste Shadows over School Cook Row'. BBC News Online (International version),, 28 March 2008, http://news.bbc.co.uk/2/hi/south_asia/7256320.stm.

Pandey, Gyanendra. 1992. *The Construction of Communalism in Colonial North India*. Oxford: Oxford University Press.

Parkin, Robert. 2003. *Louis Dumont and Hierarchical Opposition (Methodology and History in Anthropology vol. 9)*. New York: Berghahn Books.

Parry, Jonathan. 1974. 'Egalitarian Values in a Hierarchical Society'. *South Asia Review* 7: 95–124.

Parry, Jonathan. 1994. *Death in Benares*. Cambridge: Cambridge University Press.

Peter, Emrys L. 1967. 'Some Structural Aspects of the Feud among the Camel-Herding Bedouin of Cyrenaica'. *Africa, Journal of the International African Institute* 37 (3): 261–82.

Pollock, Sheldon. 2007. 'Pretextures of Time'. *History and Theory* 46 (October): 366–83.

Pollock, Sheldon. 2006. *The Language of the Gods in the World of Men: Sanskrit, Culture, and Power in Premodern India*. Berkeley: University of California Press.

Risley, H. H. 1891a. *The Tribes and Castes of Bengal: Ethnographic Glossary, Vol. 1.* Calcutta: Bengal Secretary Press.

Risley, H. H. 1891b. *The Tribes and Castes of Bengal: Ethnographic Glossary, Vols. 1 and 2.* Calcutta: Bengal Secretary Press.

Robinson, J. D. 1983. 'The Worship of Clay Images in Bengal'. PhD diss., Oriental Studies Department, Linacre College, Oxford. Unpublished.

Roy, Subhajoy. 2005. 'Call from Kumartuli'. *The Telegraph*, 4 October. http://www.telegraphindia.com/1051004/asp/calcutta/story_5302722.asp.

Rudolph, Lloyd I. and Susanne Hoeber Rudolph. (1967) 1984. *The Modernity of Tradition: Political Development in India.* Chicago: University of Chicago Press.

Russell, Robert Vane. 1916. *The Tribes and Castes of the Central Provinces of India*, Vol. 4. London: Macmillan.

Ruud, Arild Engelsen. 2003. *Poetics of Village Politics: The Making of West Bengal's Rural Communism.* New Delhi: Oxford University Press.

Said, Edward W. (1978) 1995. *Orientalism: Western Conceptions of the Orient.* London: Penguin Books.

Sanyal, Hitesranjan. 1981. *Social Mobility in Bengal.* Calcutta: Papyrus.

Sanyal, Hitesranjan. 1971. 'Continuities of Social Mobility in Traditional and Modern Society in India: Two Case Studies of Caste Mobility in Bengal'. *The Journal of Asian Studies* 30(2): 315–39.

Saraswati, Baidyanath and Nab Kirshore Behura. 1966. *Pottery Techniques in Peasant India.* Calcutta: Anthropological Survey of India, Government of India.

Searl-Chatterjee, Mary and Ursula Sharma. 1994. 'Introduction'. In *Contextualising Caste: Post-Dumontian Approaches*, edited by Mary Searl-Chatterjee and Ursula Sharma, 1–24. Oxford: Blackwell Publishers/The Sociological Review.

Sengupta, Nitish. 2001. *History of the Bengali-Speaking People.* New Delhi: UBS.

Simmel, Georg. 1978. *The Philosophy of Money.* Translated by Tom Bottomore and David Frisby. London: Routledge & Kegan Paul.

Sharma, Brijendra Nath. 1978. *Festivals of India.* New Delhi: Abhinav Publications.

Sherring, Matthew Atmore. (1872) 1974. *Hindu Tribes and Castes.* New Delhi: Cosmo Publications.

Shripamtho. 2003. *Smritir Pujo.* Calcutta: Punoshcho.

Shryock, Andrew. 1997. *Nationalism and the Genealogical Imagination: Oral History and Textual Authority in Tribal Jordan.* Berkeley: University of California Press.

Thompson, Paul. 1988. *The Voice of the Past: Oral History.* Oxford: Oxford University Press.

Uberoi, Patricia. 1993. 'Introduction'. In *Family, Kinship and Marriage in India*, edited by Patricia Uberoi, 1–44. Delhi: Oxford University Press.

Varma, K. M. 1970. *The Indian Technique of Clay Modelling.* Santiniketan: Proddu.

Venkatesan, Soumhya. 2009. *Craft Matters: Artisans, Development and the Indian Nation.* New Delhi: Orient BlackSwan.

Wachtel, Nathan. 1990. 'Introduction'. In *Between Memory and History*, edited by Marie-Noëlle Bourguet, Lucette Valensi and Nathan Wachtel, 1–18. New York: Harwood Academic Publishers.

Waldrop, Anne. 2002. *A Room with One's Own: Educated Elite People in New Delhi and Relations of Class.* Doctoral dissertation in social anthropology, University of Oslo.

Ward, W. 1811. *Account of the Writings, Religion, and Manners of the Hindoos: Including Translations from Their Principle Works*, Volume 3. Serampore: Mission Press.

Wittrock, Björn. 2005. 'Modernity: One, None, or Many'. In *Multiple Modernities*, edited by Shmuel N. Eisenstadt, 31–60. New Brunswick: Transaction Publishers.

Wolf, Eric R. (1982) 1997. *Europe and the People without History.* Berkeley: University of California Press.

Woodside, Alexander. 2006. *Lost Modernities: China, Vietnam, Korea, and the Hazards of World History.* Cambridge: Harvard University Press.

INDEX

www.ingramcontent.com/pod-product-compliance
Lightning Source LLC
Chambersburg PA
CBHW022355280326
41935CB00007B/188